White Balance

Studies in United States Culture

Grace Elizabeth Hale, *series editor*

Studies in United States Culture publishes provocative books that explore U.S. culture in its many forms and spheres of influence. Bringing together big ideas, brisk prose, bold storytelling, and sophisticated analysis, books published in the series serve as an intellectual meeting ground where scholars from different disciplinary and methodological perspectives can build common lines of inquiry around matters such as race, ethnicity, gender, sexuality, power, and empire in an American context.

White Balance

How Hollywood Shaped Colorblind Ideology
and Undermined Civil Rights

•••

JUSTIN GOMER

The University of North Carolina Press Chapel Hill

Set in Charis by Westchester Publishing Services
Manufactured in the United States of America

The University of North Carolina Press has been a member
of the Green Press Initiative since 2003.

Library of Congress Cataloging-in-Publication Data
Names: Gomer, Justin, author.
Title: White balance : how Hollywood shaped colorblind ideology
    and undermined civil rights / Justin Gomer.
Other titles: Studies in United States culture.
Description: Chapel Hill : University of North Carolina Press, 2020. |
    Series: Studies in United States culture | Includes bibliographical
    references and index.
Identifiers: LCCN 2019057955 | ISBN 9781469655796 (cloth) |
    ISBN 9781469655802 (paperback) | ISBN 9781469655819 (ebk)
Subjects: LCSH: Post-racialism—United States. | Racism in popular
    culture—United States. | Motion picture industry—United States—
    History—20th century. | Stereotypes (Social psychology) in motion
    pictures. | United States—Race relations—History—20th century.
Classification: LCC PN1995.9.N4 G66 2020 | DDC 791.43/6552—dc23
    LC record available at https://lccn.loc.gov/2019057955

For Adrienne,
for doing the heavy lifting

Contents

Illustrations

Acknowledgments

To say it took a village to complete this book is to drastically understate the amount of mentorship, love, and support I required during the years it took to write it. This book began on the sixth floor of Barrows Hall, in the African American Studies Department at the University of California, Berkeley. There, Leigh Raiford—my mentor, undergraduate thesis adviser, dissertation chair, and Jedi master—encouraged me to pursue a PhD in African American studies before I had even considered it. She then spent the better part of a decade helping me develop the critical-thinking skills, writing and research tools, and habits of mind required to have a shot at a career in academia. Similarly, Ula Taylor sees a better scholar in me than I ever will. She's invested far more time in my development and in this project than I deserve, but which I've shamelessly taken. To this day, the question, What would Leigh and Ula think? informs my research and writing. Additionally, Michael Cohen was a consistent sounding board for this project's argument, scope, and analysis. In many ways, the pages that follow are an earnest but woefully inadequate attempt to repay the debt I owe Leigh, Ula, and Michael. Whatever scholarly contributions this book contains are a testament to their generosity, mentorship, and brilliance. The book's shortcomings, on the other hand, are my own. My people taught me better, I assure you.

Leigh, Ula, and Michael are just three members of the community of scholars that cultivate and nourish the academic community on the sixth floor of Barrows. That so many people on the sixth floor are better human beings than they are scholars is as hard to fathom as it is true. I had the privilege of attending graduate school with some of the most gifted young minds in my field. I benefited greatly from the company of Ron Williams II, Shaun Ossei-Owusu, Petra Rivera-Rideau, Ryan Rideau, Jasmine Johnson, Ianna Owen, Christopher Petrella, Mario Nisbett, Ameer Loggins, Jasminder Kaur, and Reggie Royston. Moreover, the sixth floor's graduate adviser, Lindsey Villarreal, supported my family whenever life got in the way of graduate school. She found us money when we couldn't make ends meet and never faltered in her faith in my academic journey. My thanks also to Darieck Scott, Brandi Wilkins-Catanese, and Percy Hintzen for their support.

Outside the sixth floor, Scott Saul is an invaluable mentor and was fundamental to this project from its conception to its completion. Collectively, the brain trust of this book—Leigh, Ula, Michael, Scott, and me—feels like the academic equivalent of the 2017 Golden State Warriors. I am not sure who is Stephen Curry, Klay Thompson, Kevin Durant, or Draymond Green in this analogy, but I am certain that I am Zaza Pachulia.

Kathleen Moran, the associate director of UC Berkeley's American Studies Program, kept a roof over my family's head and dinner on our table for most of my seven years in graduate school and two more thereafter. More importantly, she, along with Michael Cohen and Christine Palmer, taught me how to teach.

Outside UC Berkeley, I'm fortunate to participate in a writing group with Erica Ball, Sharla Fett, and Tyler D. Parry. Erica, Sharla, and Tyler read drafts and offered detailed feedback on most of the chapters in this book. I'm not quite sure why they, all far more accomplished than I, asked me to join them, but I'll continue to draw the lion's share of the group's benefit as long as I am allowed to stay.

I'm very lucky to work in the American Studies Program at California State University, Long Beach. My director, Brett Mizelle, made sure my transition from graduate school to assistant professor was a smooth one. I admire the culture he has built in our program, one rooted in kindness and collegiality and grounded in academic rigor. In addition, my CSULB American Studies colleagues Preeti Sharma, Linda Maram, Charlie Ponce de Leon, Brande Jackson, and Larry Hashima are all examples of the professoriat at its best.

At UNC Press, Brandon Proia is as good an editor as an author could ask for. I am grateful for his expertise and unwavering faith in this project. I am honored that this book is part of UNC Press's illustrious list and grateful to the rest of the UNC Press team.

Finally, my family. My parents, Elaine and Bob Gomer, worked too hard in jobs they didn't like for too many years so that I wouldn't have to. Moreover, they made sure that their unconditional love was so ubiquitous that their children could not help but take it for granted. My brother, Bryant, and my sister, Kelly, are better testaments to my parents' selflessness than I am. I relied greatly on their love and friendship as a child, and I continue to do so to this day. My siblings-in-law—Lauren, Todd, and Conor—have each found ways to add love and happiness to an extended Gomer family that I doubted could take any more.

My three immaculate children—Belle, Leo, and Dashiell—have rendered obsolete what I thought were the bounds of joy and happiness. As Joan Didion writes, "Once [they were] born, I was never not afraid." Raising my kids has brought me a deep connection to the notion of purpose. It is my greatest honor and pleasure to fall short each day trying to be the father they deserve.

Lastly Adrienne, my wife, to whom this book is dedicated. She deserves to have her name alongside mine on the cover. We did this thing together, just as we have done everything since we were teenagers. Over the course of completing this book, Adrienne has served as my editor, therapist, champion, friend, critic, and partner, all while sacrificing her own career ambitions so I could prioritize mine. She is also a superior parent to our three children. Sharing my life with her is, and will continue to be, the most generative experience of my time on this earth. As the Brandi Carlisle song goes, "Even when I was flat broke, you made me feel like a million bucks."

White Balance

Introduction

The racial ideology of colorblindness governs a great deal of the way Americans legislate, discuss, and think about issues of race. The Supreme Court routinely uses colorblind logic to nullify race-conscious admissions policies at many of the nation's leading universities, and race-neutral ballot initiatives typically win significant voter majorities. Moreover, many insist explicit mentions of someone's racial identity violate the terms of civil discourse, and those who appear to see beyond an individual's racial identity are often lionized in popular culture.

However, the term has meant a number of different things over the last 120-plus years. The notion of a "colorblind" approach to matters of race begins with Supreme Court justice John Marshall Harlan's lone dissent to the *Plessy v. Ferguson* decision in 1896. Justice Harlan opposed the court's overwhelming support of the "separate but equal" doctrine, writing, "Our Constitution is color-blind and neither knows nor tolerates classes among citizens."

Yet, as Ian Haney López explains, Harlan's dissent in *Plessy* should in no way be misconstrued as his commitment to colorblind justice. In the same paragraph in which he uses the term "colorblind," Harlan writes, "The white race deems itself to be the dominant race in this country. . . . So, I doubt not, it will continue to be for all time." Harlan did not oppose white supremacy, nor did he object to race conscious language in law. He merely took issue with the express mention of race in this particular case and, as López writes, the "extreme civic exclusion" the law under review mandated.[1]

A half century later, colorblind rhetoric was routinely used by civil rights lawyers like Thurgood Marshall in the nation's highest courtrooms to challenge Jim Crow segregation. As a result of their efforts, the Supreme Court overturned the *Plessy* decision in *Brown v. Board of Education* (1954), concluding that "the doctrine of 'separate but equal' has no place." In 1963, Martin Luther King Jr. delivered his landmark "I Have a Dream" speech, setting the high-water mark of colorblind rhetoric in the civil rights movement. However, King's speech would unexpectedly provide the source material for the antiblack ideology of colorblindness a decade later, which would work to undo the very victories for which King fought.

Although similar in language, *colorblind rhetoric* is markedly different from the *ideology of colorblindness*. Colorblind rhetoric, like that used by King, has deep historical roots and was used to defend a wide range of political positions—from integrating America's public schools to defending housing discrimination—prior to the 1970s. The ideology of colorblindness, on the other hand, is a politically expedient "race-neutral" ideology that cherry-picks and co-opts language from the civil rights era, specifically from Martin Luther King Jr.'s "I Have a Dream" speech—that "All men are created equal" and should be judged not "by the color of their skin but by the content of their character"—in order to reinvent and reinforce white supremacy in the post–civil rights era. By the middle of the 1970s, the racial ideology of colorblindness would turn King's words against him and the movement he led in order to dismantle its legal victories and shore up white supremacy for the next four decades. In the years between King's "I Have a Dream" speech and the coherence of the ideology of colorblindness in the mid-1970s, the divergent political perspectives of those who either mobilized colorblind rhetoric or scoffed at the notion of a post-racial America reveal an ideology in its infancy, not yet bound to a single political agenda. Those, on the other hand, who espoused colorblind rhetoric did so to advance an array of political agendas. Nearly a decade after King's speech, there was significant ideological diversity in the deployment of colorblind rhetoric. Black Power leaders debated its existence, the Supreme Court was skeptical of its constitutionality, and large numbers of Americans recognized its absurdity only a few years after the civil rights movement.

The racial ideology of colorblindness grew out of these competing interests and united in the middle of the 1970s as the issues of court-ordered busing and affirmative action aroused increasing backlash among whites.[2] School integration opponents, for example, increasingly cited Martin Luther King to justify their anti-busing position; in Boston they even sang "We Shall Overcome" during a march protesting their neighborhood's integration order.[3] The Supreme Court also handed down its first colorblind anti–affirmative action ruling in *DeFunis v. Odegaard*, foreshadowing how the court would more regularly legislate matters of race thereafter. Colorblind rhetoric provided a unifying framework that united whites, both liberal and conservative, behind their opposition to school integration and affirmative action. By the end of the 1970s, those programs were decimated. The dismantling of civil rights programs required white opponents to defend white supremacy within civil rights compliant language. As Robyn Wiegman notes, "Integration, no matter how failed in its utopian projections of a nation beyond race division, nonetheless powerfully suspended the acceptability of white supremacy's public display."[4] Reframing support for segregated neighborhood schools as opposition to "forced busing" in the 1970s was one way to do so; justifying resistance to the racial integration of colleges and universities and trade and law enforcement unions as opposition to "reverse discrimination" was another. The key for either strategy was that colorblindness provided the rhetorical framework for the seemingly civil rights friendly opposition to racial integration. By the mid-1970s, integration and affirmative action foes increasingly defended their opposition by affirming an unwavering commitment to colorblindness.

Furthermore, colorblindness was built on the critiques of liberalism and the longer postwar intellectual trend of an individualistic approach to analyzing racism.[5] Beginning in the 1970s, the ideology offered an inherently antistatist, individualistic, hands-off "solution" to the "problem" of government intervention in matters of race. Because it prohibits the consideration of race in social policy, colorblind logic inhibits the government's ability to intervene in matters of racial inequality. In other words, how can the government address unequal racial access to economic, social, or political resources if it cannot consider race in the process? As the second half of the 1970s unfolded, colorblindness was increasingly positioned as the solution to the problem of government overreach in pursuit of racial integration. Unlike the varying uses of colorblind rhetoric prior to the mid-1970s, colorblind discourse increasingly borrowed the language of the civil rights movement to mobilize against its legal legacy. Colorblindness enabled whites to oppose the victories of the civil rights movement without offending post–civil rights political decorum.

The Colorblind Screen

Hollywood movies proved instrumental in organizing colorblind rhetoric around a unified ideology that disguised white backlash politics beneath a veneer of pro–civil rights rhetoric. As race-conscious language was expelled from public discourse, Hollywood offered the race-conscious visuality left ambiguous by race-neutral colorblind discourse. In the early 1970s, Hollywood films helped unify disparate colorblind rhetoric around an anti–civil rights agenda and won consent among its audiences by offering a space to dramatize and sort out those contradictions. By the middle of the decade, an increasingly influential colorblind ideology began to substantively roll back the victories of the civil rights movement and assert a new form of white supremacy. Beginning with the 1976 blockbuster *Rocky*, Hollywood movies decoded the colorblind dog whistles of busing and affirmative action, linking them directly to racialized bodies on-screen. By the middle of the decade, Hollywood offered white audiences visual narratives of who unfairly benefited and who undeservedly suffered under civil rights enforcement without direct verbal reference to race.

Colorblindness entered the oval office with the election of Ronald Reagan in 1980, nearly a century after Harlan's *Plessy* dissent. Reagan was no friend of civil rights. He had steadfastly opposed racial equality since his days campaigning for the governorship of California in the mid-1960s. Once in the White House, Reagan's administration used colorblindness to try to convince the Supreme Court to eliminate affirmative action and school integration orders. When the court proved uncooperative, Reagan signed the Martin Luther King Jr. federal holiday bill and began to routinely position himself as a supporter of King and a disciple of his supposed colorblind philosophy in order to bolster his assault on civil rights. For the remainder of his presidency, Reagan and his Justice Department routinely countered allegations of their opposition to civil rights as just the opposite—an unwavering commitment to King's colorblind philosophy. Reagan did so as he implemented his draconian War on Drugs and restaffed nearly half of the federal judgeships with appointees who shared his anti–civil rights position. By his second term, Reagan's anti–civil rights agenda found more success in the Supreme Court, and the president continued in earnest to eliminate the victories of the civil rights movement, including key voting rights protections won by activists in the 1960s.

On the heels of the Reagan presidency, Hollywood picked up where the president left off in trying to reframe black freedom struggles in the context of a colorblind past. Hollywood produced an unprecedented number of films that inserted fictional white heroes into the center of black freedom struggles. Abolition movies like *Glory* (1989) and *Amistad* (1996) and civil rights dramas like *Mississippi Burning* (1988), *The Long Walk Home* (1989), and *Ghosts of Mississippi* (1996) recast black freedom struggles in American memory as driven by an ethos of colorblind white heroism. With no evidence in the historical record, Hollywood constructed a fictional archive that provided "proof" of a colorblind past in order to justify the colorblind assault on civil rights in the present.

By the middle of the 1990s, colorblindness had won over most Americans, as citizens voted overwhelmingly in favor of colorblind ballot initiatives like California's Proposition 209, which eliminated race-conscious affirmative action programs. The initiative, titled the California Civil Rights Initiative, legally reconstituted racial injustice as overwhelmingly a white issue of "reverse discrimination," thus marking the hegemonic moment in the life of colorblindness. In the wake of Proposition 209 and similar anti–affirmative action bills throughout the country, colorblindness produced an entirely new film genre, as audiences flocked to see "teacher films" like *Dangerous Minds*—released the same year Californians voted on Proposition 209—in which white women rid urban black and Latinx neighborhoods of their "culture of poverty."

Hollywood did not merely reflect the rise of colorblindness; rather, it fundamentally constituted the ideology. As the work of scholars like Michael Rogin, Jacqueline Najuma Stewart, and Ed Guerrero demonstrate, since its inception, Hollywood movies have actively shaped white supremacy and antiblackness. In his seminal work, *Framing Blackness: The African American Image in Film*, Guerrero writes "In almost every instance, the representation of black people on the commercial screen has amounted to one grand, multifaceted illusion. For blacks have been subordinated, marginalized, positioned, and devalued in every possible manner *to glorify and relentlessly hold in place* the white-dominated symbolic order and racial hierarchy of American society [emphasis added]."[6] The work of film (and visual representation more generally) reproduces the very racialized categories it reveals. As Stuart Hall has noted, "The very obviousness of the visibility of race convinces me that it functions as a signifying system, as a text we can read."[7] And while the social construction of race may not require its visual manifestation, visual mediums like photography and film "*produced* race as a visualizable fact."[8] In this regard, colorblindness works less to inhibit our ability to "see" race than it does to prohibit the discussion, analysis, study, or legislation of matters of racial inequality. The excommunication of race from public discourse and policy, however, did little to obstruct our ability to see racialized bodies represented and racial discourse reproduced on-screen. The visual medium of film, and Hollywood in particular, crafted the political ideology of colorblindness by offering a key site where white audiences could confront racial conflict, assuage racial anxieties, and satisfy racially charged anger without vocalizing the race-conscious attitudes most would deem offensive at a moment when civil rights opponents were expunging race-conscious rhetoric from public discourse. Beginning in the 1970s, film enabled audiences to visualize what they could no longer vocalize.

Movies mythologized colorblindness. Barthes describes myth as "a type of speech," "a system of communication," and "a mode of signification" that "transforms history into nature."[9] Audiences "consume myth innocently" because they do not "see it as a semiological system but as an inductive one." "Any semiological system," according to Barthes, "is a system of values; now, the myth-consumer takes the signification for a system of facts: myth is read as a factual system, whereas it is but a semiological system."[10] Moreover, I draw my contention regarding Hollywood's mythologizing function from Will Wright, who argues in his book on the Western that through movies, "the [Western] myth has become part of the cultural language by which America understands itself."[11] Furthermore, according to Wright, the structure of myth is fluid because "within each period the structure of the myth corresponds to the conceptual needs of social and self-understanding required by the dominant social institutions of that period; the historical changes in the structure of the myth correspond to the changes in the structure of those dominant institutions."[12] With the collapse of de jure racial discrimination in the 1960s, white supremacy had to be rearticulated along race-neutral lines. Hollywood proved fundamental in sorting out these "conceptual needs" in the aftermath of the civil rights movement.

My insistence of the centrality of Hollywood in the articulation of colorblindness is the primary scholarly contribution of this book. Extant scholarship on colorblindness falls within three broad categories. The crucial work of scholars like Ian Haney López, Eduardo Bonilla-Silva, and Michelle Alexander reveal the enduring influence of white supremacy despite efforts to eradicate overtly racist rhetoric and attitudes from public discourse and the law.[13] Second, social historians of the New Right, like Matthew Lassiter and Kevin Kruse, emphasize the suburban origins of colorblindness in the 1970s.[14] Third, recent texts by Sarah Nilsen and Sarah E. Turner and Catherine Squires have begun to explore colorblind aesthetics and representations in film and television, revealing how colorblind and "post-racial" ideologies work in fluid and often contradictory ways.[15] This book links the sociopolitical project of colorblindness to the cultural and aesthetic one, emphasizing the symbiotic relationship between the two. By emphasizing the role of Hollywood, *White Balance* reveals how the reassertion of white supremacy under the mantle of colorblindness was not merely the product of white backlash. Instead, colorblindness marks a new racial formation that united white liberals and conservatives and the "national popular" behind their "possessive investment in whiteness."[16]

The title of this book, *White Balance*, plays on the photography term of the same name. White balancing sets the proper color temperature of a film or video camera and ensures that the colors of the images appear natural. The process involves filming a pure white image and adjusting the camera accordingly. White balancing, in other words, dictates how the rest of the color spectrum appears to spectators. I find this concept useful for understanding how Hollywood shaped colorblind racial ideology in two ways. First, white balancing speaks to the ways in which movie cameras actively shape how we see color—or, in this case, racialized bodies. Second, and perhaps more importantly, white, or whiteness, was always at the center of this process. In the post–civil rights era, Hollywood movie cameras shaped colorblind ideology, undermined civil rights, and reinforced white supremacy.

The emergence of colorblindness in the decades following the civil rights movement constituted what Michael Omi and Howard Winant define as a "racial formation." Omi and Winant define racial formations as "the sociohistorical process by which racial categories are created, inhabited, transformed, and destroyed. . . . Racial formation is a process of historically situated *projects* in which human bodies and social structures are represented and organized."[17] Moreover, racial formations are constructed through the process of articulation. While the term can mean "to utter, to speak forth, to be articulate," in this case, Hall uses *articulation* in the English sense, as in

an "articulated" lorry (truck): a lorry where the front (cab) and back (trailer) can, but need not necessarily, be connected to one another. The two parts are connected to each other, but through a specific linkage, that can be broken. An articulation is thus the form of the connection that *can* make a unity of two different elements. It is a linkage which is not necessary, determined, absolute and essential for all time. . . . So the so-called "unity" of a discourse is really the articulation of different, distinct elements which can be re-articulated in different ways because they have no necessary "belongingness." The "unity" which matters is a linkage between that articulated discourse and the social forces with which it can, under certain historical conditions, but need not necessarily, be connected.[18]

This second definition reveals two key features of ideology. First, that the cohesion of the individual features of an ideology are arbitrary—they have no connection to one another but come to be connected under "certain historical conditions." And second, that given their arbitrariness, ideologies are not essential and are therefore mutable. Thus, the decades after the civil rights movement resulted in the adaptation and rearticulation of white supremacy as the new racial formation of colorblindness.

The struggle over the articulation of ideology then becomes a struggle for what Antonio Gramsci called *hegemony,* or "common sense." As Hall explains, Gramsci defined common sense as the moment "when and where philosophical currents enter into, modify and transform the practical, everyday consciousness or popular thought of the masses."[19] Hall goes on to say that common sense is not coherent but fragmented, and its importance lies in the fact that "it is the already formed and 'taken-for-granted' terrain, on which more coherent ideologies and philosophies must contend for mastery; the ground which new conceptions of the world must take into account, contest and transform, if they are to . . . become historically effective."[20] A shift in hegemony occurs, then, at the point in which common sense changes.

In their work *Camera Politica: The Politics and Ideology of Contemporary Hollywood Film,* film scholars Michael Ryan and Douglas Kellner bring together the relationship between film and larger questions of racial formation, ideology, articulation, and hegemony through what they call "discursive transcoding." "Films transcode discourses of social life," they write, "into cinematic narratives. Rather than reflect a reality external to the film medium, films execute a transfer from one discursive field to another. As a result, films themselves become part of that broader cultural system of representations that construct social reality. That construction occurs in part through the internalization of representations." Thus, the "internalization" of cultural representations means that movies "play an important role in determining how social reality will be constructed."[21] Therefore, "discursive transcoding," as the link between film and racial formations, provides the key theoretical framework for how I read cinematic representations as historical evidence of racial formation.

White Balance examines the central role of Hollywood in the articulation and hegemonic rise of the racial formation of colorblindness, from its emergence as a coherent racial ideology in the years after the civil rights movement to its dominant influence in social policy in the 1990s. Beginning in the second half of the 1970s, Hollywood developed its own set of colorblind narratives and tropes. Moreover, Hollywood was not only central to the articulation of the ideology; it also depended on colorblind themes to attract audiences to theaters in the post–civil rights era. The research for this book draws heavily on the archival production histories of the films examined in these pages. I also closely read the films themselves in order to illuminate the synergy between the politics on-screen and off, and how the visual politics of the cinema shaped the politics outside theaters. Furthermore, I draw substantially on the use of the term *colorblind* to discuss matters of race in major newspapers, including the *New York Times*, the *Washington Post*, the *Los Angeles Times*, and the *Wall Street Journal*. I use newspapers as a site of public discourse to uncover the evolving logic of colorblind rhetoric from the 1970s through the 1990s. The reportage of popular newspapers, as well as their op-ed pages and letters to their editorial boards, enables the examination of how political leaders, public intellectuals, and ordinary Americans used colorblind rhetoric, and to what political ends.

This book is organized into six chapters that cover the period from the 1970s to the mid-1990s. Chapter 1 traces the emergence of colorblindness from a collection of post–civil rights utterances in the late 1960s to the beginning of its coherence in the early 1970s. Unlike its previous iterations, the colorblind rhetoric of the 1970s borrowed the language of the civil rights movement to mobilize against many of its gains. Yet colorblindness was preceded by and built on an ethos of anti-liberalism that emerged in the early years of the decade. In many ways, colorblindness was positioned as the solution to the problem of government overreach in the latter half of the decade. Through an analysis of the films *Dirty Harry* (1971) and *Coffy* (1973), I demonstrate how Hollywood developed new narrative conventions and refashioned existing ones that both shaped the antistatism of the first half of the 1970s and prescribed colorblindness as its antidote in the second.

Against the backdrop of the increasing cohesion of the racial ideology of colorblindness, chapter 2 examines the 1974 film *Claudine*. I analyze the film through three lenses. The first is the film's production studio, Third World Cinema, which modeled itself on a vision of civil rights unionism. The second is a close analysis of the film, focusing on how it offered a black nationalist critique of the welfare state, including a direct rebuke of colorblindness. Yet while that critique sought progressive reform, it would, by the end of the 1970s, be co-opted by the New Right to destroy the welfare state and reinforce white supremacy. Finally, the film's marketing catered to colorblind sentiments, thereby contradicting the racial critique of the film.

More importantly, it foreshadowed the trajectory of colorblind ideology. Rather than read these inconsistencies as evidence of the film's shortcomings, I argue that *Claudine* encompasses the swirling contradictions of the early 1970s, as colorblindness was increasingly moving into the mainstream. Therefore, *Claudine* proved fundamental in the articulation of an emerging ideology. In the early 1970s, colorblind hegemony was on the horizon, and we can read the different aspects of this film as evidence of a new racial formation *in process*.

In chapter 3, I trace the articulation of colorblindness around the issues of busing and affirmative action in the years between 1974 and 1978. *Rocky* (1976) highlights the manner in which film can offer race-conscious images and implications to colorblind political discourse. Just as the political struggles over integration produced a coherent colorblind ideology, they also, through *Rocky*, marked the first appearance of Hollywood's colorblind aesthetics. Rocky Balboa was therefore Hollywood's first hero in the age of colorblindness. Chapter 3 also examines the intersection of colorblindness and neoliberalism. Ultimately, I argue that neoliberal thought gained momentum in the 1970s because it offered solutions to both the economic sluggishness of the decade and the problem of excessive government intervention in matters of racial inequality. I examine Milton Friedman and other neoliberal economists' writings on civil rights, which highlight the intersection of neoliberal market logic with the antistatist social politics of colorblindness. I then offer a close analysis of *Blue Collar* (1978), a film about the struggles of three Detroit autoworkers with their corrupt union. *Blue Collar* ultimately marks the destruction of Hollywood's ability to narrate collective struggle, thereby signaling the manner in which Hollywood, a culture industry whose medium is inclined toward narrating the plight of individuals, became integral in cohering and disseminating neoliberal ideology.

Ronald Reagan's first presidential term, the rise of the War on Drugs, and *Rocky III* (1982) serve as the basis for chapter 4. Reagan took office hopeful that he could ban affirmative action and stop school desegregation orders by reframing racial discrimination as an individual rather than a group issue. With this, Reagan's Justice Department developed a politics of colorblind neoliberalism. Reagan also ramped up the War on Drugs, which targeted low-income black communities and relied on resurrecting popular media representations of urban blacks as animalistic criminals in need of discipline and punishment by the state. *Rocky III* engages Reagan's War on Drugs and, in so doing, reveals that although colorblindness in many ways represented a new racial discourse in America—one based in racially neutral language and neoliberal notions of individualism—beginning in the 1980s it increasingly relied on very old tenets of antiblackness.

Alongside a spate of civil rights and slavery dramas produced in the late 1980s and 1990s—most notably *Glory* (1989), *The Long Walk Home* (1990), *Forrest Gump* (1994), and *Amistad* (1997)—the penultimate chapter considers the evolution of the Reagan administration's position on the federal Martin Luther King Jr. holiday. In one sense, chapter 5 aims to deepen our understanding of movies commonly labeled "white savior" films. While such a framework is useful in certain regards, white savior critiques often miss the deep historical context and intricate role Hollywood has played in anti–civil rights maneuverings. Beginning in the latter half of the 1980s, both Reagan and the movies frequently represented civil rights and abolition as driven by a colorblind white ethos. For Reagan, the efficacy of this position was clear; for Hollywood, perhaps less so. Yet together, the reimagination of colorblind black freedom struggles by both factions proved integral to the growing influence of colorblindness, which had become and would continue to be the driving force behind the dismantling of key civil rights programs in the post–civil rights era. As colorblindness became increasingly influential, Hollywood performed the vital task of reimagining an American past in which colorblind white heroes were at the center and colorblindness was responsible for the abolition of slavery and the victories of the civil rights movement. Reimagining the historical record, of course, is as old as Hollywood itself. As Michael Rogin notes, in *The Birth of a Nation*, director D. W. Griffith—along with Thomas Dixon, who wrote the novel on which the film is based, and then-president Woodrow Wilson, who enthusiastically endorsed the film—offered the film "as the screen memory, in both meanings of the term, through which Americans were to understand their collective past and enact their future."[22] I argue that the connections between Hollywood and the White House were as strong in the Reagan years as they were in the Wilson ones. Like President Reagan, Hollywood dramatizations of black freedom struggles in the late 1980s and 1990s positioned colorblindness as an enduring quality of American whiteness and insisted that colorblind logic should inform the country's legislative future.

The final chapter examines teacher films, those movies in which a (typically) suburban white woman accepts a job teaching students of color in low-income urban neighborhoods. Although the late 1980s and 1990s certainly do not mark the first instances of teachers as protagonists in American cinema, it was during these years that films centered around white teachers and their inner-city nonwhite pupils became increasingly popular and developed specific themes and tropes that were inherently informed by the logic of colorblindness. I situate my analysis of this genre, most notably the 1995 film *Dangerous Minds*, within the context of the War on Drugs, urban blight, the dismantling of affirmative action, and, most importantly, neoliberal educational reform in arguing that colorblindness ultimately produced entirely new film genres that are inherently colorblind.

In this book, I make three arguments. First, colorblindness is the racial project of neoliberalism. The 1970s were characterized by an antigovernment ethos that extended across racial and political lines, used by neoconservatives in the 1970s to attack issues like affirmative action and busing as part of a movement intent on dismantling the welfare state. Out of these struggles emerged a neoliberal notion of individual colorblind freedom that neoconservatives, beginning in the mid-1970s, successfully sold as the antidote to the reverse discrimination of government mandated group rights. The growing popularity of neoliberal economics in the 1970s was not merely the result of the seeming failure of Keynesianism to cure stagflation. Rather, the mounting opposition to the "overreach" of the federal government in terms of busing and affirmative action was fundamental in building the appeal of a return to uncompromising laissez-faire economics.

Second, colorblindness, although post racial in theory, has served as a politically expedient tool for whites to realign and reconstitute white supremacy in the post–civil rights era. Beginning in the late 1970s, whites increasingly used colorblind discourse to attack race-conscious programs intended to promote racial equality. This was a multifaceted political project that linked Republicans to Democrats, "ordinary" Americans to Nobel Prize–winning economists, and the White House to Hollywood. Together, these efforts only exacerbated racial inequality.

Third, *White Balance* asserts that film served as a key battleground for the culture wars out of which the ideology of colorblindness formed. Just as colorblindness needed film to form its cultural cohesion, film needed colorblindness to reinvent itself in the desperate economic times of the post-classical era. In the wake of the civil rights movement, movies capitalized on the volatile racial, social, and economic struggles that shaped colorblindness and have continued to appeal to colorblind sentiments for profit. By the end of the 1980s, Hollywood had taken over the project begun in the

Reagan White House of imagining colorblind white heroes at the center of historic black freedom struggles—abolition and civil rights, specifically. And by the 1990s, an entirely new colorblind film genre emerged at the moment when colorblind ballot initiatives began to roll back civil rights policies.

It is to those concerns that I now turn.

1 The Law Is Crazy!

Antistatism and the Emergence of Colorblindness in the Early 1970s

On the steps of the Lincoln Memorial in August 1963, nearly a decade after the *Brown* decision, Martin Luther King Jr. delivered the seminal address of the civil rights movement. King's "I Have a Dream" speech, told of his dream of a world in which "all men are created equal" and his dream that his "four little children will one day live in a nation where they will not be judged by the color of their skin but by the content of their character."[1] Although King's speech and the efforts of civil rights lawyers drew on the goal of a colorblind nation, they did so in an effort to topple state-sponsored white supremacy. The political motivations behind the use of colorblind rhetoric fundamentally changed in the period after the modern civil rights movement.

It would take more than a decade after King stepped off the dais in the nation's capital before the racial project of colorblindness, which would cherry-pick and distort the post-racial rhetoric of the civil rights movement to mobilize against its very gains, cohered. In the decade or so between King's "I Have a Dream" speech and the emergence of the racial project of colorblindness, many radical political leaders, judges on the nation's highest court, and ordinary Americans scoffed at the notion of a colorblind society. Stokely Carmichael (later known as Kwame Ture)—Black Power leader and head of the Student Nonviolent Coordinating Committee—had grown critical of the colorblind politics of the civil rights era that lingered as the decade ended. As he and Charles V. Hamilton note in their renowned *Black Power: The Politics of Liberation*, "While color blindness *may* be a sound goal ultimately, we must recognize that race is an overwhelming fact of life in this historical period. There is no black man in this country who can live 'simply as a man.'"[2] As late as October 1971, the Supreme Court refused to consider challenges to Nixon's Philadelphia Plan, a program begun in 1969 requiring contractors to hire a certain percentage of nonwhite workers for federally financed building projects, on the grounds that it "violated the concept of a color-blind constitution."[3] Further, many of those who agreed with colorblindness in theory defended affirmative action policies like the Philadelphia Plan as necessary to produce a colorblind future.[4]

Those, on the other hand, who did espouse colorblind rhetoric did so to advance an array of positions across the political spectrum. Eldridge Cleaver, exiled in Algiers in 1969, criticized the black nationalist politics of Kwame Ture in an open letter, stating that suffering is "colorblind" and that suffering people needed a unity based on revolutionary principles rather than skin color.[5] This statement in no way meant Cleaver was an advocate of a colorblind approach to the pursuit of racial justice. Nevertheless, his willingness to invoke the term "colorblind" in 1969 reveals that in the late 1960s, colorblind discourse had not yet coalesced, and colorblind rhetoric had yet to become the rhetorical cudgel of white backlash politics. On the other end of the political spectrum, one year after Cleaver's letter, southern lawyers on the right mobilized the *Brown* decision's language of colorblindness to try to undo court-ordered busing mandates, which were ordered in over half of the nation's one hundred largest school districts and would draw considerable outrage by the mid-1970s.[6] And somewhere in the middle, in January 1971, South Carolina governor John C. West, a moderate Democrat, promised racial minorities "no special status other than full-fledged responsibility in a government that is totally color-blind."[7] There was, in other words, significant ideological diversity in the deployment of colorblind rhetoric in the early 1970s.

However, there was also a growing contingent of whites who increasingly adopted the moderate language of South Carolina's governor as they became sympathetic to the political agenda of what would become known as the "white backlash" of the 1970s. A July 1972 letter written to the editors of the *New York Times* by a man named David B. Simpson chastised "self-proclaimed 'liberals'" like then presidential candidate George McGovern for their support of affirmative action programs. Simpson characterized affirmative action as "an absolute betrayal of the principle that our Constitution and our political process is, should be and is intended to be 'color blind' in the fullest sense." Simpson went so far as to call McGovern a "racist" for his intention to appoint blacks to the Supreme Court.[8] Although typically not as hostile as Simpson, numerous letters decrying affirmative action programs appeared in newspapers like the *New York Times* beginning in the late 1960s. One man wrote a letter in 1969 denouncing the "racial quota system" that was "coming into fashion." After qualifying the letter by insisting that he has "tried to help eliminate racial discrimination," he cited Justice John Marshall Harlan's sole *Plessy v. Ferguson* dissent—which stated that the Constitution is "colorblind"—to argue that the so-called racial quota systems erected in the aftermath of the civil rights movement were no less unconstitutional than the Jim Crow laws that followed the *Plessy* decision.[9] The man's rhetorical commitment to civil rights and need to distinguish his opposition to policies benefiting blacks from prejudicial attitudes toward them illustrates an important development in the white backlash discourse in the post–civil rights era.[10]

The increasing investment in colorblindness in the early 1970s arose amid a widespread ethos of antistatism.[11] By "antistatism," I refer to an acute skepticism of, or outright hostility to, government—a rampant belief in the 1970s that the government was not only incapable of alleviating social inequities but in fact to blame for the problems Americans faced. Broadly speaking, events in the 1960s, like civil rights activists' push for federal legislation to dismantle Jim Crow segregation and Lyndon Johnson's "Great Society," demonstrated some faith among the American public in the government's ability to address racial inequality. By the end of the 1970s, however, much of the country—black, white, conservative, liberal—not only distrusted the government's capacity to promote racial progress but cited the government as the cause of heightened racial tension. I use "antistatism" to define this ethos of the decade, which extended far beyond the issue of race. Interestingly, this antistatist ethos, especially among conservatives, is often contradictory. On the one hand, it holds that the state must be as small as possible—and ever shrinking—in terms of regulating commerce and protecting the civil rights of individuals and the environment. On the other hand, it accepts that the state can be monstrously big when it comes to warfare, policing, and corporate subsidies. Nonetheless, in the early 1970s, black, white, left, right, center, liberal, conservative, radical, or otherwise believed that whatever their issues were, and no matter how contradictory they were to those of their political opponents, the government was somehow to blame. On the left, Black Power organizations crafted black nationalist politics to address the inadequacies of the civil rights movement and widespread police brutality and oppression at the hands of the state.[12] On the right, the issue of race continued to fuel white backlash against the welfare state.

As the 1970s dawned, the contradictory diagnoses of the government's exploitative practices and inability to alleviate suffering mirrored the ideological diversity of colorblind rhetoric. When dealing with issues of race, activists, politicians, and suburban homemakers across the political spectrum often gave voice to their political agenda by linking colorblindness and antistatism. Some Black Power advocates linked the discourses to promote racial inclusivity in the battle for racial justice, while conservatives turned to colorblind language to defend their opposition to civil rights programs against charges of bigotry and to insist that government overreach was the sole motivator of their opposition.

In this political climate, film provided a pivotal arena in which to dramatize and make sense of the divergent discourses of colorblindness and antistatism. The early 1970s coincided with the era of "New Hollywood."[13] A series of antitrust rulings by the Supreme Court, combined with television's increasing siphoning of movie audiences, brought the Hollywood studio system, which had made movies the country's largest mass culture industry for nearly four decades, to its knees by the mid-1960s. By the 1970s, the film industry saw its average weekly box-office receipts sink to their lowest mark ever—$15.8 million in 1971, compared to a post–World War II high of $90 million.[14] The dire economic conditions produced by the forced disintegration of the Hollywood studio system beginning after World War II made Hollywood studios far more willing to explore new subject matter and push the formal boundaries of the classical era in an effort to remain economically viable.

The economic strife of the movie business created the conditions for the emergence of an "American Film Renaissance." As Peter Biskind writes, led by a new generation of American filmmakers that included Martin Scorsese, Francis Ford Coppola, and Robert Altman, "New Hollywood was a movement intended to cut film free of its evil twin, commerce, enabling it to fly high through the thin air of art."[15] On the other hand, dwindling profits made Hollywood producers desperate and therefore more willing to explore controversial material—as long as it brought audiences into theaters. Race was one such subject. The historical timing of the more or less concurrent collapse of the Hollywood studio system and Jim Crow enabled film to shape racial discourse in an unprecedented fashion in the post–civil rights era. As Derek Nystrom argues, while New Hollywood is typically understood as a renaissance of American art cinema, the movement was in fact rooted in exploitation films.[16] The enormous amount of exploitation films, B movies, and avant-garde cinema created new opportunities for African Americans, who constituted a disproportionately large share of movie audiences, to appear both in front of and behind the camera. Most importantly, the economic uncertainty of the business in the late 1960s and early 1970s enabled filmmakers to make films that explored the nascent discourses of colorblindness and antistatism, which audiences themselves were trying to make sense of.

This chapter examines the intersection of colorblindness and antistatism in New Hollywood exploitation films of the early 1970s. Focusing on *Dirty Harry* (1971) and *Coffy* (1973), I argue not only that the disintegration of the Hollywood studio system offered greater opportunities for the production of films dealing explicitly with race but also that the success of New Hollywood relied in part on its ability to function as a laboratory for the development of colorblind ideology. The economic distress in which the movie industry found itself pushed it to produce films that would appeal to different communities in order to avoid bankruptcy. On the one hand, this led to the emergence of genres like blaxploitation; on the other hand, appealing to the increasingly mainstream white backlash politics of the 1970s through the rhetoric of colorblindness became a reliable revenue stream for Hollywood. While scholars appropriately credit the film industry's resurgence in the mid-1970s largely to the rise of the blockbuster, one cannot ignore that a substantial amount of Hollywood's profits derived from movies dealing explicitly with race.[17] These films helped shape the logic of colorblindness, forming the necessary cultural cohesion for the ideology long before its social or legal one.

Most importantly, this chapter charts the emergence of what I call Hollywood's "colorblind aesthetics." Both *Coffy* and *Dirty Harry* make deliberate efforts to appeal, rhetorically, to colorblind sentiment. Yet both films are visually saturated with race. The racialized bodies on screen subvert any shallow appeals to post-raciality. This is not a failure on these films' part, as it is precisely how colorblindness functions. This dynamic, in which race-conscious rhetoric is scrubbed from the script, while racialized bodies abound on the screen, is the central component of Hollywood's colorblind aesthetics and is the modus operandi of colorblind ideology.

What follows are close examinations of *Dirty Harry* and *Coffy*—two films from the early 1970s. While others have written about the right wing, racist, and sexist politics of *Dirty Harry*, I am interested in the film's yoking of antistatism and colorblindness.[18] The vast literature on blaxploitation has yet to consider a film like *Coffy* in this context.[19] Together, these films, similar in genre but marketed to vastly different audiences, reveal the disparate ends colorblind rhetoric served in the first half of the 1970s. Both appealed to emerging colorblind sentiments and helped shape the antistatist ethos of the early decade while reinforcing popular and dehumanizing notions of blackness. That ethos was a fundamental precondition for the emergence of colorblindness; it provided the necessary foundation on which colorblindness would gain traction in the ensuing years. Positioning the ideology as a neoliberal solution to the problems of the invasive liberal welfare state on-screen in the early 1970s was a pivotal step in the emergence of the racial project of colorblindness. While the discourse lacks the coherence it would develop in the latter half of the decade, the divergent deployments of colorblindness on and off the silver screen illustrate the appeal of colorblindness long before the issues of affirmative action and busing fully moved to the forefront of American politics.

"Harry Hates Everybody"

Released in December 1971, *Dirty Harry* follows a rogue San Francisco Police Department inspector named Harry Callahan on his vigilante pursuit of an elusive serial killer known as Scorpio, loosely based on San Francisco's real-life Zodiac Killer. The detective drama serves as a metaphor for the larger national political war between the New Left and the silent majority, or what would eventually become the New Right. Over the course of the film, Callahan enacts revenge on the entire New Left and the legal system that coddles them in pursuit of the "hippie" serial-killer Scorpio. The lionization of Callahan, therefore, is indicative of a country that was lurching rightward in the early 1970s. *Dirty Harry*'s malevolent New Left was formed through a sacrilegious alliance between liberal politicians, judges, and hippies. The "threat" to civilization in this film is less about individual leftist groups than about the support their coalition receives from the state.

The white backlash politics embodied by Callahan are the product of a multitude of progressive movements in the late 1960s in places like Berkeley, Chicago, and New York City: the often violent antiwar protests; student radical groups like the Youth International Party telling young people to "kill [their] parents"; the Weather Underground blowing up bombs in Manhattan's Greenwich Village in 1970; the armed conflicts between black nationalists and police in places like San Francisco, Oakland, Houston, and Chicago; and the riots between police and gay rights activists at Stonewall in 1969.[20] The original script for *Dirty Harry* sets the action in New York City, home of the Stonewall Inn, but San Francisco—the epicenter of 1960s counterculture—proved too enticing to director Don Siegel and the backlash aesthetics he sought.

Race plays an essential role in this confederation and in the film as a whole. Many reviewers criticized the film's racism upon its release. Vincent Canby took particular issue with the bank-robbery scene in which Callahan brazenly kills several black nationalist types.[21] In fact, throughout the film one finds consistent evidence of Harry's antiblack bigotry. A subtle but significant reference lies in one of the film's first scenes, in which Harry meets with the mayor of San Francisco. After assigning Callahan the Scorpio case, the mayor warns, "I don't want any more trouble like you had last year in the Fillmore district, understand? That's my policy." In the period after World War II, San Francisco's Fillmore district served as the heart of the city's black community. As hundreds of thousands of African Americans fled the racial violence of the Jim Crow south and moved to the West Coast in search of economic opportunity, the overwhelming majority of those that landed in San Francisco settled in the Fillmore district and other Western Addition enclaves as well as Japantown. While these new black San Franciscans may have otherwise struggled to find vacant apartments in the densely populated city by the Bay, the Fillmore and its surrounding neighborhoods were awash with vacancies, as the previous Japanese American tenants found themselves forcibly interned in the country's interior for the duration of the war. This new black population helped create a vibrant business and cultural enclave, which former mayor Willie Brown dubbed a "Harlem of the West." However, beginning in the 1960s, the impious combination of urban renewal and gentrification began forcing out the primarily working-class black residents of the Fillmore, earning the district the nickname "the No More." By 2010, the black population of the district was half that of 1960.[22] Thus, while neither the mayor nor Callahan ever identifies the racial identity of the victim (or victims) Harry gunned down in the Fillmore, the insinuation is clear. Callahan, in other words, has a history of legally dubious, if not murderous, interactions with San Francisco's black community.

If one goes along with this assumption, then the group of black bank robbers Callahan guns down in the next scene are not the first African Americans to find themselves on the wrong side of Callahan's .44 Magnum. Additionally, Callahan's exchange with the mayor immediately establishes an antagonistic relationship between Callahan and both the mayor's office (i.e., the state) and the city's black community. Moreover, as with the "trouble" in Callahan's past, there is no racial identification of the bank robbers. Callahan, in fact, utters only a single word—"Halt!"—prior to his iconic "Do I feel lucky?" monologue. The scene is therefore colorblind in one sense, as it makes no mention of race. Yet just as the history of San Francisco racializes the dynamics of Harry's previous "trouble," the montage of a white man with "the most powerful handgun in the world" gunning down three black

Harry Callahan (Clint Eastwood) points his .44 Magnum at a group of black bank robbers.

men, killing two of them, racializes the scene's construction of criminality and those who combat it.

The entire shoot-out sequence sets up the confrontation at the scene's conclusion. Callahan stands over the only perpetrator left alive, pointing a gun down at him and almost directly into the camera before telling him, "You've got to ask yourself one question, Do I feel lucky?" The payoff of the entire sequence for the audience, then, is to have a white police officer kill two black men, wound a third, and render him helpless at the end of the barrel of his gun. Just over a year prior, in a courthouse a short drive across the Golden Gate Bridge, a young Jonathan Jackson, who occasionally worked security for Black Power intellectual Angela Davis, entered the Marin County courthouse with three guns, freed several prisoners from their holding cell, and took a number of people hostage in an attempt to get the Soledad Brothers—three black men, including his brother, black revolutionary and intellectual George Jackson—freed from prison. The resulting shoot-out left Jonathan Jackson, two of the prisoners, and the white judge dead. Less than three years before the Marin County courthouse incident, on the other side of the San Francisco Bay, Black Panther leader Huey Newton was involved in a shoot-out with police that left a white officer dead. Harry's shoot-out, coming on the heels of two high-profile incidents in the same metropolis that left a white judge and a white law enforcement officer dead, serves as filmic revenge for a white audience moving rightward politically that would, the following year, reelect the "law and order" president Richard Nixon.

There are other moments in the film that reveal the nuances of Callahan's racial attitudes and speak to the complexity of the post–civil rights racial climate into which the film debuted. After his boss assigns Callahan a new Latino partner, Chico Gonzales, Gonzales, familiar with Callahan's prejudices, asks Callahan why he hates Hispanics, to which a white officer responds, "Harry hates everybody: limeys, micks, hebes, dagos, niggers, honkeys, chinks, you name it." Gonzales follows up with, "How about Mexicans?" and Callahan answers, "Especially spics," and then winks at the other officer, a gesture Gonzales does not see. Although Callahan's wink suggests that the scene may be little more than a comedic break—that Callahan is kidding and merely goading his new partner—I argue otherwise. Callahan's portrayal as an equal opportunity bigot distinguishes him from Hollywood's other backlash heroes of the early 1970s, who proudly wear their antiblack bigotry. Take, for example, the title character of John Avildsen's 1970 film *Joe*, about a white-collar bigot who teams up with an Upper East Side plutocrat to kill a commune full of "hippies."[23] Joe first appears on-screen ranting about "niggers" and "welfare": "All you gotta do is act black and the money rolls in," he opines.[24] Callahan, on the other hand, hates everybody. One could even argue that his hatred is ultimately not about race, as white ethnic slurs are included in his laundry list of loathing, but about a general disdain for the citizenry of San Francisco, a population that had proven to be one of the country's most progressive and socially liberal over the previous century.[25] In either case, we see, as in the bank-robbery scene, a moment that is at once colorblind and yet totally reliant on race consciousness.

More significantly, the only person we ever see Callahan act kindly toward is his black doctor, whom he visits immediately after his shoot-out with the black bank robbers. This small detail further distinguishes Callahan from other backlash heroes in films like *Joe*. Callahan is as violently right wing and hateful of liberals as Joe, but his interaction with his black doctor deliberately makes it difficult to characterize Callahan's shoot-out with the group of black bank robbers as motivated purely by antiblack bigotry. During his doctor's visit, the doctor even remarks, "Us Potrero Hill boys have to stick together," suggesting both that Callahan is not racist and, more importantly, that neighborhood allegiances supersede racial ones. The fact that Callahan and his doctor grew up in the working-class Potrero Hill neighborhood of the 1930s and 1940s is important when considered in contrast to the film's other representations of working-class or poor blacks in its reference to the Fillmore district and the Black Panther–like bank rob-

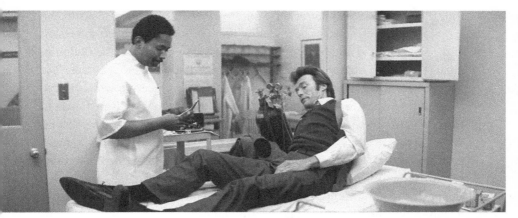

Harry's black friend (unnamed), a doctor he grew up with in the Potrero Hill neighborhood of San Francisco.

bers.[26] The class similarities between the black doctor and the black bank robbers imply that the divergent lives the black characters lead in this film are largely if not entirely the result of personal choice, thereby reaffirming "bootstraps" ideology and belying systemic racism. More specifically, this implication echoes the newly emergent "culture of poverty" thesis of the late 1960s in which sociologists and politicians like Daniel Patrick Moynihan argued that the urban black poor suffered not from racism but from a "pathological" culture that liberal social policies like welfare only exacerbate, and that black mothers pass these inferior "traits" to their offspring.[27] The allusion to the similar class backgrounds of the white inspector, the black doctor, and the black criminals in *Dirty Harry* makes a diagnosis of racial prejudice difficult, suggesting that class may be the more salient distinction, and "cultural values" rather than race may play a more influential role in socioeconomic (im)mobility.

A careful examination of the film's production history adds further insight into the manner in which the film makes deliberate efforts to safeguard its protagonist from charges of bigotry. A February 1971 version of the script, written only ten months before the film's release, describes the doctor merely as a "nameless intern," without any mention of his race. Furthermore, the "Us Potrero Hill boys" line does not appear in this *or* the final version of the script, nor does any other dialogue that would imply that the two were friends or that the doctor is black. The early script does introduce the doctor's more limited dialogue with Callahan as "speaking to a familiar customer," but the implication is not that the two are friends but that they know each other as a result of Callahan's frequent visits to the hospital due to his reckless behavior on the job. Similarly, the final version of the script makes no mention of the doctor's race or that he and Callahan are old friends.[28] Furthermore, the February version of the script does not contain the "Harry hates everybody" line from the scene in which Harry meets his new partner.[29] It appears, therefore, that the friendship between Harry and his doctor, the race-conscious casting of the doctor as black, and dialogue that occludes charges of bigotry and positions neighborhood as a stronger bond than race were all late additions to the film. These decisions reveal the manner in which the filmmakers—be it director Don Siegel, screenwriter John Milius, or star Clint Eastwood himself—actively sought to soften the perception of Callahan's racial politics among viewers in minor scenes throughout the film.

Moreover, the 1971 draft assigns Callahan's Latino partner, Chico Gonzales, an entirely different backstory. In the film, Gonzales and Callahan meet each other for the first time when their sergeant assigns them as partners (although Gonzales is already familiar with Callahan's "Dirty" reputation). However, in the 1971 draft, the same one that identifies the black doctor as a "nameless intern," Gonzales and Callahan have a prior history. "Don't I know you?" Callahan asks upon meeting Gonzales. His new partner responds by explaining that on a street corner ten years ago Harry broke up a gang fight, in which he spanked one of the gangsters. Gonzales reveals that he received the spanking but then credits Harry for putting him on the "right path."[30] Perhaps the filmmakers believed that this backstory's anecdotal evidence of Callahan's positive effect on the life of a young Latino man was outweighed by the act of spanking—yet another example of Harry's physical assault of people of color. While it is difficult to determine, it is possible that the elimination of this version of Gonzales's backstory and the addition of the friendship between Callahan and his black doctor were connected. Whether or not that was the case, the edits to Gonzales's backstory between the script and the film, along with the edits that transformed the "nameless intern" to Callahan's black friend, function to soften Callahan's racial prejudice.

Callahan's black doctor-friend, along with his Latino partner, transform the film into an interracial "buddy" picture, like *The Defiant Ones* (1958) and *In the Heat of the Night* (1967). Moreover, the "friend of color," which functions to offer purported proof of white innocence, is an old racist trope dating back to at least *Huckleberry Finn*. As film scholar Donald Bogle notes, Sidney Poitier, in films like *The Defiant Ones* and *Guess Who's Coming to Dinner,*

Harry and his Latino partner, Chico Gonzales.

"was the model integrationist hero." "In all his films," Bogle continues, "he was educated and intelligent. He spoke proper English, dressed conservatively, and had the best of table manners. For the mass white audience, Sidney Poitier was a black man who had met their standards." James Baldwin, writing about the contradiction between white audiences' desire for images of black respectability vis-à-vis Poitier's roles and those of the burgeoning Black Power and black arts movements, which sought very different representations of black life, wrote, "White Americans appear to be under the compulsion to dream, whereas black Americans are under the compulsion to awaken."[31] The doctor's function here is not, as was typically the case, to allay white anxiety about black masculinity but to ease heightened white fear of accusations of bigotry in the years immediately following the civil rights movement. In other words, Callahan is not racist because we can clearly see that his best friend is black. The ability of the audience to *see* the doctor's black body—and the race-conscious visual politics of the film, more broadly—is essential to the colorblind racial politics of Callahan and the colorblind aesthetics in this film. According to film historian Ed Guerrero, the buddy films of the 1960s would be reconstituted in the 1980s as buddy-cop films, most notably starring Eddie Murphy. The interracial partnership between Callahan and Gonzales prefigures the 1980s "buddy formula," which, according to Guerrero, "reveals all the strategies by which the industry contains and controls the black filmic image and conforms it to white expectations."[32] The "black buddy" film not only contains black bodies and conforms them to white expectations but in fact contains and conforms them to white desire. *Dirty Harry*, therefore, combines the buddy roles of the 1960s and 1980s: the black doctor plays the Sidney Poitier role, and the Latino partner plays the Eddie Murphy role.

That Callahan has a black friend and a Latino partner, along with the film's efforts to sarcastically characterize Callahan as an equal-opportunity bigot in order to undermine the charge, paired with the timing of these revisions in the filmmaking process, suggests that the writers, director, and producers were concerned as to how viewers would characterize Callahan's racial attitudes in the volatile early 1970s. The last-minute choices to give Callahan a black friend and make it clear that he "hates everybody" indicate that the filmmakers wanted to make Callahan appeal to the white racist backlash of the times while also distancing him from its most vitriolic antiblack sentiments. That balance hinges on the colorblind politics of the film's dialogue and the color-conscious politics of the images on-screen.

This tension, moreover, reveals traces of a nascent colorblind ideology that would increasingly gain cohesion both on- and off-screen as the decade unfolded. This is not to say that the criticisms of this film's racial politics or its portrayal of black nationalists, for instance, are misguided. However, I do think that one cannot ignore the subtle but important differences between Callahan and other heroes of early 1970s backlash films that lionize white racists who attack blacks and hippies. While Callahan has much in common with these heroes—hatred of the Left, proclivity for violence, and anti-elitism—he also has important differences. Callahan shares the white-backlash animus toward African Americans, but the subtleties of this hatred distinguish it from the antiblack racism of on-screen characters like Joe and off-screen bigots like George Wallace. If Joe is George Wallace, Callahan is Richard Nixon, stoking the racial fears of the silent majority without violating the rules of post–civil rights standards of respect and decency, won through hard-fought battles by civil rights activists.

These distinctions reveal the emergence of efforts both on-screen and off to use civil rights–friendly discourse in the interest of backlash politics aimed at undoing the very gains of the movement from which the rhetoric is borrowed. The racial politics of Harry Callahan are complex. On the one hand, they are often explicitly race conscious, yet Callahan's moments of boorish racial impropriety ultimately work to frame the film's protagonist as racially unbiased, if not exactly colorblind. The antihero Callahan, therefore, embodies the emerging white conservative backlash, a backlash that would have to learn to frame its racial anger in a colorblind fashion in order to gain supporters as the decade progressed.

"The Law Is Crazy!"

Equally important to the nuanced racial politics of Harry Callahan is the film's uncompromising acrimony for the state. From its opening frame, *Dirty Harry* aligns itself with the white backlash politics of the late 1960s and early 1970s. The movie begins with a shot of the marble inscription in the lobby of San Francisco's Hall of Justice, which reads, "In tribute to the Police Officers of San Francisco who gave their lives in the line of duty." The camera then pans upward to an image of a San Francisco police shield before scrolling downward through the inscribed names of slain officers, while the shield remains in the center of the frame, double exposed behind the officers' names. At the end of a decade awash with reprehensible police actions—police dogs and fire hoses in Birmingham, cops murdering civilians in Watts and Newark, officers beating antiwar demonstrators during the 1968 Democratic Convention in Chicago—police were arguably the biggest enemy of the New Left.[33] Cops were a symbol to many of how repressive the U.S. government had become, especially to African Americans, whose long history of suffering under police brutality only intensified during the 1960s.[34] *Bullitt*, a 1968 film centered around another San Francisco cop, Frank Bullitt, ends much as *Dirty Harry* begins—with a shot of a bumper sticker that reads "Support Your Local Police."[35] However, the villains of the civil rights movement are the heroes of *Dirty Harry*. For the film's star, Clint Eastwood, the film is "not about a man who stands for violence. It's about a man who can't understand society tolerating violence."[36] As Eastwood's comments reveal, the film pairs a strident defense of police officers with an equally harsh indictment of a society that "tolerat[es] violence." Eastwood's remarks refer not simply to the liberalization of American social and political life in the 1960s but more specifically to the correlating changes in the legal system, most notably the *Miranda v. Arizona* (1966) decision, which expanded the rights of persons suspected of criminal behavior. John Milius, an uncredited screenwriter of the film, echoes Eastwood's sentiments: "The police seemed helpless to prevent riots. . . . People were angry with a certain erosion of justice . . . erosion of a sense of the law protecting them."[37] Eastwood's and Milius's statements succinctly encapsulate white backlash politics: it was not the police who acted inappropriately in Birmingham, Newark, or Chicago; rather, it was the civil rights protesters, black urban rioters, and antiwar youth who were out of line, all the while enabled by the "liberal" government and courts, which protected the rights of these "criminals."

The sequence of scenes surrounding the capture but eventual release of the film's villain—Scorpio—highlights the film's critique of the "nanny" state. Near the end of the film, Harry chases Scorpio through Kezar Stadium, where Scorpio lives in the groundskeeper's apartment. After the killer ignores Callahan's orders to halt, Harry shoots Scorpio in the leg, crippling him in the middle of the football field. As he reaches Scorpio, Harry demands the location of his latest kidnapping victim, a young white girl he has buried alive. "Where's the girl?" he repeatedly demands, to which Scorpio responds, "I have the right to a lawyer. . . . I want a lawyer. . . . I have rights!" Harry then presses the heel of his shoe into Scorpio's gunshot wound in an effort to force the killer to reveal the girl's location. In the following scene, the district attorney summons the proud Callahan to his office. Director Don Siegel introduces the office with an establishing shot of the building's exterior, over which the eerie extra-diegetic sound of a sustained minor chord played on a synthesizer foreshadows the injustice about to unfold. Inside, the San Francisco district attorney chastises Harry for his illegal police procedure, which will ultimately force law enforcement to release Scorpio. Using the same language as Scorpio, the DA scolds Callahan: "You're lucky I'm not indicting you for assault with intent to commit murder. . . . Where the hell does it say you've got the right to kick down doors? Torture suspects? Deny medical attention and legal counsel? Where have you been? Does *Escobedo* ring a bell? *Miranda*? I mean, you must have heard of the Fourth Amendment. . . . That man had rights!" *Escobedo* and *Miranda* were 1960s Supreme Court decisions that ensured the rights of accused criminals to legal counsel, thereby raising the standards of admissibility of evidence and testimony acquired during an arrest. The DA continues, "As soon as he's well enough to leave the hospital, he walks." Noticing Callahan's dumbfounded reaction, the DA explains, "The problem is that we don't have any evidence," yet the murder weapon, Scorpio's hunting rifle, rests atop the adjacent table. "Inadmissible as evidence," the DA explains when Harry asks about the rifle. "And who says that?" asks Callahan. "It's the law," the DA answers. "Well, then, the law is crazy!" replies Callahan.

The DA's colleague, Judge Bannerman, a professor of constitutional law at the nearby University of California, Berkeley, validates the DA's claims. Bannerman tells Harry that because he did not obtain a search warrant, all the evidence he acquired, including the murder weapon, is inadmissible. "The suspects rights were violated . . . under the Fourth and Fifth, and probably the Sixth and Fourteenth Amendments," Bannerman concludes. An enraged Harry responds, "And Ann Mary Deacon, what about her rights? I mean, she's raped and left in a hole to die. Who speaks for her?" After lecturing Harry about the illegality of his actions, the judge rises from a couch and stands across the desk from the DA. The film cuts to a low-angle wide shot that sandwiches Harry between the two lawyers. The positioning of Harry in the background and the lawyers in the fore make Harry, the tallest man of the group, appear smaller than the others. He is visually dwarfed by the two state employees in this shot, just as his commitment to justice and ability to apprehend criminals is overpowered by misguided liberal legal technicalities. In this particular case, bureaucratic delays, due process, and the constitutional coddling of the accused prevent law enforcement from prosecuting a known serial killer already in custody. The concern of the DA and judge lies solely in the frivolous laws violated in the process of apprehending the known killer, not with the victims of his horrific crimes. The law and justice are diametrically opposed, according to these scenes, and these lawyers care only about the former. In so doing, they have abandoned the innocent civilians who were subjected to Scorpio's terror. Thus, the law, not the serial murderer Scorpio, is the ultimate villain of this film. Distilling this dynamic in the film, cultural studies scholar Paul Smith writes, in *Dirty Harry*, "civic justice obstructs natural justice."[38]

Callahan must therefore do more than stop a serial killer who rapes, tortures, and murders young women and children. He must also bring down the liberal government and courts, which pass laws that prevent bringing degenerates like Scorpio to justice.[39] Despite Scorpio's obvious guilt, the police release him due to the aforementioned legal technicalities. That Callahan captures Scorpio but then must release him to kill again shows not only that the government coddles suspected criminals (who, in backlash films like *Dirty Harry*, are *always* guilty) but that this coddling threatens the innocent lives of white girls and thereby threatens the police's ability to maintain "law and order." Moreover, this idea of the erosion of the fabric of "law and order" and the peril in which it placed the future of American democracy was a foundational component of Nixon's 1968 Southern Strategy.[40] Commenting on the legal system at the time the film was made, Eastwood recounted in 2008, "All of the bureaucracies and everything was favoring [the accused]. The *Miranda* decision had come down a few years earlier. . . . Everybody was just sort of sick of worrying about the accused. And [we] said 'how about the, how about let's worry about the victims for a while.'"[41] Eastwood's commentary echoes the film's ideology. According to conservatives in the late 1960s and early 1970s, the liberal Warren Court, through decisions like *Escobedo v. Illinois* (1964) and *Miranda v. Arizona* (1966), placed the rights of criminals above those of their victims. The vigilante Callahan, therefore, is the only person left to defend the vulnerable innocents abandoned by the state.

What's This "Dirty" in *Dirty Harry*?

Harry's noble commitment to justice raises questions as to why the film assigns the pejorative moniker "Dirty" to its hero. Harry is "dirty" not because he climbs atop garbage bins to spy on unsuspecting women while they undress or because, as Harry himself claims, "he gets stuck with all the dirty jobs" or even, as his partner argues, "because he always gets the shit end of the stick." Harry is "dirty" because he, and he alone, is willing to do what is necessary to enact justice, which includes tactics the alleged criminal-coddling Warren Court prohibits and a depraved 1960s America misconstrues as "dirty." In this perversely liberalized legal system, the lone puritan is easily mistaken for "dirty." The nickname, and the film's title, is not meant as a pejorative but as irony that supplies further evidence both of Harry's martyrdom and of the film's indictment of the state. Callahan's pursuit of justice requires him, albeit from different motivations, to become much like the villain he loathes. This trope, of a hero becoming like the enemy in order to win, is not only central to several classic Hollywood Westerns, such as *The Searchers* and *The Dirty Dozen*, but a common element in Clint Eastwood's film roles.[42] Moreover, the trope of the bureaucracy-despising hero has roots outside Hollywood; it is essential, for example, in the genre of detective fiction. In fact, Callahan elicits comparisons to Mike Hammer, the protagonist in much of Mickey Spillane's anticommunist detective fiction beginning in the late 1940s. As historian Stephen J. Whitfield explains, although Mike Hammer "chose not to become a cop because a 'pansy' bureaucracy was emasculating policemen with its rules and regulations, his real contempt is reserved for the professional and intellectual classes."[43] The film, therefore, relies on well-established filmic and literary elements of the antihero to speak directly to the antistatism of the early 1970s.

To stop Scorpio, Harry must ultimately kill him, because the legal system refuses to lock him up even after Harry delivers him in handcuffs. Murdering Scorpio is, therefore, the only way to protect the innocent. As noted earlier, it was not until the script's final draft that the action of *Dirty Harry* was set in San Francisco, a change that reinforces the anti-counterculture message of the film.[44] In *Dirty Harry*, San Francisco in the 1960s has transformed into the new Wild West, and Callahan must therefore become John Wayne in order to enact justice and restore civility. Minutes before their shoot-out, after Scorpio hijacks a school bus full of children, the film cuts to a wide shot of a herd of buffalo grazing in a large field of grass, an image very closely associated with the American frontier, before panning right to reveal a highway and eventually the bus. The imagery of the West continues in the climactic shoot-out between Callahan and Scorpio, which takes place in a rock quarry, absent any signs of the urban metropolis.

J. Hoberman argues that *Dirty Harry* is a Western, although an urban and inverted one.[45] Whereas the typical Western formula pits the civilized garden against the savage wilderness, in *Dirty Harry* it is civilization that is monstrous and savage, specifically the New Left of the 1960s.[46] It is up to Harry Callahan to become John Wayne, perhaps specifically Wayne's role as Davy Crockett in *The Alamo*, and clean up and civilize, or re-civilize, the "mess" of hippies, black nationalists, and the liberal Supreme Court. Furthermore, the casting of Eastwood—fresh off of starring in Sergio Leone's Man with No Name trilogy, and only a few years from playing the title role in the Western classic *The Outlaw Josey Wales* (1976)—further supports the notion that *Dirty Harry* functions much like a Western. Moreover, the racist language Callahan uses in the film, whether jokingly or not, aligns closely with the racial attitudes of the Western's greatest film star—John Wayne. Roughly seven months before *Dirty Harry* hit movie screens across the country, Wayne told *Playboy* magazine, "I believe in white supremacy until blacks are educated to a point of responsibility." Pivoting to Native Americans, Wayne continued, "I don't feel we did wrong in taking this great country away from the Indians. There were great numbers of people who needed new land, and the Indians were selfishly trying to keep it for themselves."[47]

After shooting Scorpio, Callahan removes his police shield from his pocket and, torn by the irreconcilability of his commitment to justice and duty to the law, throws the star into the lake, where Scorpio's corpse bobs. The ending mirrors that of the classic Western *High Noon* (1952), in which the protagonist, Marshall Will Kane (played by Gary Cooper), must discard the law and his star (which he removes and throws on the ground before leaving town with his wife) in order to enact justice and defend the town's innocents.[48] The connections between these two finales extend beyond the action on-screen. As historian Richard Slotkin argues, while there are both leftist and rightist readings available in *High Noon*, either reading shares "a common ideological structure that 'devalues' democracy as an instrument of progress and declares that the only effective instrument for constructive historical action is a gun in the hands of the right man."[49] *Dirty Harry's* conclusion, in which Harry cannot arrest but must kill Scorpio and cut all ties with law enforcement, is the *only* way to avenge Scorpio's victims. Obtaining justice through a legal system in a lawless world, be it on the frontier or in San Francisco in the late 1960s, is futile. Justice is possible only to those authoritarian vigilantes committed to "natural," rather than "civic," justice, irrespective of legal impediments to it. The film's conclusion illustrates how misguided and unaccountable the state has become to the society it supposedly serves. By the time the credits roll, immediately after Harry discards his police star, the audience understands not just that justice is irreconcilable with the "criminal-coddling" legal system of the Warren Court but also that the two cannot coexist. Either the supposed liberal excrescence must be removed from the law, or it will continue to withhold justice from innocent victims, as police are handcuffed by technical procedure and liberal courts cannot help but find loopholes to exonerate the guilty. The antistatist vigilantism of Callahan and his complicated racial politics form the two pillars of Callahan's character and his heroism for an audience lurching rightward in the early 1970s.

"I Don't Care about Black, Brown, or Yellow. I'm in It for the Green."

The socioeconomic and political climate of the early 1970s, combined with the dire economic situation of Hollywood, gave rise to a host of low-budget, racially charged B-movie genres—including white backlash movies like *Dirty Harry*—that drew audiences back to movie theaters by speaking to the racial anxieties of the period. Blaxploitation was another important genre in this regard. Though scholars debate the precise number, blaxploitation refers to the roughly sixty to one hundred black action films produced in the first half of the 1970s, often consisting of a "pimp, gangster, or their baleful female counterparts, violently acting out a revenge or retribution motif against corrupt whites in the romanticized confines of the ghetto or inner city."[50] As with white backlash films, engagement with nascent colorblind sentiment along with antistatism—albeit for drastically different reasons—are essential components of the blaxploitation genre. Whereas backlash films like *Dirty Harry* blame the state for the erosion of law and order via the prioritization of civic over natural justice, the impoverishment and overpolicing of urban black communities by repressive governments and corrupt police fuel the antistatism of the blaxploitation genre. More-over, in the case of *Coffy*, race-conscious visuality is blended with colorblind rhetoric to distinguish its heroes from its villains, as in *Dirty Harry*. Yet un-like *Dirty Harry*, colorblind pronouncements in *Coffy* are not evidence of one's heroism but of one's villainy.

As film historian Ed Guerrero argues, blaxploitation emerged out of the rise of the Black Power movement in the late 1960s, whose leaders de-manded, as part of their larger political activism, new representations of African Americans that challenged the one-dimensional images of blacks in classical Hollywood films, which amounted to little more than what film historian Donald Bogle succinctly referred to in the title of his history of blacks in Hollywood as "Toms, Coons, Mulattoes, Mammies, and Bucks." In the midst of the Hollywood economic crisis of the 1960s, the film indus-try's trade journal, *Variety*, estimated that while blacks made up less than 15 percent of the nation's population, they made up more than 30 percent of moviegoing audiences. *Ebony* readers alone spent an estimated $450,000 weekly on movie admissions. The combination of Black Power politics, the demands for new representations of blackness, the dire economic condi-tions, and a reliable black moviegoing audience proved irresistible to Hol-lywood. After the economic success of the independently produced *Sweet Sweetback's Baadasssss Song* (1971), Hollywood studios began pumping out blaxploitation films at a rapid pace, beginning with *Shaft* in 1971.[51] Blax-ploitation films found fleeting success among black audiences. As Amy Abugo Ongiri explains, "On the one hand, Blaxploitation's narrative of ghetto despair deliberately spoke both to the mass news media's inflamma-tory coverage of events such as the Watts rebellion and to the general cov-erage of a post–civil rights expression of Black race in the Black Power era. . . . On the other hand, however, the powerful images of African Amer-ican masculinity in Blaxploitation films directly responded to Hollywood's problematic history in representing African American masculinity."[52]

By 1972, the Black Panthers began using the pages of its newspaper, the *Black Panther*, to denounce blaxploitation films. However, they took a round-about path to opposition, and this opposition itself was contradictory. The Panthers' minister of defense, Huey P. Newton, devoted an entire issue of the *Black Panther* to Melvin Van Peebles's *Sweet Sweetback's Baadasssss Song*, the movie that inspired the blaxploitation boom in June 1971. New-ton hailed the film as "the first truly revolutionary Black film ever made" because it put forth the communal "love," "sacredness," and "unity" African Americans "so desperately need."[53] Yet as the genre quickly devolved into bastardized Hollywood imitations often directed by whites, the Panthers' support for the genre faded. Less than eighteen months after the movie's release, the *Black Panther*'s editors put a photograph from a demonstration protesting blaxploitation films in the Panthers' hometown of Oakland, California, on the cover of the October 7, 1972, issue. The feature article from that edition, titled "Blaxploitation," condemned the increasingly popular B-movie genre: "By turning our oppression into fantasies, by making Black people look like fun-loving, love-making, hustling freaks, Hollywood would have us walk away from the theatre feeling that all of the problems we saw were of our own cause. The dehumanization of our communities comes in black and white, or Technicolor, as the mad dog moguls of Hollywood grind out negative images of Black people, destroying the positive ones."[54] Ten days prior, party chair Bobby Seale released a statement condemning the blaxploitation genre and its estimated hundred-plus films: "Using our oppression as a twisted story line, using our inexperience in the film-making industry to underpay us, and by collecting our money at the box offices as a 'reward' for finally putting us on the silver screen, the formula for big capital gain is complete."[55]

The Panthers' change in attitude toward the blaxploitation genre was not merely a flip-flop. While the article in the organization's newspaper is critical of these films' content, particularly their depiction of black nationalists— they "usually portrayed Black youths with outdated rhetoric, [and] the 'revolutionaries' come across as stumbling fools, with no program to serve the community and obviously controlled by others"—perhaps its harshest critique had to do with the production of such films by overwhelmingly white-run studios and crews. In this regard, Seale's statement came with the following demands: "We demand that Black actors, writers, directors, cameramen and all of our people whose talents are used in the profitable film-making industry be paid at least an equal amount to their white counterparts. We further demand that a large percentage of the millions of dollars now going in the pockets of rich, white businessmen be put into the hands of the Black community for our benefit."[56] Ultimately, as cultural theorist Cedric Robinson argues, blaxploitation amounted to a "degraded cinema," one that "in lieu of a deliberate interrogation of the political and moral dilemmas which attended the failures of an integrationist activism . . . trivialised (*sic*) the troubled activists of the [Black Power] movement into the now familiar male counter-revolutionary creatures."[57] More importantly, as Seale's statement illustrates, it did so without integrating the production process, which comprises the vast majority of Hollywood jobs. As a caption that accompanied a collage of blaxploitation posters published with the aforementioned article summed up, "We believe that from Stepin' Fetchit to *Superfly* is a great leap to nowhere."[58]

Among the hundred or so films Seale directed his criticisms toward was *Coffy*, which premiered in 1973 after the initial breakout of blaxploitation.[59] As a result of the success of *Shaft*, studios cranked out dozens of copycats in search of similar box-office yields.[60] By the time *Coffy* premiered, however, blaxploitation had entered the twilight of its existence due largely to diminishing audience interest. By 1973, Hollywood studios had already released numerous blaxploitation films featuring female superheroes played by black actresses like Pam Grier, who stars in *Coffy*; Rosalind Cash; and Tamara Dobson.[61] On the one hand, the "Bad Black Woman" subgenre offered a rare example in the first half of the 1970s of what Sherrie A. Inness might call "tough girl" alternatives to the tough masculine portrayals that dominated Hollywood movie screens in films like *Dirty Harry* and *Rocky*.[62] As Donald Bogle writes, "In her films Pam Grier always came across as a fiercely aggressive, tough, resilient, hot, and surprisingly funny black woman on the move."[63] Nonetheless, female-driven blaxploitation films exacerbated the problematic gender politics of blaxploitation. As Ongiri argues, "Blaxploitation as a genre was primarily focused on beautiful Black phallocentric masculinity," which personified Frantz Fanon's "conflation of Black masculinity and phallocentric power."[64] While Huey Newton praised this dynamic in *Sweetback*, such sentiments quickly wore on black audiences and were, in part, responsible for the short-lived favor the genre won among urban black audiences.[65] The move toward female leads in the genre's twilight further problematized blaxploitation's relationship between its black protagonists and their sexuality. Cedric Robinson argues that the roles of blaxploitation stars like Pam Grier were largely "eroticisations" of Angela Davis and her political activism. These "Bad Black Woman" films "transported Davis' form from a representation of a revolutionist to that of an erotic Black Nationalist, largely devoid of historical consciousness. This was achieved by eviscerating the original's intellectual sophistication, political and organizational context, doctrinal commitments, and[,] most tellingly, her critique of capitalist society and its employment of gender, race and class."[66] Black revolutionaries in the early 1970s were not immune to the misrecognition of eroticism as power. Huey Newton's article praising *Sweetback* also fetishizes the film's naked "women with their large breasts" and describes their numerous sex acts as integral to the process of transforming black boys into black men and liberators.[67] The female body in these films becomes a receptacle for "all the libidinal desire and social pathology of America's urban classes" that attempt to substitute revenge narratives enacted solely for the purposes of voyeuristic pleasure for political action.[68] As Ongiri argues, *Sweetback* provided "the opportunity to maintain, and even potentially enhance, its view of African American masculinity as threatening, sexually potent, and extremely dangerous."[69] Consequently, as we shall see in chapter 2, given that the "Bad Black Woman" subgenre emerged amid the early 1970s ethos of antistatism, these films offer an opportunity to further demonize, police, and control "threatening" hypersexualized black femininity.

In some ways, *Coffy* and *Dirty Harry* are quite different from each other. In fact, the bank robbers Harry kills on the streets of San Francisco are the exact "buck" caricatures that were the heroes of most blaxploitation films. Film historian Donald Bogle defines the initial years of the blaxploitation boom as "*the age of the buck*, a period when a band of aggressive, pistol-packing, sexually-charged urban cowboys set off on a heady rampage, out to topple the system and right past wrongs."[70] *Coffy*, and the blaxploitation genre more generally, amounted on the surface to Hollywood's black liberal counterpunch to white backlash films like *Dirty Harry*. Nonetheless, both films mobilize the antistatism of the decade. In each film, the protagonists must venture outside the law to obtain justice. Coffy and Callahan are both, in other words, vigilantes.[71] In *Coffy*, Pam Grier embarks on a murderous rampage to eliminate an organized crime network composed of drug dealers, gangsters, pimps, police, and politicians that pumps drugs into her community, ruining the lives of black children including Coffy's kid sister, who lives in a mental hospital as a result of brain damage caused by heroin use.

Furthermore, despite their fundamental differences and antithetical politics, the racial politics of *Coffy*, like those of *Dirty Harry*, reveal an incipient colorblind ideology. After Coffy's politician boyfriend Howard delivers a speech about the "vicious combination of big business and government" that comprise the "white power structure," the audience learns that Howard is, in fact, part of that corrupt power structure. He arranges a deal, along with his city's Latino mayor and an Italian mob boss, to take over the drug trade in their congressional district after his election. Therefore, while the dialogue in the film refers to the racially exclusive "white power structure," what one sees on-screen is the buttressing of that structure by opportunistic, self-interested people of color. However, one should not confuse the integration of this cartel as evidence of racial progress. George Lipsitz argues that the dialectic of public policy and individual bigotry has produced a "possessive investment in whiteness" that is responsible for the reproduction of racial inequality in the post–civil rights era. The social and economic advantages afforded to whites encourage them to "invest" in their racial identities in ways that have severe repercussions for people of color. Yet on an individual level, in the period after civil rights, persons of color are not wholly excluded from the largesse of white privilege. As Lipsitz writes, "nonwhite people can become active agents of white supremacy as well as passive participants in its hierarchies and rewards."[72] So while Howard may individually benefit through his place among the leadership of this drug cartel, his profiteering in no way mitigates the larger retrenchment of racial inequality on which his campaign relies.

More importantly, when Howard meets with the mayor and members of the mob, a black gangster, nervous about Howard, opines that "all blacks stick together," to which Howard responds, "I don't care about black, brown, or yellow. I'm in it for the green." Shortly thereafter, the mob boss applauds the group's cross-racial cooperation, albeit in an illegal venture. In the context of the genre, one may read Howard's colorblind endorsement of capitalism as merely further proof of his corruptible character—a man whose greed causes him to sell out his community and his race for his own monetary gain. That several Black Power organizations, including the Black Panthers, were, in fact, socialist organizations supports such claims. Nonetheless, that the scene mobilizes colorblind rhetoric, if only to reinforce the sordid nature of the character, further reveals a racial ideology in its infancy, disconnected from a singular political ideology.

Despite the occasional colorblind dialogue, other lines in the film are racially explicit. In fact, throughout the vast majority of the film, race-conscious dialogue saturates the script, as in most blaxploitation films. One scene depicts the lynching of the film's pimp, King George, who has a noose tied around his neck and his hands bound before he is dragged behind a car driven by two white men, predating the similar lynching of James Byrd Jr. in Jasper, Texas, by twenty-five years.[73] The men hold King George's black driver at gunpoint and force him to watch the lynching from the back seat. At one point, one of the white men, while dragging King George, remarks, "This is the way we lynch niggers." Furthermore, the visual images of this sequence are laden with references to Jim Crow—an epoch in American history in which race consciousness was the letter of the law.

In addition, archival notes related to the movie's marketing racializes *Coffy* in ways that perpetuate stereotypical notions of black vernacular. One slogan idea reads, "She's Black, She's Hot, She's Coffy." Additionally, advertisements commonly dubbed Coffy the "Godmother of Watts." Yet in the studio notes, someone, presumably an advertising executive, crossed out the second "o" and the "er" in "Godmother" and replaced it with a "u" and an "a" so that the tag reads "Godmutha of Watts."[74] While that slogan never made it into an actual advertising campaign, the notes shared among the advertising team highlight the race-conscious appeal they sought. The racial discourse informing the advertising, combined with much of the film's dialogue and, most importantly, the visual politics of the film, are laden with race. Here again, as with *Dirty Harry*, one finds the paradox of these early iterations of Hollywood's colorblind aesthetics in the first half of the 1970s—colorblind dialogue paired with a heavily racialized screen. The protagonists in *Coffy* and *Dirty Harry* are both outsiders, and each film employs colorblind aesthetics, albeit to attract different audiences. The similarities between these two films, despite their divergent political positions, mirror the political diversity of colorblind discourse outside movie theaters, which was not tied to any one political ideology, and reveal how colorblindness was beginning to cohere across political lines.

"The Law Is in for a Piece of the Action"

Like *Dirty Harry*, *Coffy* characterizes American society in the early 1970s as rife with societal ills. Although the two diverge substantially over the nature of the problems plaguing the country, both films cite law enforcement as the primary enabler and perpetrator of corruption and moral depravity. *Dirty Harry* blames liberal governments and the decisions of the Warren Court for prioritizing the rights of alleged criminals over those of their victims, thereby inhibiting the police's ability to maintain law and order. *Coffy*, on the other hand, depicts an apparatus of corruption in which government, pimps, and drug dealers are all complicit in organized criminal activity that preys on innocent black children and impoverishes and criminalizes black communities.

These two films also have opposing attitudes toward law enforcement. In *Dirty Harry*, cops are the lone state actors driven solely by a moral commitment to justice. In *Coffy*, the police are not only part of the corrupt state apparatus but at the root of its corruption. In one scene, Coffy and her friend Carter—the lone upstanding police officer who is eventually left brain dead after fellow cops order a hit on him after he threatens to expose their corruption—ride back to their homes after visiting Coffy's sister in a methadone clinic. Coffy, who has already killed a drug kingpin and one of his street-level dealers, asks Carter about the moral justification of killing a known drug dealer:

> *Carter*: What, to kill some pusher who's only selling so he can get money to buy for himself? What good would that do, Coffy? He's only part of a chain that reaches back to some poor farmer in Turkey or Vietnam. What would you do, kill all of them?
>
> *Coffy*: Well, why not? Nothing else seems to do any good. You know who they are. Everybody knows who they are. Now, you're a cop. Why don't you just arrest them?
>
> *Carter*: It's not that simple, Coffy. *The law can't do that.*
>
> *Coffy*: You bet it can't. And I know why it can't, too. Because *the law is in for a piece of the action.*
>
> *Carter*: Not all of it. Not yet. [emphasis added]

Here, as with *Dirty Harry*, the law is ineffectual. Known criminals parade in plain view of police, who do nothing. Yet while Carter offers a vague explanation similar to that of Harry Callahan's colleagues, implying that the "law can't do" anything because of legal technicalities and government bureaucracy, Coffy goes further, blaming the lack of arrests on the accusation that police are "in for a piece of the action," a charge Carter, in absolving himself, only confirms. In addition, whereas Callahan, as a morally righteous public servant, must circumvent state bureaucrats in his pursuit of justice, Carter, the *only* righteous police officer, is severely beaten by his corrupt colleagues.

Later in the film, Coffy's boyfriend Howard films a campaign video as part of his congressional campaign. Walking through a park with his index finger holding a sport coat slung over his shoulder, accompanied by a handful of hired black supporters, Howard panders to his audience, "So you see this vicious combination of big business and government has kept our sisters prostituting and our brothers dope-peddling." The loose black nationalism of Howard's monologue elicits comparisons to Black Power activists who ran for political office in the first half of the 1970s. Only a month before the film's June release, Black Panther leaders Bobby Seale and Elaine Brown ran, unsuccessfully, for political office in Oakland, California. Their campaign speeches made similar appeals to those of Howard. In late March 1973, for example, only a few months before *Coffy* debuted, Bobby Seale spoke of assembling a coalition of people of color who would serve as "freedom fighters" and "liberators." "What you're going to have to do," Seale explained, "is commit yourself to change the system, vote them (incumbents) out, use the system they already have."[75]

After explaining an encounter with a "junkie" who has a $100-per-day habit, Howard continues:

> Our power structure has given this man no reasonable alternative. . . . Why would a power structure deliberately create addicts? I ask you, where do you think that one hundred dollars a day goes? Sure, part of it goes to black pushers and distributors, but the main part of it, the really big part goes to those white men who import the narcotics, and the big part goes to those white men who corrupt our law enforcement agencies. . . . This whole thing becomes a vicious attempt of the white power structure to exploit our black men and women in this society.

The 1960s saw a sharp increase in the amount of heroin users, especially among black and Latinx communities.[76] As the baby-boomer generation came of age in the early part of the decade and America's urban centers— New York, Chicago, Detroit, Philadelphia—became overwhelmingly populated by blacks and Latinx folks, many of them poor, there was a surge of heroin use among these populations.[77] By the end of the decade, the number of heroin addicts in New York City had doubled, with at least sixty thousand users living in the city.[78] This uptick produced a trend toward more draconian jail sentences among state governments, most notably the Rockefeller laws. This, along with the popularity of heroin among American troops in Vietnam, prompted Richard Nixon, in 1972, to declare a "war on drugs."[79]

Given the social context of the early 1970s, especially the growing popularity of heroin along with the harsher penalties for users, Howard's choice to campaign on the government's inability or unwillingness to address the heroin epidemic in America's urban centers is not surprising. It was, in fact, a central issue to many black political organizations in the late 1960s and early 1970s. For example, in 1970 the Black Panthers released an eleven-page pamphlet titled *Capitalism Plus Dope Equals Genocide*, which, like Howard's speech, criticized not drug users but the government's inability to stop the flow of heroin into the United States and its inability to adequately treat drug addiction, which its author describes as "a monstrous symptom of the malignancy which is ravaging the social fabric of this capitalist system."[80] More specifically, the view expressed by Howard—that the government was complicit in pumping drugs into America's inner cities—was a popular belief among many blacks in the late 1960s and early 1970s.[81] In fact, Howard's entire speech is remarkably similar to the Panther's aforementioned pamphlet, which states, "As long as the [heroin] plague was confined to the ghetto, the government did not see fit to deem it a problem. But as soon as college professors, demagogic politicians, money-crazed finance capitalists and industrialists discovered that their own sons and daughters had fallen victim to the [heroin] plague, a virtual 'state of national emergency' was declared."[82]

Although the details of the corruption differ in each film—in *Dirty Harry*, government bureaucrats prioritize criminals' rights over justice for their victims, thereby enabling criminal activity, whereas in *Coffy*, cops and politicians are the primary perpetrators of crime—both films ultimately blame the state for the societal problems each identifies. In *Dirty Harry*, the government's backward priorities endanger the innocent. In *Coffy*, the government itself is part of the criminal enterprise that funnels drugs into black communities and then profits off their sale. Nonetheless, in pointing the finger at the state, these films demonstrate an antistatist consensus that stretched across race, class, and political affiliation by the early years of the 1970s and formed the foundation on which a more cohesive colorblind ideology would be built as the decade progressed.

Coffy's tethering of the state to criminal enterprises is a feature of many, if not most, blaxploitation films. *Super Fly* (1972), *The Mack* (1973), *Cleopatra Jones* (1973), and *Sweet Sweetback's Baadasssss Song* (1971), to name just a few, all contain corrupt cops and similar story lines centered around a black vigilante protagonist. This implicit anti–law enforcement criticism of the genre resonates with larger motivations of Black Power politics, although strictly in a commodified form. As Ture, a key architect of Black Power ideology and political thought, said, "Black Power means black people coming together to form a political force and either electing representatives or forcing their representatives to speak their needs [rather than relying on established parties]." Black Power was a "struggle for the right to create our own terms through which to define ourselves and our relationship to the society, and to have these terms recognized."[83] It "is a call for black people in this country to unite, to recognize their heritage, to build a sense of community. It is a call for black people to begin to define their own goals, to lead their own organizations and to support those organizations. It is a call to reject the racist institutions and values of this society. . . . The goal of black self-determination and self-identity—Black Power—is full participation in the decision-making process affecting the lives of black people, and recognition of the virtues in themselves as black people."[84] Consider, also, the first entry in the Black Panther Party's Ten Point Program: "WE WANT FREEDOM. WE WANT POWER TO DETERMINE THE DESTINY OF OUR BLACK AND OPPRESSED COMMUNITIES. We believe that Black and oppressed people will not be free until we are able to determine our destinies in our own communities ourselves, by fully controlling all the institutions which exist in our communities."[85]

Black Power activists promoted the idea of black self-determination. This philosophy, on the one hand, was the product of skepticism regarding the state's ability, or willingness, to eradicate racial injustice after the shortcomings of the civil rights movement a decade prior. On the other hand, self-determination was the product of the state's coordinated efforts to undermine and murder Black Power activists. On December 4, 1969, for example, an FBI agent, working with agents from the Cook County State's Attorney's Office and officers of the Chicago Police Department, murdered Fred Hampton, chair of the Illinois chapter of the Black Panther Party, and Mark Clark.[86] Moreover, as Ture and Hamilton make clear, self-determination offered black activists an opportunity to close ranks and develop democratic parallel institutions of their own before entering the larger political arena and served as a safeguard against becoming overwhelmed by white allies. This philosophy of self-determination, however, did not equate to a wholesale abandonment of state engagement. Black Panther leaders Huey Newton, Bobby Seale, and Elaine Brown, for example, all ran for public office in Oakland, California, in the 1970s. Similarly, despite the fact that *Dirty Harry* and *Coffy* disagree over who is to blame for society's ills, they both have serious doubts about the state's ability to address social injustice.

Additionally, if we understand the standard blaxploitation formula as revenge narratives that draw on a distorted idea of Black Power ideology and aesthetics, then the antistatist ethos of the 1970s was integral to the emergence of the genre. Given the historical context of the late 1960s and early 1970s, and given the reliability of black urban audiences, it is easy to understand why Hollywood looked to cater to, albeit in problematic ways, Black Power themes and iconography during the industry's economic crisis of the immediate post–civil rights era. Moreover, revenge narratives centered around black protagonists allowed Hollywood to combine the aesthetics of black nationalism with the pervasive ethos of antistatism, a combination that attracted audiences in the early 1970s. Antistatism was therefore fundamental to the production of the blaxploitation genre.

Whether it was blaxploitation films using the discourse to slander race traitors on-screen, or Black Power leaders fighting for racial justice off it, colorblindness found its way into both black nationalist rhetoric and the bastardized Hollywood versions of its aesthetics. Similarly, Hollywood used the combination of antistatism and colorblind aesthetics—which combines colorblind rhetoric with race-conscious visuality—to appeal to white backlash sentiment in films like *Dirty Harry*, while trying to distinguish Callahan's racial politics from those of Jim Crow segregationists like George Wallace. Therefore, white backlash and blaxploitation films of the early 1970s each contributed to the rampant antistatist ethos that would come to define the decade. This ethos would provide the foundation on which a more cohesive colorblind ideology would be built as the decade unfolded. More importantly, both *Dirty Harry* and *Coffy* reveal early, though incomplete, iterations of Hollywood's colorblind aesthetics, which would continue to develop throughout the decade and ultimately prove paramount to the rise and influence of the ideology.

Hollywood did not, however, monopolize the American film industry in the early 1970s. Independent film afforded black artists the potential to make movies that addressed the dehumanizing representations of black life in front of Hollywood cameras and the economic inequality behind them. Thus, the 1970s saw the maturation of a generation of black independent filmmakers, formally trained in film schools like the University of California, Los Angeles. The economic model of New Hollywood also afforded established black Hollywood actors to exercise greater autonomy over their careers and the opportunity to write, direct, or produce their own films. One such group, along with other actors and writers of color and a white producer ally, formed their own film company in an effort to produce new images of blacks on-screen and increased opportunities for black workers off it. But, like Hollywood, they had to grapple with both the decade's ethos of antistatism and the nascent ideology of colorblindness. This elixir of cultural, economic, and political ambition led to the creation of Third World Cinema and its first film, *Claudine* (1974).

2 Keep Away from Me, Mr. Welfare Man

Claudine, Welfare, and Black Independent Film

• •

Sometime in 1970, as colorblind discourse imbued public discourse around the political spectrum, screenwriters Tina and Lester Pine pitched an idea for a film to their friend, producer Joyce Selznick, the niece of legendary Hollywood producer David O. Selznick. Selznick spent the next several years trying to get the Pines' film made, and in May 1974, *Claudine* premiered. However, the film that debuted at the Hollywood Pacific Theatre on May 16 and would earn an Academy Award nomination had little in common with the Pines' original idea. The Pines had conceived a story "about a white woman who seeks homes for her six fatherless children before she dies of cancer."[1] The actual film, shot around 116th Street and Lenox Avenue in Harlem, became a love story about a black sanitation worker named Rupert, or "Roop," played by James Earl Jones, and Diahann Carrol in the title role of Claudine—a black mother of six subsisting off welfare. The film follows the two as their "courtship and marriage plans are complicated and frustrated by the regulations and red tape involved in the child support funds she receives from the welfare department."[2]

The metamorphosed script—from a story about a terminally ill white woman to one about a single, black welfare mother—became the first production of the newly formed Third World Cinema Corporation. Modeling itself on a vision of civil rights unionism, Third World Cinema (TWC) sought to counter popular representations of blackness on Hollywood movie screens and integrate the film industry's labor unions.[3] TWC was part of a multifaceted effort among independent black filmmakers to address the racial inequities in Hollywood amid the blaxploitation boom, both in front of and behind the camera. As film historian David A. Cook notes, "The American film industry changed more between 1969 and 1980 than at any other period in its history except, perhaps, for the coming of sound."[4] The collapse of the Hollywood studio system in the 1960s wreaked havoc on the movie industry and catalyzed the complete reconstitution of the film business. *Claudine* and TWC more generally were products of this instability.[5]

TWC's story begins at the end of the 1960s with a journalist turned television and film producer named Hannah Weinstein. Weinstein left the United States for Europe in the early 1950s amid the anticommunist purges in the film industry and produced a handful of television series abroad, hiring many blacklisted Hollywood writers. In 1969, when she was back in the United States, Weinstein teamed up with actors Ossie Davis, Diana Sands, James Earl Jones, and Brock Peters (and eventually Rita Moreno and writer Piri Thomas), and together fought to integrate film production unions. Thereafter, the company they formed, Third World Cinema, sought to increase opportunities for blacks and Puerto Ricans in the movie business.[6] An inscription containing the familiar Chinese proverb "Give me a fish and I eat for a day. Teach me to fish and I eat for a lifetime" hung on the wall in Third World Cinema's Manhattan office, which exemplified its philosophy as a corporation. By the time TWC was officially established in 1971, the group had won union cards for over two hundred new technical workers. TWC then expanded its efforts on-screen and sought to produce films that would serve as a counterweight to blaxploitation films like *Coffy*, which largely monopolized the representations of African Americans in Hollywood in the early 1970s.

Claudine was the group's first project, and it put the organization's philosophy into practice both in front of and behind the camera. All but one in the cast were black, and twenty-four of the thirty-seven crew members were black or Puerto Rican, seven of those trained directly by TWC. The film's white director, John Berry, had previously directed Orson Welles's stage production of Richard Wright's *Native Son* in 1942, and was a member of the Hollywood blacklist.[7] During *Claudine*'s production, Cliff Frazier, a black actor involved with Third World Cinema, explained, "Too many [movies] have been made for purely commercial purposes with little regard for the effect on the viewing public. . . . The movie [industry] has a tremendous influence on thought processes—for good or bad. Black movies have concentrated on crime and violence with an almost complete absence of warm human relationships. The impact on young black kids is obvious."[8] Echoing Frazier's sentiments, Gordon Armstrong—national publicity director for 20th Century Fox—said of the film, "The super-jive, super-spade, cocaine desperado image of the ghetto that has been flashing across the screen in superabundance of late is given its rightful place in the Harlem of 'Claudine'— off in the shadows."[9] Armstrong's revelation that TWC made *Claudine* to counter the immensely popular blaxploitation genre, which dominated

Hollywood representations of blackness in the early 1970s, highlights the uphill battle TWC faced in producing a film like *Claudine* and reveals that the film would likely not have been made without the existence and excess of the blaxploitation genre.

Yet unlike the emerging LA Rebellion—a collection of UCLA-trained black independent filmmakers, including Haile Gerima, Julie Dash, and Charles Burnett, that developed a new and deliberately anti-Hollywood aesthetics of black independent film—Third World Cinema was not wholly anti-Hollywood. Instead, TWC sought to change Hollywood's race problems through reform—more people of color in front of and behind movie cameras and more "respectable" representations of those communities on-screen. Thus, TWC's first film, *Claudine*, occupies a unique middle ground between black independent film and the Hollywood mainstream in early 1970s film. It was critical of Hollywood's limited and dehumanizing representations of African Americans yet understood itself as both a part of and a reforming influence on its future.[10]

More importantly, because TWC was both apart from and a part of Hollywood, *Claudine* offers a knottier picture of the inchoate racial ideology of colorblindness in the early 1970s than one finds elsewhere on movie screens. As TWC began filming *Claudine*, colorblind rhetoric was scattered across the political spectrum, untethered from a single political ideology. Yet the racial ideology of colorblindness was finding a widening purchase with politicians and the (white) public alike. In the years after *Claudine's* release, a nearly hegemonic colorblind ideology began to substantively roll back the victories of the civil rights movement and assert a new form of white supremacy, marking the reestablishment of what Michelle Alexander refers to as a "racial caste system" in the post–civil rights era.[11] As we shall see in chapter 3, as colorblindness emerged as a racial project that cherry-picked the rhetoric of the civil rights movement to attack its very gains, Hollywood would play an increasingly influential role coalescing the ideas and developing the aesthetics of colorblindness.

This chapter examines TWC's first film, *Claudine*, within the context of the emerging colorblind ideology and widespread antistatism of the early 1970s. I begin with an overview of the racialization of welfare discourse beginning in the 1960s. Welfare was one of the most divisive policies in the country in the late 1960s and early 1970s. As we saw in chapter 1, anti-liberalism characterized the early 1970s, both on- and off-screen. There was perhaps no other social policy that inflamed antistatist anger more than welfare. Antistatism was also a central theme of films from the early 1970s.

Blaxploitation films like *Coffy* and white backlash ones like *Dirty Harry* take on the corruption of government and law enforcement explicitly, particularly the complicity of cops and politicians in illegal activity. *Claudine* takes a different look at antistatism, exploring the effects of the bondage of welfare on the lives of ordinary African Americans trying to reconcile love and the need to make a living.

I then turn to *Claudine*, analyzing the film through three lenses. The first is TWC's larger philosophy, rooted in the integrationist ethos of the civil rights movement. The second is a close analysis of the film itself, focusing on how the movie offers a black nationalist critique of the welfare state and Lyndon Johnson's Great Society that includes a direct rebuke of colorblindness; *Claudine*, in fact, is one of the first films to critique it. Yet while this black nationalist critique sought progressive reform of the welfare state, by the end of the 1970s it would be co-opted by the New Right to destroy it. Finally, despite TWC's civil rights origins and the film's race-conscious black nationalist politics, the film's marketing catered explicitly to colorblind sentiments, thereby contradicting the racial critique of the film. Moreover, *Claudine*'s marketing minimizes the importance of race in the dehumanizing treatment of welfare recipients in a manner that foreshadows the forward trajectory of colorblind ideology. Rather than read these inconsistencies as evidence of the film's shortcomings, I argue that *Claudine* encompasses the swirling contradictions of the early 1970s as colorblindness increasingly moved into the mainstream. Therefore, *Claudine* proved fundamental in the articulation of an emerging ideology. In the early 1970s, colorblind hegemony was on the horizon, and we can read the different aspects of this film as evidence of a new racial formation in process.

"The Welfare Man, That's My Husband"

While TWC drew heavily on the philosophy of the civil rights movement off camera, its first film aligns with contemporary black nationalist critiques of welfare and of Lyndon Johnson's Great Society more generally. *Claudine* takes up the "crisis" of the black family and the high incidence of single-black-female-headed households, and ultimately blames invasive and disruptive government welfare policies for that suffering. The *Los Angeles Times* promoted *Claudine* as "a movie that deals seriously with a real inner city problem—the dilemma of a black couple who are caught in the insidious web of the welfare state."[12] An April 1974 review in the *Hollywood Reporter* said of the film: "*Claudine* sorts out the circular, schizophrenic logic of the welfare syndrome with clarity."[13] A similar review in the June 1974 issue of *Playboy* magazine praised the film for its portrayal of the "degrading inequities of welfare rules."[14] In *Claudine*, the government requires and maintains broken black families through senseless stipulations that keep black men out of households and prohibit recipients from earning a living wage. Due to these government technicalities, Claudine must choose between welfare, without which she cannot house, feed, or clothe her children, and marrying the man she loves. Through the telling of this story, *Claudine* highlights the government's role as the primary force behind the breakdown of low-income black families.

The film's critique of the dehumanizing effects of welfare compliance and the racialized implications of welfare policing garnered critical acclaim at a moment in which welfare reform was a central part of the political platform of black nationalist groups like the Black Panthers. Leaders of the Black Panthers characterized welfare as exploitative and argued that the program further entrenched black families in poverty rather than alleviate its pain. In 1967, when Stokely Carmichael wrote, "People must no longer be tied, by small incentives or handouts, to a corrupting and corruptible white machine," he was primarily referring to welfare.[15] The Black Panthers frequently published articles about the inhumanity of the program in their weekly periodical—the *Black Panther*. In a seventeen-month period between July 1971 and December 1973, the *Black Panther* published no fewer than five articles criticizing welfare policy.[16] One particularly revealing feature from September 1972 about cuts to California's welfare system under Governor Ronald Reagan wrote that the program "is humiliating, degrading and inhuman. . . . It is the goal of the welfare system to keep welfare recipients as poor as possible, and to give the public false ideas that those on welfare are almost all black, receive too much money, and are lazy."[17] Similarly, in the newspaper's final issue of 1972, an article titled "Our Challenge for 1973" lists welfare as one of the eleven most pertinent issues for the organization in the upcoming year. The article characterizes California's state-level welfare policy as a "fascist form of slave labor which forces welfare recipients to work menial jobs for no wage at all," and chastises welfare more broadly as a "vehicle by which the federal, state and city powers attempt to degrade, dehumanize, and further impoverish the poor."[18] As these statements indicate, Black Power activists like the Panthers insisted that welfare was a predatory program that bound black families to poverty and placed them under invasive government surveillance.

The Panther's critique, moreover, rebuked the conservative discourse of welfare that vilified black mothers and accused the program of nourishing an inferior female-headed familial "culture." As Robin D. G. Kelley explains, beginning in the 1960s social scientists studying urban poverty entered the "concrete jungles" of America, unanimously agreeing "that a common, debased culture is what defined the 'underclass.'"[19] These studies, most prominently the Moynihan Report, popularized notions of cultural pathology among African Americans—specifically in the ability of black women to raise children. The culture-of-poverty thesis offered an appealing scapegoat that combined civil rights backlash and economic frustration in a single figure—the black mother. As Wahneema Lubiano argues, race has so thoroughly dominated conservative attacks on welfare that the program has become synonymous with black women. Lubiano writes of the black woman: "She is the agent of destruction, the creator of the pathological, black, urban, poor family from which all ills flow; a monster creating crack dealers, addicts, muggers, and rapists—men who become those things because of being immersed in her culture of poverty."[20] By the 1970s, the image of lazy black women refusing to work and deliberately producing children to enhance their monthly government "handout" had taken hold of much of white America's imagination. Individual states went so far as to sterilize welfare recipients.[21]

Claudine draws directly on the overwhelming frustration of black nationalist organizations with welfare. In a scene that is repeated later in the film, Claudine and her eldest daughter, Charlene, iron and fold laundry in their kitchen while Curtis Mayfield's "Mr. Welfare Man," written for the film and performed by Gladys Knight and the Pips, plays off-screen. Claudine's son Paul then rushes into the room and informs his mother that their social worker is "coming up the stoop." The entire family breaks into a well-choreographed and presumably often-repeated drill, hiding all household items their social worker may deem too fancy for a family on government relief. Claudine hurriedly unplugs her new iron and stashes it under the stove while Charlene replaces it with a much older one. Claudine and her children then proceed to hide the new coffee pot, toaster, and living room rug from view. Only then is Ms. Kabak, the family's social worker, invited in as the family hides a few final personal effects. As Ms. Kabak enters, patronizingly deferential tones and meek demeanors replace the family's obstreperous behavior and vulgar language. The scene is played for comedy, yet the audience is left with the irony of a comedic routine that is also

Claudine (Diahann Carroll) and her children rush to hide housewares before the arrival of their social worker, Ms. Kabak.

troubling in the way that the children and their mother must hide their natural dispositions and ordinary conveniences of modern life for fear that if discovered, their caseworker will cut off their food stamps. This family is, after all, a bunch of "welfare cheats," a point reiterated in the film's finale, when the entire family jumps into the back of a moving paddy wagon. And yet there is no Cadillac in their driveway, only a new iron on the board and a new coffee pot atop the stove.

After asking Claudine about her recent work history, Ms. Kabak begins to badger her about the man she is dating, despite the fact that Claudine has not informed her of the new relationship. After Claudine protests, accusing Ms. Kabak of spying on her, Ms. Kabak asks, shamelessly, if Claudine is having sex with a man and, picking up a newer-looking olive-green undergarment out of the wicker laundry basket, reminds Claudine that if a man is "giving you things . . . I have to know." "Do you sleep with a man?" Claudine responds. An offended Ms. Kabak responds that such a question is none of Claudine's business. Claudine replies that her sex life is none of Ms. Kabak's business either, to which Ms. Kabak replies, "You're wrong! It is our business. This man may be bringing things into your home which you are not deducting [from your welfare benefits]." As a state employee, Ms. Kabak refuses to respect any boundaries of privacy Claudine tries to erect between her private life as a sexually active woman and her public life as a welfare recipient. The forfeiture of the right to privacy in order to receive welfare benefits underlines the feminist politics of the film; the personal is explicitly political in Claudine's life, as it is for the thousands of black women on welfare she represents.

This scene, the first of Ms. Kabak's two visits to Claudine's home, underlines the "humiliating, degrading, and inhuman" system the *Black Panther* described two years before the film's release. Ms. Kabak discards Claudine's right to privacy as she wanders freely through the apartment, inspecting its contents without permission, interrogating Claudine about her sex life, and unapologetically acknowledging she spies on her. The meticulousness with which Ms. Kabak surveils Claudine's family and searches in every nook and cranny, determined to find "contraband" to deduct from Claudine's welfare check or to disqualify her from the program entirely, indicates her prejudgment of the family as cheats. Yet even the full welfare disbursement is woefully insufficient, forcing Claudine to work in secret, hidden from Ms. Kabak's and therefore the state's view, in the home of a rich white couple far out in the suburbs. The price, then, that Claudine must pay in order to barely feed, clothe, and house her six children (in a four-room apartment) requires a complete forfeiture of privacy and propriety, careful concealment of job and man, and absolute subjugation to state surveillance.

A later scene restores some of the feminine agency stripped from Claudine through welfare compliance, illuminating the manner in which the assertion of black femininity is possible only when hidden from view of the state. After asking her secret lover Rupert to take her home, Rupert replies that because of the covert nature of their affair, dating Claudine is like dating a married woman, to which Claudine responds that she is married: "The welfare man, that's my husband. Makes me beg for them pennies. Starvation money. And if I can't feed my kids, that's child neglect. Go and get myself a little job on the side and don't tell him, then I'm cheatin'. If I stay at home, I'm lazy. You can't win. . . . I'd do anything to divorce that bastard." Much of Claudine's monologue in this scene is shot in a shallow-focused close-up, which, although Diahann Carroll does not look directly into the camera, creates a sense of direct address and intimacy with the spectator that heightens the emotional impact of her testimony regarding the dehumanizing effects of welfare compliance. The close-up also enables the audience to compare Claudine's face in this scene to her face in the scene with

Claudine gets dressed and laments about the burdens and restrictions of welfare compliance.

Ms. Kabak. In contrast to the bare face and pulled-back hair during the social worker's visit, her made-up face and styled hair restore a sense of feminine beauty denied Claudine in her confrontation with the state via Ms. Kabak. Her slightly tousled hair reveals a woman who has just had sex with a man she cares deeply for, thereby asserting a feminine agency, sexuality, and autonomy prohibited by the state and routinely pilloried in public discourse. Yet it is only in Rupert's bedroom, outside her state surveilled household, that Claudine can claim this agency.

A subsequent scene highlights the manner in which welfare compliance precludes the involvement of black paternal figures. When Ms. Kabak returns unannounced to Claudine's home, "Mr. Welfare Man" again plays along with a similarly choreographed rush to hide the family's modest belongings. Ms. Kabak discovers Rupert hiding in the coat closet, and as she and Claudine begin to argue, Rupert asks, "You supposed to give aid to dependent children. Why don't you just go ahead and give aid to dependent children instead of worrying about who the mother is keeping company with?" As their quarrel continues, Claudine interjects, confessing that Rupert did buy her a television and a few other housewares. Claudine's children then add a toaster and a coffee pot to the table of "contraband" from Rupert, physical items that represent the traditional roles of husband and father as provider. Rupert's position on the couch in front of Claudine and two of her sons, her youngest daughter on his lap, his outstretched arm across the couch's back, creates a physical barrier between Claudine and her children and Ms. Kabak. Rupert's attempt to fulfill the traditional roles of father and husband require that he literally protect them from the state, personified again here by Ms. Kabak. Yet doing so will nullify the family's welfare eligibility, throwing them deeper into poverty and therefore threatening Rupert's masculinity by undermining his ability to provide financially.

Claudine and Rupert's sneaking around to avoid Ms. Kabak, and Rupert's reluctance to move in with Claudine, is the direct result of man-in-the-house or substitute-father rules. Like suitable-home laws, man-in-the-house laws, enacted in many states, disqualified a woman from welfare benefits if a man lived in the home.[22] Such stipulations were subject to considerable criticism by groups like the Black Panthers, who drew on similar critiques from civil rights leaders a decade prior.[23] Black men in this film find themselves in a catch-22: either they abandon their "duty" as father and husband so their spouses can receive welfare benefits, or they stay in the home and disqualify themselves from resources their children desperately need. As Rupert and Ms. Kabak's argument continues, the social worker explains:

Ms. Kabak: We know that children need a man in the house, a woman needs a man in the house. We don't insist people be married.
Rupert: You mean, you'd help a man move in if he's not married to the mother?
Ms. Kabak: That's right.
Rupert: That's immoral. . . . What kind of example is that to set for the children?

This scene, along with the previous one, reiterates the black nationalist critique of the invasive and humiliating cost of welfare's "starvation money," as Rupert puts it. There is no war on poverty in *Claudine*. Government intervention in this film undermines economic and familial stability. While Ms. Kabak acknowledges the importance of cohabitation for both the children and the parents, she also admits that doing so without marrying is perhaps the most economically beneficial choice for the two of them. It is the government, then, not a "culture of poverty," that threatens poor black families in *Claudine*.

The punitive impact on low-income black families who inform the state of new romantic relationships plays out in the second act of the film. After their encounter with Ms. Kabak, Claudine broaches the possibility of making their relationship more official. She tells Rupert, "I want to be with you, and I want to know that you're there." Angry, Rupert responds, "Uh-oh, Goddamnit! Claudine, don't try to put me on welfare!" Claudine then explains that although formalizing their relationship would require Rupert to register with the welfare office, he would remain a "non-recipient," but her children would retain their benefits. An unhappy Rupert declares, "Claudine, they'd cut my balls off, and you'd look at me and you'd hate my guts!" Here, the film magnifies welfare's emasculation of black men and objectification of black women. Importantly, this exchange occurs as Rupert and Claudine lie in bed, Rupert smoking a postcoital cigarette. The symbolic castration to which Rupert alludes occurs immediately after he exercises his masculine vitality, reinforcing the state's undermining of black men's ability to provide for their spouse and children. The bedroom becomes the only place, therefore, where Rupert can "be a man," but even that must be done in secret—in Rupert's but never Claudine's apartment, hidden from government view.

As Rupert registers with the welfare office in the next scene, the film reemphasizes his emasculation. Rupert sits slumped at the social worker's desk, meek postured and head bowed, which forces the broad-shouldered, six-foot, two-inch Rupert to look up at the two female social workers, with a raised brow and sad droopy eyes that emphasize his powerlessness now that he is back under state surveillance. Rupert and Claudine's new cohabitation places a host of limitations and obligations on Rupert's finances, leaving him financially vulnerable and potentially unable to provide for Claudine and her children. In other words, by following the welfare rules and placing himself under government supervision, Rupert jeopardizes the financial security of this newly blended black family, compromises his ability to fulfill traditional gender roles, places increased stress on Claudine and his relationship, and threatens the stability of the family unit.

In *Claudine*, not only does the state deny black men and women the opportunity to fulfill conventional gender roles in the manner they desire, but welfare technicalities destroy each of the lives in this black family by influencing the reproductive and relationship choices for both parents and children. Once Rupert registers with the welfare office, hardship befalls all of the film's major characters. Now registered with the government, Rupert receives a court order charging him of willful neglect of his own children from a previous relationship. Despite Rupert's belief that he paid the entirety of his child support obligation, court documents reveal that he did not. The government begins garnishing Rupert's wages, and his reduced take-home pay is not enough to subsist. This sends Rupert into an angry alcoholic binge. He misses the Father's Day party Claudine throws him and disappears until the end of the film, failing to uphold his emotional and economic obligations as a husband and father. Claudine's children fare no better. Claudine's teenage son Charles has a vasectomy, a "small operation" in order to, according to him, limit the amount of poor black children in the world. Charles's younger sister Charlene becomes pregnant. The inadequate support welfare provides forces Claudine to secretly find extra work, taking her away from raising her children, who, without proper parental influence, make poor choices. Furthermore, the welfare income cap destroys Claudine and Rupert's relationship. Therefore, it is the invasive state, not black women, that manufactures the female-headed "culture of poverty" in America's urban ghettos. As Mayfield's lyrics read, "Though I've made some mistakes for goodness sakes, why should they help mess up my life?" *Claudine*'s portrayal of the suffering that welfare compliance imposes on low-income black families was an integral part of the larger black nationalist critiques of the social program in the 1970s. Welfare criticism was a central element of the broader anti-liberal ethos across the political spectrum, from left to right, that characterized the early decade. Moreover, that ethos provided the foundation on which colorblindness would take hold in subsequent years, as the race-neutral neoliberal language of the market itself was increasingly positioned as the solution to the socioeconomic "problems" of the 1970s.

Claudine Just "Happens to Be Black"

While *Claudine* primarily offers a black nationalist critique of welfare, the film also takes up the possibility of a colorblind alternative for black families, ultimately finding little reason for optimism. *Claudine* is therefore one of the first films to rebuke the emerging ideology of colorblindness. Roughly halfway through the film, Rupert asks Claudine's youngest child, Francis, about his future. Francis answers that when he grows up he wants to be "invisible." As the child picks up a pad and pencil to draw, Rupert asks what he is drawing. Francis responds, "A house in the country. A mom and a daddy." When Rupert asks to see the sketch, Francis shows him a blank page. When a confused Rupert asks, "Where is everybody?" Francis replies,

Claudine's youngest son, Francis, draws "A house in the country. A mom and a daddy," but they're "invisible."

"Invisible." Drawing on previous black intellectual critiques of the white gaze by writers like W. E. B. Du Bois, Ralph Ellison, and Frantz Fanon, the metaphor of invisibility here is Janus faced. On the one hand, it represents the desire of this black child to exist out of view of the panopticon of the state, whose constant surveillance impoverishes and torments his family. On the other hand, the empty page represents the impossibility and emptiness of the American dream—embodied here as a house in the country and a two-parent household—for poor black children begat by welfare laws. The best Francis can hope for, then, is invisibility, because his only other option is hypervisibility at society's bottom. This, then, is the best colorblindness can do for poor blacks in the early 1970s. There are no delusions in *Claudine* of post–civil rights racial harmony or an unadulterated race-neutral meritocracy. The colorblind desire for invisibility of the black child in this film amounts to the wholesale disregard and abandonment of the black poor through a tragic alternative to the constant harassment and monitoring of the state through predatory welfare policies.

A second scene reiterates the abandonment of black youth by the state. After Rupert fails to show up for the Father's Day party Claudine and her children prepared, Paul rides his bike through the busy Harlem streets, while Francis sits on the handlebars. The two brothers zigzag through traffic, unprotected by helmets or other safety gear, racing to see if Rupert is at his apartment, perhaps having lost track of time. The bike ride is edited as a montage that cuts between the black emotionless faces of the boys, riding inches from cars driving at high speeds, and point-of-view shots of the boys weaving in and out of traffic, barely avoiding a collision at each maneuver. Like Francis's blank drawing, this scene works as an extended metaphor for the future confronting black youth, riding unprotected through a life full of constant threats to their well-being. Here, again, colorblind solutions that fail to address the specific injustices these children face as young black men—living in a low-income black neighborhood of Harlem, impoverished by a century of race-conscious housing discrimination and policing—offer little relief and no protection for the racialized society these children must navigate.

On-screen, *Claudine* disavows colorblindness and racializes the dehumanization of welfare compliance. Whether it is the film's topic or corresponding dialogue, such as Rupert's reference to the Moynihan Report that "if I do go on the welfare, I'm just another lazy ass nigger living off the taxpayer"; the location of the film in the predominantly black neighborhood of Harlem; or the black nationalist awakening of Claudine's oldest son, Charles, *Claudine* proudly identifies itself as a "black film." The fact that this was the first picture produced by Third World Cinema, a film company founded specifically to increase the opportunities of persons of color in the movie business—both on- and off-screen—further corroborates this fact. Moreover, the production history of the film, which began as an idea about a terminally ill white single mother not on welfare, along with TWC's philosophy, discredits any claims that TWC wanted audiences to view *Claudine* as anything other than a story of urban black life in the early 1970s.

However, the manner in which TWC promoted the film catered directly to colorblind sentiments. The film's star, James Earl Jones, and others involved in the film's production sought to attract white audiences by framing the film in ways that aligned with the emerging popularity of colorblindness among whites. In one interview, Jones described the film as a "very gentle love story of people we all know, working people, who happen to be black."[24] Gordon Armstrong, the national publicity director of 20th Century Fox, characterized the film as "the first motion picture to combine the elements of a love story, a survival story, a family drama and a soul comedy into a story of the ghetto meant for everyone, no matter who."[25]

Critics concurred. An untitled review in the May 25, 1974, issue of the *New Republic* called *Claudine* "one of the most enjoyable romances of any kind, black or white, since *For Love of Ivy* (1968)."[26] Additionally, a *Product Digest* review from the same month had the following to say: "Not since "A Raisin in the Sun" has there been a film about black family life in the U.S. as funny and touching as 'Claudine.' And not since that 1961 release has there been one with such high potential to please a white audience as well as those blacks who are fed up with the distortion of their experiences in the sex-and-violence melodramas that have been so prolific recently."[27]

The colorblind advertising strategy of *Claudine* marks a significant departure from that of blaxploitation films of the same era. As we saw in chapter 1, American International Pictures' advertising strategy for *Coffy* leveraged stereotypical notions of black vernacular in an effort to appeal directly to urban black audiences. By contrast, the colorblind marketing strategy of *Claudine* aimed to sell a "black" film to a white audience in a manner that dovetailed with emerging audience trends in Hollywood in the early 1970s. As Ed Guerrero explains, the blaxploitation boom in Hollywood was an effort to attract black audiences, which made up a disproportionate percentage of Hollywood moviegoers, in the aftermath of the independent success of *Sweet Sweetback's Baadasssss Song* (1971). However, by 1972, through movies like *The Godfather,* Hollywood learned it did not need a predominantly black cast to draw black audiences. By 1974, blaxploitation films were on the decline, and the belief that black-oriented films needed "cross-over" appeal increasingly persuaded Hollywood producers.[28] As the history of *Claudine* reveals, film producers believed that one of the most effective ways to do so was to appeal directly to the emerging popularity of colorblindness.

That many associated with *Claudine*'s production thought the film could serve as an antidote to the typical blaxploitation representations of blackness by presenting a colorblind drama of people "who just happen to be black" in order to attract white viewers highlights the distinctive nature of the film itself and the complicated racial politics of both the film and the early 1970s. Although the film and its production history may not elicit obvious colorblind connections, its promotion indicates that the film's producers could not avoid, or perhaps were even drawn to, inchoate colorblind discourse and sought to position the movie in a way that would appeal to colorblind sentiments and attract a broader audience. This paradox mirrors the convoluted nature of colorblindness in the early 1970s. It also, more importantly, illuminates the racial ideology of colorblindness on the verge of cohesion. The active erasure of race in the promotion of *Claudine* may amount to little more than marketing strategy in one sense, but the inclination to do so among the film's producers reveals an understanding of a larger (white) social ethos that was increasingly drawn to colorblindness as an effective way to frame its opposition to civil rights in the decade after the civil rights movement. In this regard, colorblindness in Hollywood functioned not merely as a matter of aesthetics but as a production practice in the 1970s.

Claudine sits on the brink of colorblind hegemony, at a moment when political activists, artists, and ordinary Americans across the political spectrum were still parsing the political utility of colorblind rhetoric. The story of *Claudine*, therefore, attempts to reconcile a transitional moment in American racial politics whereby competing social and political interests were debating the utility of colorblindness while highlighting the uselessness of the discourse in the pursuit of racial justice, yet not wholly unable to avoid appealing to the very colorblind sentiments it aims to critique. Just a few years before the film's release, few took arguments for a colorblind approach to racial inequality seriously; just a few years after, colorblind discourse would cohere around the opposition to two civil rights issues—affirmative action and court-ordered busing—and the racial project of colorblindness would emerge. As it grew, colorblind hegemony would begin to dismantle many of the legal victories of the civil rights movement and reinforce white supremacy in the post–civil rights era. Using the very language of the civil rights movement, white backlash activists petitioned the nation's highest courts to dismantle some of the very programs the movement had fought so hard to implement on the grounds that it, like Jim Crow segregation, violated a colorblind approach to the law. In the op-ed pages of the nation's most popular newspapers, columnists sought to win support for the white backlash by appealing to colorblind sentiments. And in movie theaters across the country, audiences would flock together to watch a relatively unknown actor—Sylvester Stallone—play a down-and-out, cannot-catch-a-break, blue-collar amateur boxer take a shot at the heavyweight title against a rich, overconfident, and undeserving black champion, on a ring decorated like the American flag on the country's bicentennial, becoming Hollywood's first hero in the age of colorblindness.

3 He Looks Like a Big Flag

Rocky and the Origins of Hollywood Colorblind Heroism

[Affirmative Action] is, by whatever name, reverse discrimination. . . .
[It] violates the principle that the law should be colorblind.

—George Will, *Washington Post*, 1976

In the early 1970s, colorblind rhetoric had yet to cohere behind a singular political agenda. Political activists both conservative and progressive mobilized colorblind discourse to serve their political ends. The nascent colorblind aesthetics on Hollywood movie screens matched the inconsistent political deployment of colorblind rhetoric. In other words, there was no united colorblind ideology in the early 1970s. That would change by the decade's end. As the seventies unfolded, colorblind discourse provided a unifying framework that united whites in opposition to school integration and affirmative action. Hollywood movie screens proved instrumental in this process. Popular films like the 1976 blockbuster *Rocky* provided the race-conscious visuality left ambiguous by race-neutral colorblind discourse. Hollywood offered white audiences visual narratives of who "unfairly benefited" and who "undeservedly suffered" under civil rights enforcement. Hollywood movies decoded the colorblind dog whistles of busing and affirmative action. The result was the coherence of the racial project of colorblindness, which co-opts the race-neutral language of the civil rights movement to undermine its very gains and reinvent and reinforce white supremacy.

School integration and affirmative action were the two most controversial civil rights issues of the 1970s. By decade's end, both programs were decimated. The dismantling of these civil rights programs required white opponents to reframe white supremacy within civil rights–compliant language in the post-1960s. Reframing support for segregated neighborhood schools as opposition to "forced busing" was one way to do so. Reframing opposition to the racial integration of colleges and universities and employment sectors like trade and law enforcement unions as opposition to "reverse discrimination" was another. The key for either, however, was that colorblindness provided the seemingly civil rights friendly rhetorical framework for each iteration of opposition to racial integration. By mid-decade, integration and affirmative action foes increasingly defended their opposition by affirming an unwavering commitment to colorblindness.

It was in the trenches of the sociopolitical fights over busing and affirmative action that the racial ideology of colorblindness cohered. Colorblindness was built on the anti-liberal ethos of the early decade and offered an inherently antistatist, hands-off "solution" to the "problem" of government intervention in matters of race in the mid-1970s. Because it prohibits the consideration of race in social policy, it effectively handcuffs the government's ability to intervene in matters of racial inequality. Whites' successful labeling of affirmative action and court-ordered busing as "reverse discrimination" galvanized support to defeat these civil rights programs by the end of the seventies.[1] As the second half of the decade unfolded, the ideology was increasingly positioned as the solution to the "problem" of government overreach in pursuit of racial integration. Unlike its deployment earlier in the decade, colorblind rhetoric in the latter half of the 1970s increasingly borrowed the language of the civil rights movement to mobilize against its legal legacy. Colorblindness enabled whites to oppose the very victories of the civil rights movement without offending post–civil rights rhetorical standards of respect.

Hollywood proved fundamental in the articulation of a unified colorblind ideology in opposition to busing and affirmative action by providing race-conscious understanding to race-neutral political discourse, acting as translator for the coded racial dog whistles of busing and affirmative action. To that end, Rocky Balboa, protagonist of the 1976 film *Rocky*, which won the Academy Award for Best Picture, was the age of colorblindness's first Hollywood hero. Balboa was by no means the first major movie character unprejudiced by a person's skin color or the first to espouse colorblind rhetoric. For example, Sidney Poitier's Dr. John Prentice, from *Guess Who's Coming to Dinner*, beat him by nearly a decade. Rocky Balboa was instead the first post–civil rights hero to combine civil rights–friendly colorblind rhetoric with the politics of white opposition to integration. Although Balboa is not a bigot in the typical sense, the working-class redemption that this film offers comes via the reassertion of white male dominance over African Americans and the symbolic defeat of "reverse discrimination."[2] Ultimately, *Rocky* proved fundamental to the colorblind white backlash of the decade by offering race-conscious visual evidence of the racial stakes of the colorblind opposition to key civil rights programs.

In 1976, one month before *Rocky* premiered, as antibusing outrage spread across the country and the Supreme Court was halfway between its first two major anti–affirmative action cases, University of Chicago economist Milton Friedman won the Nobel Prize in Economics. His free-market fundamentalism moved from the fringes of postwar economic thought to the field's highest honor.[3] Friedman's star rose considerably in the early 1960s with the publication of *Capitalism and Freedom* in 1962. The popularity of the book brought Friedman's free-market fundamentalism to an audience outside academia, which he further cultivated in a weekly *Newsweek* column from 1966 to 1984. Moreover, as Keynesian medicine appeared an insufficient tonic for the high unemployment and inflation that characterized the stagflationary 1970s economy, Friedman's warnings regarding the discontents of government planning finally seemed vindicated.

Friedman's journey from the margins of the discipline in the 1940s to winning its top prize three decades later demonstrates the growing popularity of Friedman's antistatist, free-market fundamentalism. That Friedman's rise coincided with the economic recessions of the 1970s, the more general antistatist ethos of the decade, and mounting opposition to government intervention in matters of civil rights is no accident. Numerous scholars have linked neoliberalism and colorblindness. As education scholar Pauline Lipman writes, "From the dawn of capitalism, white supremacy was mobilized for the accumulation of capital. . . . The centrality of white supremacy to neoliberal accumulation strategies is the present-day iteration of this dynamic."[4] In other words, neoliberalism relies on the colorblind language of the free market to reinforce white supremacy. Yet like colorblindness, neoliberalism is by no means post-racial. As George Lipsitz argues, "Neoliberalism needs to disavow the idea of race, because race references historical social identities not reducible to market relations. . . . At the same time, neoliberalism needs race even more than previous stages of capitalism did. By making public spaces and public institutions synonymous with communities of color, neoliberals seek to taint them in the eyes of white working-class and middle-class people, who then become more receptive to privatization schemes that undermine their own stakes in the shared social communities that neoliberalism attempts to eliminate."[5] It is no coincidence that the neoliberal creed—that government inhibits freedom, be it in the market or in the classroom, and that freedom must be understood strictly at the level of the *individual*—found increasingly sympathetic ears among whites as the 1970s progressed and whites sought colorblind ways to kneecap the government's ability to address the racial inequality of

African Americans as a *group*.[6] While scholars like Lipman and Lipsitz have astutely noted the utility of neoliberalism in racializing the public sphere as "black" in order to justify its dismantling, I argue that white opposition to government intervention in school integration, college admissions, and hiring in the mid-1970s played a fundamental role in turning whites, especially blue-collar whites, against the state and toward the colorblind political project of neoliberalism.[7] Colorblindness and neoliberalism were mutually constitutive, and colorblindness functions as the racial ideology of neoliberalism.

This chapter begins by tracing the articulation of colorblindness as a coherent ideology around the issues of busing and affirmative action in the years between 1974 and 1978. From there, I offer a close reading of *Rocky*, highlighting the manner in which the film offers race-conscious images and implications to colorblind political discourse. Just as the political struggles over integration produced a coherent colorblind ideology, they also, through *Rocky*, reflected the first appearance of Hollywood's colorblind aesthetics. *Rocky* was instrumental in shaping colorblindness, which was fundamental in the opposition to affirmative action and busing. As scholar Jennifer Pierce argues, historians have placed too much blame on the role of the economic decline of the 1970s for the white backlash against welfare, affirmative action, and busing. Pierce and Matthew F. Delmont contend that the news media, as well as anti–affirmative action intellectuals, also played an important role.[8] I offer my own analysis of newspapers and anti–affirmative action intellectuals like George Will to further this point. Yet my analysis of *Rocky* highlights the integral role Hollywood played in both the white backlash of the late 1970s and the articulation of colorblindness.

I then turn to the intersection of the rise of colorblindness and neoliberalism. Ultimately, I argue that neoliberal thought gained momentum in the 1970s because it offered solutions to two problems: first, to the economic sluggishness of the decade, and second, perhaps more importantly, to the broad "problem" of excessive government intervention and to matters of racial inequality specifically. In other words, neoliberalism appealed to whites whose school districts faced busing orders or whose universities or unions implemented affirmative action programs. Many blue-collar whites proved willing to sacrifice the union power they had spent decades building to protect their "possessive investment in whiteness."[9] Certainly, the poor economic performance of the decade and the seeming failures of traditional Keynesian remedies played a role. Yet economics alone does not fully account for this transformation. As whites increasingly turned on civil rights programs, they articulated a neoliberal ideology of colorblind individualism in order to handcuff the government's ability to intervene in matters of race. Like colorblindness, neoliberalism must simultaneously deny and embrace race in order to carry out its political project. In the closing years of the 1970s, colorblindness became not the actualization of civil rights dreams but the racial politics of an emerging neoliberal nightmare.

Moreover, Hollywood played an integral role in cohering the racial politics of neoliberal colorblind individualism. The narrative conventions of the film industry, especially the centrality of the individual protagonist, are particularly predisposed to neoliberal politics. The third part of this chapter traces the emergence of colorblindness as the racial politics of neoliberalism. I examine Friedman's and other neoliberals' writings on civil rights, which highlight the intersection of neoliberal market logic with the antistatist social politics of colorblindness. I then offer a close analysis of *Blue Collar*, a film about the struggles of three Detroit autoworkers—two black, Zeke and Smokey (Richard Pryor and Yaphet Kotto), and one white, Jerry (Harvey Keitel)—with their corrupt union, which premiered in 1978, midway between the awarding of Friedman's Nobel Prize and the presidential election of Ronald Reagan, who would bring colorblindness and neoliberalism to the Oval Office. While scholars have noted the manner in which the film represents the disintegration of labor power as a result of the coming neoliberal era, the film also forebodes the ruinous effects of neoliberalism on racial justice.[10] *Blue Collar* precedes and anticipates the policy changes wrought by the Reagan administration specifically, and neoliberal thought more broadly. Moreover, the film marks the destruction of Hollywood's ability to narrate collective struggle, thereby signaling the manner in which Hollywood, a culture industry whose medium is inclined toward narrating the plight of individuals, became an integral player in cohering and disseminating neoliberal ideology.

Affirmative Action and Busing: A Historical Overview

In the 1968 presidential campaign, Richard Nixon's Southern Strategy, devised by Republican strategist Kevin Phillips, foregrounded "wedge" issues to court white Democrats frustrated with their party's position on civil rights. As GOP strategist Lee Atwater explained in 1981, "You start out in 1954 by saying, 'Nigger, nigger, nigger.' By 1968 you can't say 'nigger'—that hurts you. [It] backfires. So you say stuff like forced busing, states' rights and all that stuff."[11] Nixon's own special counsel, John Ehrlichman, made little effort to hide the campaign objective behind Nixon's opposition to busing and affirmative action. "We'll go after the racists," he stated, with "subliminal appeals to the anti-black voter."[12] As Ian Haney López argues, "'Busing' offered a Northern analog to states' rights. The language may have referred to transportation, but the emotional wallop came from defiance toward integration."[13]

In the follow-up to the landmark *Brown* ruling (*Brown II*), the Supreme Court banned racial segregation in American schools but left the time frame for integration vague, ordering the desegregation of America's schools with "all deliberate speed." By 1971, the Supreme Court decided that districts had been given more than enough time to integrate, ruling in *Swann v. Charlotte-Mecklenburg Board of Education* that busing students across district lines to achieve racial integration was an acceptable solution to those districts refusing to integrate. By the mid-1970s, white parents across the country were in violent revolt against efforts to integrate America's public schools. All told, forty-seven of America's one hundred largest school districts faced busing orders in the 1970s.[14]

It was in Boston where violent antibusing resistance reached its zenith. In June 1974, a judge issued a busing order to integrate schools in South Boston. At the beginning of the school year, half of the eighty thousand students in the affected areas were kept home from school in protest. What followed were three years of fights, stabbings, and intimidation in what historian Ronald Formisano argues "amounted to terrorism" against blacks and sympathetic whites by a group of "antibusers."[15] Within the first month, 140 people were arrested and 69 injured, and antiblack harassment as a whole was too rampant to quantify.[16] White protesters stood outside schools and pelted buses carrying black schoolchildren with rocks. The violence culminated in April 1976, when a group of white antibusers used an American flag to assault a black lawyer passing by on his lunch break.[17]

As a result, what amounted to a mass exodus of whites from the cities and into the suburbs ensued, in which parents enrolled their children either in private schools or in suburban public schools a safe distance from integration pressure. From 1968 to 1976, the percentage of white students in Boston public schools fell from 68.5 percent to 44 percent; and in cities like Detroit and Atlanta, over half of all whites left public schools.[18] Moreover, in places like Los Angeles, Pasadena, San Francisco, and Nashville, court-ordered busing led to violent resistance and even riots from white parents protesting the racial integration of America's public schools. Worst of all, in Pontiac, Michigan, in 1971, a group of five Ku Klux Klan members dynamited ten school buses just days ahead of the start of the city's busing program.

The prevailing historical narrative of busing frames its opponents as pro–civil rights moderates, or even liberals, who had simply grown to believe civil rights enforcement had gone too far, threatening the integrity of their neighborhood schools and encroaching on their rights as homeowners. However, as Matthew F. Delmont demonstrates, opposition to busing had, in actuality, little to do with transporting children significant distances to and from school. Instead, the term itself became a dog whistle for the racial integration of public schools, which enabled parents and politicians to "support white schools and neighborhoods without using explicitly racist language."[19] Moreover, opposition to school integration in "progressive" northern cities like New York predate busing orders by decades. Perhaps most revealing, northern members of Congress insisted on amending the initial language of the 1964 Civil Rights Act in order to shield northern cities with segregated schools from desegregation orders.[20] And, as Jamin B. Raskin notes, school districts facing busing orders deliberately maintained segregated schools. In other words, had all-white districts merely complied with the *Brown* decision, they would have avoided court-ordered busing mandates altogether.[21] By the time President Nixon scheduled a nationally televised address to announce a moratorium on new busing orders in March 1972, the antibusing animus was firmly entrenched in the minds of most whites. "The majority of white Americans," Delmont concludes, "never supported civil rights if it meant confronting or overturning the structures of racial discrimination that created and maintained segregated schools and neighborhoods."[22]

California offers an important case study regarding how busing enabled whites to both defend segregated schools and avoid charges of racial prejudice. California voters passed two antibusing initiatives in the 1970s. The first, Proposition 21 (1972), banned race-based assignments in California public schools, thereby halting busing orders throughout the state, including in Los Angeles County, where the proposition's sponsor, the hard-line conservative Floyd Wakefield, resided. Wakefield sold his amendment to California voters as a way to end "forced integration" and protect whites' rights. Wakefield's backlash posturing worked; 61 percent of California voters approved Proposition 21, though the Supreme Court would overturn the amendment two years later. In 1978, California voters approved another initiative—Proposition 1—which ended school integration via busing. However, this time the anti-desegregation bill's sponsor—Alan Robbins—was a self-professed liberal Democrat who insisted that his bill was best for all children. Robbins even courted support from black and Latino civil rights leaders to prove that he, unlike Wakefield, was not trying to end busing out of racial animus. Instead, Robbins argued his opposition to busing stemmed from the tax bill and burden for *all* involved. Nearly 70 percent of California voters agreed, as did the Supreme Court, which upheld the proposition and ended mandatory desegregation in the Golden State.[23] As the history of busing opposition in California demonstrates—specifically the backlash sentiments of Floyd Wakefield versus the colorblind approach of Alan Robbins—the successful dismantling of school integration through busing relied heavily on busing opponents' ability to frame their opposition to school integration in a manner that complied with post–civil rights rhetorical standards of respect.

Busing was one of two social issues that drew outrage from whites during the 1970s; the other was affirmative action. Affirmative action programs were a victory of the civil rights movement. In 1961, President John F. Kennedy issued Executive Order 10925, which required government contractors to "take affirmative action to ensure that applicants are employed and that employees are treated during employment without regard to their race, creed, color, or national origin."[24] Lyndon Johnson took the federal government's commitment to affirmative action a step further. In June 1965, in his commencement address at Howard University, the president argued that "freedom is not enough: It is not enough just to open the gates of opportunity. All our citizens must have the ability to walk through those gates. This is the next and most powerful stage of the battle for civil rights. We seek not just freedom but opportunity—not just legal equity but human ability—not just equality as a right and a theory but equality as a fact and as a result."[25]

Race-based hiring, in order to integrate segregated labor unions and workforces, became popular in the wake of the social unrest of the second half of the 1960s, when cities across the country, most notably Watts, Detroit, and Newark, ignited in riot. In the aftermath, the *Kerner Report*—written by the Kerner Commission, tasked by President Johnson with investigating the causes of the 1967 racial uprisings in Newark and Detroit—recommended, in part, jobs for poor blacks living in urban ghettos.[26] The Johnson administration responded by incentivizing trade unions seeking government contracts to hire more people of color.[27] His initial plan, to require a certain number of nonwhite workers for all companies seeking government contracts, and for those who did not meet the quota to prove that they either could not or were doing everything they could to comply, was twice thrown out by the comptroller general. Perhaps ironically, the plan was revitalized in the early days of the Nixon presidency. As demonstrated by his Southern Strategy, Nixon was certainly no civil rights ally. Yet in the late 1960s, the Nixon administration proposed an amended plan, which replaced Johnson's "quotas" with "goals," a distinction that would confound the Supreme Court for decades thereafter. Nixon's Philadelphia Plan held up in court, and the plan, first implemented in 1969, marked the beginning of federal affirmative action in employment. It is important to clarify that Nixon's goal with the Philadelphia Plan was not to endorse affirmative action; rather, the president thought the program would prove an effective wedge between unions and blacks, two key constituents of the Democratic Party. Nonetheless, colleges and universities throughout the country began enacting affirmative action policies in their admissions processes. White opposition to affirmative action, despite the fact that affirmative action programs benefited white women more than any other group, emerged as soon as the program began.[28] By 1972, 82 percent of whites opposed affirmative action.[29] Trade union members overwhelmingly opposed these programs, which both required racial integration and threatened union seniority policies.

Given the widespread white opposition to affirmative action, it was only a matter of time before the Supreme Court intervened, which it did frequently in the 1970s. The court's affirmative action rulings tried to distinguish hiring or admissions "goals," which were legal, from "quotas," which were not. By eliminating the ability to ensure racial integration (i.e., quotas), the "goals" versus "quotas" criterion was a victory for affirmative action opponents. The groundwork for this distinction was laid almost a decade earlier, when Republican opponents of the Civil Rights Act of 1964 fought tooth and nail to water down Title VII of the act—which, in theory, outlawed job discrimination—by requiring proof of discriminatory intent, rather than simply an unequal result, thereby making it nearly impossible to prove discrimination or implement effective affirmative action programs.[30] In one of the court's first major affirmative action rulings, *Griggs v. Duke Power* (1971), the court placed significant influence on *results*, not *intentions*, a ruling that would prove inconsistent with future rulings.

The *Griggs* decision was a decisive victory for affirmative action supporters. However, it was short lived. As the decade progressed, opponents of affirmative action won increasing influence in Congress, the executive branch, and the courts. In *DeFunis v. Odegaard* (1974), Marco DeFunis sued the University of Washington School of Law in 1971 after receiving a rejection letter. He claimed he was the victim of discrimination because minorities with inferior test scores were admitted while he was rejected. It was only a technicality that prevented a similar decision to that of the landmark anti–affirmative action ruling four years later. In *Regents of the University of California v. Bakke*, the court invalidated the affirmative action program at the University of California, Davis, medical school.[31] By the middle of the decade, then, significant opposition had mounted against affirmative action and was beginning to see its efforts bear fruit, both in the courts and in the attitudes of politicians.

The Birth of Reverse Discrimination

Between the years 1974 and 1976, colorblind rhetoric became increasingly popular among school integration and affirmative action opponents. Conservatives increasingly turned to colorblind discourse to mount populist opposition to the civil rights programs. Building on the antistatist ethos of the first half of the 1970s, whites sold colorblindness as a discursively tactful solution to the overreach of government in matters of race; in so doing, they set a new course for the reassertion of white supremacy. As Matthew Lassiter argues, the suburbs provided the crucible for politically centrist, middle-class colorblind ideology: "The considerable success of the civil rights movement in dismantling the legal caste system and discrediting overt racism, in combination with the rapid expansion of a suburban landscape organized around residential segregation and socioeconomic privilege, resulted in the evolution of a middle-class outlook expressed through color-blind language of consumer rights and meritocratic individualism."[32] In places like Charlotte, North Carolina, what amounted to a "populist revolt of the center," whereby middle-class white suburban homeowners mobilized against busing orders under the guise of a commitment to colorblind racial justice, spread throughout the country in the 1970s. In the case of Charlotte, suburban whites insisted that they supported busing black schoolchildren to the suburbs, but vehemently opposed busing their own children into the inner cities to integrate all-black schools. In their opposition, these middle-class white suburbanites organized around the discourse of colorblindness to protest busing, regularly referring to and aligning themselves with the language of the *Brown* decision to defend their resistance.[33] Lassiter concludes, "The 'color-blind' ideology that percolated in the Charlotte suburbs . . . ought to be understood as part of an emerging bipartisan defense of suburban autonomy and middle-class residential privilege[,] not simply from within a teleological narrative of the New Right."[34]

Similarly, white Bostonians who resorted to violence in opposition to the busing order took offense to the press's likening of them to white southerners who opposed the civil rights movement a decade earlier. Integration opponents in Boston framed themselves as just the opposite—as heroic defenders of civil rights, not its racist opponents. They were exasperated that the media represented them otherwise. "How come when Negroes have a civil rights march people pay attention, but when we do nobody stirs? Don't we have civil rights?"[35] White opponents' insistence that they were on the side of civil rights was integral to their activism. Throughout the three-year crisis in Boston, the antibusers and their supporters around the country frequently complained about the alleged antiwhite, pro-black bias of the press.

The pro–civil rights, anti-integration balancing act in places like Charlotte and Boston imbued antibusing rhetoric throughout the country. As integration opponents found voice on the pages of the nation's most widely circulated newspapers—in op-eds, letters to the editor, and so forth—colorblind discourse provided the lens through which to align their opposition to civil rights programs with the civil rights movement itself. In October 1974, for example, journalist Tom Wicker wrote a column in the *New York Times* denouncing the violence among white Boston parents and President Ford's unwillingness to intervene in Boston. He described the response as "predictable," and likened the riots of whites opposing the busing order to those in Little Rock in 1957, when nine black high schoolers integrating the city's Central High School sparked similar violent backlash from white protesters.[36] Two weeks later, a man named Henry S. Huntington published a letter in the *Times* objecting to Wicker's Little Rock comparison. As a result of the deliberate segregation in Little Rock, wrote Huntington, "the court decision there required essentially that race be ignored in assigning children to schools, reflecting recognition of the constitutional principle of color-blindness." Contrastingly, in Boston, argued Huntington, children had always been assigned to schools on a "straight color-blind basis," so the court order to bus children violated "the constitutional guidelines setting our course for a color-blind society."[37] What Huntington's letter missed, however, was the complex transfer policies in Boston school districts, which created loopholes for whites to escape district lines while preventing blacks from doing so. Nevertheless, in an effort to further bolster their position, white antibusers frequently quoted Martin Luther

King Jr. and disseminated flyers defending their version of civil disobedience as inspired by King himself. They even sang "We Shall Overcome" during a march protesting the busing order.[38]

The attempt of antibusers to align themselves with the civil rights movement, as opposed to its opposition, speaks to a fundamental transformation of racial discourse in the mid-1970s. As a result of the victories of the civil rights movement, the proud white supremacy of southern opposition to black freedom struggles in the 1960s grew increasingly unpopular, even among those who took up their cause in Boston. The post–civil rights era is characterized, in part, by a racial discourse that deems blatant espousals of white supremacy unacceptable. This is important for two reasons. First, white opposition to busing in Boston was not simply New England's version of, say, the White Citizens' Councils of Montgomery, Alabama. Instead, these were people who, in general, did not oppose the end of de jure segregation in the South. However, as Delmont argues, these parents vehemently defended de facto segregation in their own communities, maintained largely in absence of race-conscious law or rhetoric. They therefore represent the strategic reframing of white supremacy in the mid-1970s. Second, and more importantly, the rhetoric mobilized by school integration and affirmative action opponents speaks to a larger political strategy that gained increasing popularity in the mid-1970s and proved essential to civil rights opponents: the emergence of colorblindness as the antidote to the supposed reverse discrimination of busing and affirmative action. The success of opponents to affirmative action and busing relied on their ability to frame public discourse around colorblindness and reverse discrimination. As whites grew more recalcitrant, colorblindness proved irresistible to the growing number of whites raging against government "overreach" in civil rights.

By the middle of the decade, whites had successfully yoked the discourse of colorblindness with the idea of reverse discrimination. As we have seen, usage of the term *colorblindness* varied significantly during the late 1960s and early 1970s. However, by 1976, it was being used overwhelmingly to defend those opposing the supposed reverse discrimination of affirmative action and busing. The number of articles insisting that affirmative action and busing were "reverse discriminatory" and that colorblindness offered a remedy in line with Dr. King's dream increased exponentially beginning in 1976. The counterargument that affirmative action was necessary now in order to produce a colorblind future fell on deaf ears.[39] Whites positioned colorblindness as the singular legacy of the civil rights movement, which therefore mandated the eradication of "reverse discriminatory" programs like affirmative action and busing. A March 1976 article in *U.S. News and World Report* noted that whites were no longer reluctant to speak out about "reverse discrimination."[40] Eight months later, on a November edition of *Meet the Press*, one such unreluctant white man, conservative columnist George Will, asked NAACP director Benjamin Hooks if he favored reverse discrimination. In a subsequent column, Will wrote, "[Affirmative Action] is, by whatever name, reverse discrimination. . . . [It] violates the principle that the law should be colorblind."[41] Will's racial brethren agreed; a March 1977 Gallup poll found that 83 percent of respondents opposed racial preference in higher education.[42]

There was perhaps no greater advocate for the racial project of colorblindness on the pages of America's newspapers than George Will. Will frequently devoted his *Newsweek* columns to the issues of reverse discrimination and colorblindness. In July 1976, addressing the busing crisis in Boston, Will wrote, "[The *Brown* decision] seemed to mean that no child would be barred from a school because of race. Today, court orders exclude many white children from their neighborhood schools solely because they are white. . . . *Brown* held that 'separate' school *systems* are 'inherently' unequal. Obviously dual school systems had to be dismantled . . . [which] meant making the law 'color blind.'"[43] According to Will, the Boston busing order violated colorblindness, which he argued was the foundational principle of the civil rights movement. Will objected to the "blurring" of the "compulsory" (i.e., de jure) segregation of the pre-1960s Jim Crow South, which he opposes, with the unintentional (i.e., de facto) segregation under "color blind" law, which he defends. Nonetheless, a cantankerous Will found reason for optimism. Referring to a recent ruling in Pasadena, which overturned a 1970 order to maintain racial balance because "school authorities need not alter racial patterns that they do not cause," the relieved Will believed that "reason is staging a comeback." For Will, it was perfectly legitimate for the government to forcibly integrate schools, but only those that had engaged in "forcibly segregative acts." Those schools that had not, like the ones in Boston, should be left alone. "The Constitution mandates a free, not a 'racially balanced,' society," argued Will.[44] For Will, the only issue at hand was whether or not Boston had specific policies prohibiting the admission of black students. Like the Supreme Court and the conservative opponents of the 1964 Civil Rights Act, Will insisted on irrefutable evidence of discriminatory intent. Without it, no prejudice existed. By his rules, then, busing amounted to reverse discrimination.

In a subsequent column that November, Will reiterated his opposition to busing on the grounds that it violates the colorblind principles of the Constitution. "Forced busing," he writes, "involves (as does reverse discrimination) abandonment of the principle that the law should not take notice of a citizen's race."[45] Here, again, Will insists on proof of discriminatory intent, something nearly impossible to find, which thus effectively prohibits the state's ability to address racial injustice. In *Washington v. Davis* (1976), the Supreme Court officially adopted the proof-of-discriminatory-intent criteria.[46] By the mid-1970s, the courts were beginning to sway Will's way. It should not be surprising, then, that the Supreme Court's ruling in *Village of Arlington Heights v. Metropolitan Housing Development Corp.* in January 1977, which threw out a district court ruling of discrimination because the high court could find no evidence of discriminatory intent, pleased Will.[47] The columnist applauded the decision in a column titled "Common Sense on Race," calling it "refreshingly crisp." "The racially disproportionate *impact* of a policy," he concluded, "is without constitutional significance unless there is proof of a racially discriminatory *purpose*."[48]

This moment in 1976, when a growing number of whites turned to colorblindness precisely because it undermined affirmative action and busing policies, along with the Supreme Court's adoption of the discriminatory-intent criteria, marks a watershed moment in the emergence of colorblindness. The momentum gained in the mid-1970s laid the groundwork for colorblindness's first major victory in the Supreme Court and reinforced the *intent* over *results* criteria. In 1978, in *Regents of the University of California v. Bakke*, the Supreme Court reviewed whether the affirmative action policy at UC Davis's medical school, which set aside sixteen of one hundred positions for minority applicants, violated the Fourteenth Amendment's equal protection clause and the Civil Rights Act of 1964.[49] Allan Bakke, a white man in his mid-thirties, was twice rejected from the medical school. He sued, arguing that the university's affirmative action program racially discriminated against him. The *Bakke* case split the court, which eventually wrote six different opinions. The court's decision, however, ordered that Bakke be admitted to the medical school, concluding that while race could continue to play a role in college admissions, quotas were unconstitutional. In *Bakke*, the Supreme Court determined that so-called reverse discrimination merited greater constitutional protections than did actual racism.

The *Bakke* decision not only validated the arguments of people like George Will—that affirmative action constituted reverse discrimination, thereby discriminating against whites—but also sounded the death knell for any results-based civil rights programs like affirmative action. In the aftermath of *Bakke*, people challenged affirmative action policies in other states with similar success, and affirmative action would be all but extinct by the mid-1990s. De jure inequality remained illegal, but de facto inequality merely had to avoid proof of discriminatory intent to remain unaddressed. This made it virtually impossible to make serious progress toward racial equality in the years after *Bakke*. As late as the early 1970s, discriminatory *results* were sufficient to mandate government intervention, but by the end of the decade, proof of discriminatory *intent* was required, something far more difficult to prove. Colorblindness was largely responsible for this shift.

"Yo Adrian, We Did it!"

Rocky premiered in November 1976, the year of the nation's bicentennial, the same month George Will appeared on *Meet the Press* and wrote one of his many columns decrying "reverse discrimination." By then, whites were more and more vocal in their opposition to school integration and affirmative action, which they argued violated the colorblind bedrock of the nation's Constitution and the core philosophy of the civil rights movement. *Rocky* offers the tale of the humble, industrious but nitwitted Rocky Balboa (Sylvester Stallone), who does battle with the cocky, three-piece-suit wearing, Muhammad Ali–inspired black man, Apollo Creed (Carl Weathers), for the heavyweight boxing title. *Rocky* became the highest grossing picture of 1976 and won the Academy Award for Best Picture. It was rare among films in that it appealed widely to Hollywood audiences and won the accolades of the industry itself. The film was the brainchild of a young Sylvester Stallone. Stallone wrote the script after watching Chuck Wepner fight heavyweight champion Muhammad Ali in 1975. The bout was nothing more than a publicity stunt for the champ, built around the novelty of affording an average joe the opportunity to fight the greatest boxer in history. Ali and his promoter, the equally eccentric Don King, advertised the fight with the slogan "Give the White Guy a Break" imprinted on pennants and buttons. Yet Wepner, an amateur club fighter and liquor salesman, lasted fifteen rounds against the champ.[50] The fight's slogan, combined with the white working-class amateur's ability to stand toe to toe with Ali, a proud member of the Nation of Islam and one of the most vocal critics of white supremacy in America in the 1970s, proved too enticing to the young Stallone. In fact, the struggling actor went broke trying to sell it and even threatened to burn the script rather than accept less than a fair price to produce it or allow another actor to play the title role.[51]

For many white viewers, the Ali versus Wepner fight perfectly drama-tized white backlash attitudes—a humble, hardworking, and deserving working-class white man competing against an arrogant, lazy, and unde-serving black man, be it in the ring, the job market, or college admissions. Moreover, black versus white heavyweight bouts had captivated Americans— many of whom viewed them as symbolic, or even literal, battles for racial supremacy—for nearly seventy years. By the turn of the twentieth century, not only had the United States become the center of the boxing world, but the all-white roster of heavyweight champions offered "proof" of the phys-ical and mental superiority of the white race. Jack Johnson's ascent to the top of the boxing world in 1908, when he became the first black heavyweight champion in the nation's history, created a fundamental crisis of white mas-culinity. Former champion Jim Jeffries came out of retirement to fight Johnson under the moniker "Great White Hope" and restore the racial or-der of white supremacy. Jeffries returned to the ring, he said, "for the sole purpose of proving that a white man is better than a Negro."[52] He lost to Johnson handily.

It was more than Johnson's black skin that offended white audiences. Johnson was brazenly outspoken on social issues and, most abhorrent of all, married to a white woman, thereby in open defiance of the sexual mo-res of the Jim Crow era. It would take another two decades, when Joe Louis, "the Brown Bomber," won the heavyweight title, before a black boxing champion would avoid the vitriol of the white boxing world and win its em-brace. However, the attitude of white boxing fans toward Louis compared to their attitude toward Johnson had little to do with the passing of time and the easing of antiblack racism. Rather, whites found the "dignified" and "respectable" manner in which Louis conducted himself, as opposed to the brash Johnson, far more palatable. As journalist Dave Zirin writes, "Louis was quiet where Johnson had been outspoken. An all-white management team handled Louis very carefully, and had a set of rules he had to follow, including, 'never be photographed with a white woman.'"[53] As Louis him-self used to say, "My manager does my talking for me. I do my talking in the ring."[54]

Nearly three decades after Louis first won the heavyweight title, Muham-mad Ali aroused white backlash with an intensity not seen since Jack Johnson. Like Johnson, Ali spoke out about political issues like civil rights and the Vietnam War. As Ali himself noted, whites often asked why he could not behave more like Joe Louis. Yet some civil rights leaders, like Julian Bond, while not agreeing with Ali's decision to join the Nation of Islam, admired Ali's willingness to give voice to what many African Americans felt but could not articulate out of fear for their lives toward white Americans in the 1960s. Ali "sent a little thrill through you. . . . He was able to tell white folks for us to go to hell; that I'm going to do it my way."[55]

Stallone's film draws directly on the history of boxing as an arena of racial combat. He based his champion, Apollo Creed (Carl Weathers), on Ali. The eponymous Rocky Balboa, played by Stallone, was largely inspired by Wepner but shared a name with Rocky Marciano, the last white American heavyweight boxing champion before a twenty-year run of black champs in the lead up to the film. More than character inspiration and name references, the mise-en-scène of the film's climactic bout directly engages both the racial drama of boxing and, more importantly, the colorblind aesthetics of Hollywood amid the backlash politics of the mid-1970s. Balboa and Creed duke it out in a ring decorated like the nation's original Betsy Ross flag. The fight, in other words, is less a contest for a championship belt than a battle for the country itself—and who can (and cannot) claim national belonging in the 1970s. The box-office success of the film demonstrated that the film's metaphorical fight for the nation itself proved irresistible to white audiences increasingly vexed by school integration orders and affirmative action programs.

The stakes of the fight are laid bare before it even begins. Before the fight's opening bell, the champion Creed enters the arena dressed as George Washington in a re-creation of Emanuel Leutze's 1851 painting, *Washington Crossing the Delaware*. Once inside the ropes, Creed trades his navy-blue cape and tricorn hat for a stars-and-striped penguin-tailed tuxedo jacket, trunks, and top hat. Only a white beard shy of Uncle Sam, he shouts "I Want You!" while pointing to Rocky and the crowd. Once the match begins, Creed fights in American flag trunks. According to the mise-en-scène, two centuries after its founding it is African Americans who can lay claim to America; the nation belongs to them and serves their interests. Whites have been left behind, "forgotten" by their country. Unlike the American Apollo Creed, Rocky Balboa fights under the moniker "Italian Stallion," not "Italian *American* Stallion." His boxing trunks, moreover, are white with a red stripe, missing the American flag's iconic blue, which symbolizes justice. The absence of blue from Balboa's trunks visually represents the absence of justice from the lives of Balboa and his white racial brethren amid the civil rights battles of the 1970s.

Rocky Balboa (Sylvester Stallone), the Italian Stallion.

Apollo Creed (Carl Weathers) enters the ring dressed as George Washington.

Apollo Creed trades his George Washington costume for that of another American icon: Uncle Sam.

The white ethnic branding of Rocky Balboa, whose satin red and yellow robe (as opposed to the red, white, and blue of Creed) features the words "Italian Stallion" on his back, along with the rectangular patch of his sponsor, which contains a picture of a shamrock and reads "Shamrock Meats Inc.," illustrates the shift in collective white identity historian Matthew Frye Jacobson calls the "white ethnic revival" of the post–civil rights period. As Jacobson explains, the civil rights movement's critique of white supremacy made many whites uncomfortable with their racial privilege. In response, whites collectively began asserting an "Ellis Island Whiteness," which distanced whites from the slave-holding lineage of WASPs, reimagined white ethnic roots through narratives of suffering, and reframed the United States as a "nation of immigrants." As Jacobson argues, however, this rearticulation of whiteness did not "disrupt, but actually bolstered, the racial whiteness that had long held the key to American belonging and power relations."[56] Furthermore, it "blunted the charges of the civil rights and Black Power movements and eased the conscience of a nation that had just barely begun to reckon with the harshest contours of its history forged in white supremacism."[57] Here, Balboa's multiple references to "Ellis Island Whiteness" both align him with a post-civil rights politics of whiteness that sought to detach itself from histories of white supremacy and position him outside of a racialized discourse of Americanness.

The combination of the racial nationalism of Creed's costumes and Balboa's white-ethnic alias invert the racial hierarchy of American history in line with the white backlash politics of the mid-1970s.[58] Cultural studies scholar Jennifer L. Pierce contends that *Rocky* and the *Bakke* decision together reveal the popular notion of the late 1970s that "whites are disadvantaged vis-à-vis black Americans."[59] Furthermore, Creed's claims to America are largely for show, rather than reflective of a deep, heartfelt patriotism. This further fuels the audience's hatred of the black champion, both in the arena and in movie theaters across the nation. Creed's entrance and masquerade as two icons of American nationalism are largely for theatrics—the humorous gimmicks of a champion who views himself an entertainer rather than an athlete. Earlier in the film, when Creed conceives of the idea to give an unknown fighter a chance at the heavyweight title, the fight's promoter praises Creed's idea as "very American," a la Horatio Alger, to which Creed responds, "No, it's smart." Intelligence, in Creed's view, is synonymous with business acumen, not patriotism. Creed's motivation, therefore, is driven more by his desire to grow his net worth than his love of country or sport. This early scene sullies Creed's ringside references to American iconography later in the film.

Creed's actions enrage the "true patriots" in the arena and in theaters—the left-behind white men, the "Italian Stallions" who want nothing more than, as Balboa puts it, their "shot" at the American dream their country has stripped from them by granting "preferential treatment" to African Americans in school assignments, college admissions, and hiring. Creed's prefight routine is not comedy but tragedy. By playfully claiming ownership of America, he mocks it. At the country's bicentennial, the American dream is on its deathbed, in desperate need of rehabilitation as African Americans undeservedly benefit from its largess at the expense of the deserving white working class. If Jim Jeffries was the first "Great White Hope," the film offers Rocky Balboa as its last. As historian Jefferson Cowie argues, the film uses the boxing ring as "a setting for hope and possibility" to "prove that a white working-class hero could go the distance with a black superstar."[60] Sylvester Stallone put it similarly: when people in the film or watching the film "cheer for Rocky[,] they are cheering for themselves."[61]

Most importantly, the backlash politics of the film operate entirely within Hollywood's colorblind aesthetics. While spectators *see* the stark contrast

Rocky and Apollo fight in a ring decorated like Betsy Ross's American flag.

between a black champion who refuses to train or take his opponent seriously and mocks iconic American symbols, and a blue-collar white challenger who literally puts his blood, sweat, and tears into his one "shot," the film does not contain a single race-conscious line of dialogue. In other words, the script is colorblind. The film's juxtaposition of Rocky and Apollo—of hero versus villain, deserving versus undeserving, hardworking versus lazy, authentic versus disingenuous—comes without explicit reference to race. Thus, the backlash politics of *Rocky* are decidedly different from those of, say, George Wallace, who infamously intoned, "Segregation now, segregation tomorrow, segregation forever," in opposition to school integration over a decade prior. Unlike Wallace, Balboa expresses no signs of antiblack prejudice. He trains in an integrated gym, high-fives black supporters as he enters the ring, and even defends Creed during a conversation with his local bar owner. Balboa's defense of Creed foreshadows the close friendship the foes will develop in the subsequent three *Rocky* films. As with Harry Callahan's Latino partner, Creed will become Rocky's sidekick and friend, again perpetuating the "friend of color" trope discussed in chapter 1. Lastly, Rocky's racial politics stand in direct contrast to those of his friend Paulie. According to Stallone, Paulie is "a symbol of the blue collar disenfranchised, left-out mentality, a man who feels life has given him an unfair amount of cheap shots."[62] If Paulie symbolizes the white backlash politics of the 1960s, Rocky typifies the seemingly civil rights friendly backlash of the 1970s.

If Hollywood's colorblind aesthetics pairs colorblind dialogue with race-conscious visual aesthetics, *Rocky* is the first film to perfect these aesthetics. While the dialogue elides race, the screen is saturated with race-conscious specifications for the exhaustive dog-whistle dialogue around hard work, laziness, and deservingness that continuously contrast the determined "true" American Balboa and the smooth-talking, gilded Creed. The film therefore reveals the articulation of a colorblind white backlash that pairs race-neutral dialogue with race-conscious visual aesthetics that together highlight the racial stakes of the colorblind opposition to civil rights. Several writers note that the film serves as one giant *Bakke* metaphor on the silver screen—a dramatization of the first major anti–affirmative action Supreme Court ruling two years after the film's release.[63] Indeed, the affirmative action metaphor pervades the entire film with little subtlety or nuance. Rocky loses his gym locker to a less experienced black fighter over whom he holds six years seniority. Moreover, although most of the second act dramatizes Rocky's intense training regimen, not once does the audience see Creed spar, work a speed bag, throw a punch, or lift a single dumbbell before fight night. Furthermore, the bout between the down-and-out, bumbling working-class white brute and the wealthy, handsome, and "articulate" black man pulls no punches in piling on the affirmative action metaphors. The unjust split-decision result was as obvious to the spectators in the Philadelphia Spectrum as it was to those in theaters around the country, whose patronage made the film the year's highest grossing film. Rocky clearly wins the fight by dominating the later rounds. In at least two instances, the bell saves a nearly defeated Creed from a knockout punch. Rocky, on the other hand, never needs the bell to protect him. Instead, he relies on his own resiliency, picking himself up off the mat each time Creed knocks him down. As the credits roll, the audience is left with the triumphant tale of an industrious working-class white male who defeats the arrogant undeserving but over-privileged black champion in a test of grit, endurance, and brute strength.

By the time the film debuted, affirmative action and busing had become the country's two biggest social issues. By mid-decade, whites increasingly believed the federal government was prioritizing the needs of African Americans at their expense, therefore subjecting them to "reverse discrimination."[64] *Rocky* marks not the beginning of white backlash on-screen but the

Rocky loses his locker to a less experienced black boxer.

movement of its politics to the mainstream. In Rocky Balboa, whites found
a hero who embodied their underdog narrative and went the distance with
the beneficiary of their "oppression." By the time the film left theaters,
whites overwhelmingly opposed the civil rights policies of affirmative action and school integration, the Supreme Court increasingly sided with
white civil rights opponents, and the civil rights friendly rhetoric of colorblindness became the justification for these positions. Colorblindness offered a solution that both appealed to the antistatist anger of whites and
satisfied post–civil rights rhetorical standards of respect. Conservatives like
George Will were, as they framed it, merely continuing the work of Dr. King.
By 1976, whites had begun turning the language of the civil rights movement against itself in order to undermine and undo many of its gains. With
Rocky, Hollywood made an important contribution to that transformation.
Rocky marks not just the movement of backlash politics to the white mainstream but also the maturation of Hollywood's colorblind aesthetics. As we
have seen, a politically and racially diverse group of people espoused colorblind rhetoric at the beginning of the decade. Yet it was those who argued
that colorblindness was the antidote to the reverse discrimination of race

conscious policies that increasingly became, as George Will argued, "common sense." As Will wrote in February 1979, eight months after the *Bakke* ruling, Sears Roebuck and Co.'s resistance to affirmative action was a "non-rebellion."[65]

The (Colorblind) Hand of the Free Market

Sylvester Stallone's journey from struggling actor to Academy Award–winning movie star in less than two years was as improbable as the journey of the character he played in *Rocky*. Perhaps more unlikely was economist Milton Friedman's voyage from the margins of his profession to its highest honor less than five weeks before *Rocky* premiered. Friedman's unwavering commitment to free-market fundamentalism became the basis of the economic philosophy of neoliberalism. *Neoliberalism* is a term that is overused and undertheorized. It is commonly thrown around in criticisms of capitalism in the period following the dismantling of the Keynesian welfare state in the 1970s. The "neoliberal state" began to emerge in the early 1970s as embedded liberalism seemed inadequate to deal with the stagflationary U.S. and British economies. The United States responded by deindustrializing its economy and deregulating its financial markets. Labor power was curbed, and a largely service-based economy in the nation's Sunbelt (built, it is important to note, on massive state largesse) replaced the predominantly blue-collar Northeast. In addition, federal and state governments made massive cuts to social safety-net programs like welfare.

David Harvey defines neoliberalism as a "theory of political economic practices proposing that human well-being can best be advanced by the maximization of entrepreneurial freedoms within an institutional framework characterized by private property rights, individual liberty, unencumbered markets, and free trade."[66] Neoliberalism, in theory, posits maximizing economic efficiency by expanding, wherever possible, the influence of economic markets in order to reduce the wasteful inefficiency of the public sector. Stuart Hall explains, "Neo-liberalism is grounded in the idea of the 'free, possessive individual.' It sees the state as tyrannical and oppressive. The state must never govern society, dictate to free individuals how to dispose of their property, regulate a free-market economy or interfere with the God-given right to make profits and amass personal wealth."[67] While scholars like Harvey and Jamie Peck define neoliberalism as a political project aimed at the restoration of class power, I argue, alongside others, that neoliberalism is a *racial* project accomplished through the repurposing, rather than the elimination, of the state.[68]

Many scholars lament the overuse of the term and the inability to distinguish the neoliberal logic of capitalism from capitalist ideology itself. Loic Wacquant, Jamie Peck, and others have asked: What is "neo" about neoliberalism? For Carolyn Hardin, the term often has no meaningful distinction from classical liberalism in much of its use. Instead, she argues that the "neo" in neoliberalism relates primarily to the supremacy of the corporation, whose importance—through, for example, Supreme Court decisions like 2010's *Citizens United v. Federal Election Commission*—now supersedes that of the individual. Hardin contends, "It seems that the epistemological project of neoliberalism refigures society as an economic system of corporations. Individuals are refigured as corporations or entrepreneurs and corporations are treated as individuals."[69] Similarly, Colin Crouch argues that neoliberalism is characterized not by a free market but by the omnipotence of the corporation. Most recently, Wendy Brown distinguishes neoliberal reason through its conversion of "the distinctly *political* character, meaning, and operation of democracy's constituent elements into *economic* ones."[70] The conduct of the business firm therefore becomes identical to that of the state and the individual. All other government responsibilities are secondary to economic growth. Considering Barack Obama's 2013 State of the Union address, Brown notes that while the president covered a multitude of topics that seemingly had little to do with the U.S. economy—expanding Medicare, eliminating sex discrimination, and implementing education reform—each was advocated through its economic benefit. Creating classes in K–12 education that focus on STEM education, for example, will better develop "the skills today's employers are looking for. Immigration reform will attract "entrepreneurs" and "grow our economy." Economic growth would even cure domestic violence, offering battered spouses financial independence from their abusers, argued the president.[71]

Criticisms of neoliberalism focus primarily on its erosion of democracy and its manufacturing of unprecedented wealth inequality. Henry A. Giroux writes, "Wedded to the belief that the market should be the organizing principle for all political, social, and economic decisions, neoliberalism wages an incessant attack on democracy, public goods, and non-commodified values."[72] "Neoliberal ideology," Giroux elaborates, "on the one hand, pushes for the privatization of all non-commodified public spheres and the upward distribution of wealth. On the other hand, it supports policies that increasingly militarize facets of public space in order to secure the privileges and benefits of the corporate elite and ultra-rich."[73] Harvey ultimately summarizes neoliberalism as a system of "accumulation by dispossession," which aims to privatize and commodify public goods, create markets where there previously were not, and task the state with the upward redistribution of wealth.[74]

In practice, the neoliberal state rarely comports with its espoused antistatist free-market fundamentalism. As Peck argues, "Capturing and transforming the state was always a fundamental neoliberal objective. . . . Notwithstanding its trademark antistatist rhetoric, neoliberalism was always concerned—at its philosophical, political, and practical core—with the challenge of first seizing and then retasking the state."[75] In other words, neoliberalism, "in its various guises, has always been about the capture and reuse of the state, in the interests of shaping a pro-corporate, freer trading 'market order.'"[76]

While the maturation of the neoliberal racial political project would decimate low-income black communities in the 1980s, the rise of the neoliberal racial state depended on the racial project of colorblindness. As Michael Omi and Howard Winant argue, "Neoliberalism was at its core a racial project as much as a capital accumulation project. Its central racial component was colorblind racial ideology."[77] As both Eric Williams and Cedric Robinson note, the histories of capitalism and white supremacy are inextricably linked.[78] Building on this idea, Pauline Lipman and George Lipsitz both note that neoliberalism is the latest, and most acute, episode of that ontology.[79] Colorblindness provides the racial logic of neoliberalism. Neoliberalism's rise in the United States was built on a foundation of antigovernment sentiment that had increasingly solidified among Americans as the seventies progressed. Contributors to this ethos included, on the one hand, the stagflationary economy of the 1970s, which classical Keynesianism seemed incapable of curing. Another, more important factor was the ideological racialization of the "public" as black and therefore "bad" in the minds of whites, who became, as a result, far more willing to support its divestment.[80] However, equally significant was a growing animus toward the state as a result of legal and social battles over civil rights programs in the mid-1970s—affirmative action and court-ordered busing, in particular. It is no coincidence, in other words, that a significant portion of the American public became sympathetic to neoliberalism's small-government ideology at precisely the moment when many of them, whites in particular, felt that the government was doing too much to enforce black civil rights. Colorblind discourse provided the rhetorical ammunition for opponents of black civil rights; it allowed whites the opportunity to oppose busing and affirmative action while aligning themselves with the legacy and language of the civil rights movement. They were not racists, so the logic went; they merely supported Martin Luther King's dream of a society in which people were judged "not by the color of their skin, but by the content of their character." Yet colorblindness provides more than a political discourse that obliged post–civil rights rhetorical standards of respect while opposing racial equality. By prohibiting considerations of race in addressing racial inequality it aims to eliminate the government from racial matters altogether. In its place, as with neoliberalism's prescription for economic policy, colorblindness offers white supremacy through race-neutral market logic as the solution to government intervention.

Milton Friedman and Race

Milton Friedman wrote a series of essays on civil rights and racial discrimination that linked his free-market fundamentalism to the racial ideology of colorblindness. Most notably, he devoted an entire chapter of his influential book *Capitalism and Freedom* (1962) to the topic of racism. He begins the chapter, titled "Capitalism and Discrimination," by stating, "It is a striking historical fact that the development of capitalism has been accompanied by a major reduction" in discrimination.[81] He continues by contending that "discrimination against groups of a particular color or religion is least in those areas where there is the greatest freedom of competition." These two quotes, which begin and end the opening paragraph in the chapter, outline Friedman's basic neoliberal notion of civil rights: that capitalism is inherently democratic and colorblind, making racial discrimination entirely the product of government interference in the free market.

Not surprisingly, Milton Friedman opposed the landmark Civil Rights Act of 1964, passed two years after *Capitalism and Freedom*'s publication. In fact, while advising Barry Goldwater's presidential campaign in 1964, Friedman called the Arizona senator's opposition to the act "excellent." His only criticism, in fact, was that the candidate did not express his opposition sooner.[82] Goldwater had, in fact, made his opposition to federal civil rights legislation known in his book *The Conscience of a Conservative*, published four years before the passage of the Civil Rights Act.[83]

In place of federal civil rights legislation, Friedman advocated a simpler solution. By removing the government from matters of race, which entailed not merely eliminating de jure discriminatory laws but also eliminating provisions like the Civil Rights Act and the Voting Rights Act, an unencumbered free market would produce a colorblind freedom-maximizing utopia. How, exactly, the elimination of civil rights protections would eliminate discrimination resided in the supposed magic of the free market. The market punishes discrimination, according to Friedman, because bigots who refuse to work alongside, buy from, or sell goods to African Americans limit their choices and therefore depress their wages or artificially inflate the price they must pay for goods.[84] Under the market mechanism, therefore, individuals are encouraged to discard racial prejudices in search of the highest wages and the lowest prices. Friedman could not imagine, for example, that whites might be willing to pay a premium to eat at a segregated lunch counter. In Friedman's view, the free market is a colorblind arbiter of equality, which naturally rewards racial equality and punishes racial discrimination by increasing the cost of goods and deflating the wages and profits of bigots.

Although he never uses the term *colorblind*, in large part because he published *Capitalism and Freedom* over a decade before the term entered the national lexicon, maximizing wages and guaranteeing the lowest price of goods requires an inherently colorblind approach to the economy. Race for Friedman functions no differently than, say, unions (which Friedman vehemently opposed); both place artificial restrictions on the free market, tamper with the price mechanism, and require an excessively large role of the government at the expense of the economy. The elimination of government from matters of race, then, not only helps optimize the economy but also promotes colorblind equality. Important here is Friedman's distinction between freedom and equality. The government, according to Friedman, was wrong in trying to impose equality. Such efforts, in his view, were doomed to failure and would actually inhibit freedom. However, by promoting freedom (of the market, first and foremost), including the freedom to discriminate, equality would follow. Equality, in Friedman's view, is the by-product of freedom. As he stated in 1980, "A society that puts equality before freedom will get neither. A society that puts freedom before equality will get a high degree of both."[85] Yet as David Harvey notes, freedom under neoliberalism "degenerates" into merely the freedom of the market.[86]

For Friedman, discrimination is merely a matter of "taste," which, like differences in wine, film, or music preference, is to be respected and absolutely should not, under any circumstance, be regulated by the government. He writes,

It is hard to see that discrimination can have any meaning other than a "taste" of others that one does not share. We do not regard it as "discrimination"—or at least not in the same invidious sense—if an individual is willing to pay a higher price to listen to one singer than to another, although we do if he is willing to pay a higher price to have services rendered to him by a person of one color than by a person of another. The difference between the two cases is that in the one case we share the taste, and in the other case we do not. Is there any difference in principle between the taste that leads a householder to prefer an attractive servant to an ugly one and the taste that leads another to prefer a Negro to a white or a white to a Negro, except that we sympathize and agree with the one taste and may not with the other?[87]

After qualifying these remarks by stating that he himself deplores racism, he continues, "In a society based on free discussion, the appropriate recourse is for me to seek to persuade them that their tastes are bad and that they should change their views and their behavior, not to use coercive power to enforce my tastes and my attitudes on others."[88] Here Friedman advocates the market's inherent ability to *discourage* discriminatory behavior as a preferable solution to government intervention. In Friedman's view, the government has no business interfering in matters of civil rights.

Friedman's student Thomas Sowell, the retired black conservative economist who served as the Rose and Milton Friedman Senior Fellow on Public Policy at Stanford University's Hoover Institution, devoted no fewer than three books—*Race and Economics* (1975), *Markets and Minorities* (1981), and *The Economics and Politics of Race* (1983)—to the relationship between racial equality and the free market between 1975 and 1983. Each book argues essentially the same thing: that discriminatory actions depend exclusively on the "*costs* of doing so. Where those costs are very high," Sowell argues, "even very prejudiced or biased people may engage in little or no discrimination."[89] The reason for this, Sowell elaborates, is because "the marketplace puts a price on incorrect generalizations, as it does all sorts of other incorrect assumptions behind economic decisions."[90] In Sowell's view, like that of Friedman, the market punishes prejudice. In other words, because the costs the seller incurs through discriminatory hiring and selling practices threaten his business, the seller will eventually stop discriminating in order to maximize his profit margins. The free market implicitly demands equal treatment of all participants. It is, in other words, colorblind. Sowell, in conjunction with his mentor, ultimately blames the government, even its attempts to eradicate racial discrimination and inequality, for the existence of both: "Discrimination has always been most prevalent where it costs discrimination the least—in government employment, in regulated utilities, or in non-profit organizations. That was true throughout the pre–civil rights era, just as reverse discrimination is generally strongest in such organizations today. . . . Yet those who wish to fight against discrimination often try to move employment decisions and other decisions out of the marketplace and into the hands of people who pay no price—politicians, bureaucrats, and judges."[91] In Sowell's view, because the market mechanism does not dictate (as it should, in his and Friedman's opinion) its actions, governments are therefore more susceptible to engage in discriminatory, and "reverse discriminatory," behavior, because it suffers no economic penalty to do so.

However, as legal scholar Daria Roithmayr details, free-market ideologues like Sowell and Friedman, who believe that market competition eliminates racial discrimination, overlook the historical function of "racial cartels" in America. For economists, cartels refer to "a group of actors who work together to extract monopoly profits by manipulating price and limiting competition."[92] The conduct of racial cartels, according to Roithmayr, "helps to explain why markets did not successfully eliminate discrimination during Jim Crow. Cartel conduct disrupted the forces of the market, as whites engaged in cartel conduct for their own economic gain."[93] Moreover, after World War I, increased government support enhanced the influence of racial cartels in areas like housing, labor unions, and the New Deal. The state support of racial cartels continued into the post–World War II era through organizations like White Citizens' Councils, the Ku Klux Klan, parent-teacher associations, homeowners associations, and white political parties.[94] In short, partly due to the influence of state-supported racial cartels, the free market has proven entirely ineffective at producing racial equality.

Although Friedman did not write regularly about social issues in his *Newsweek* column, the controversy over affirmative action and busing programs in the 1970s prompted a response from the economist. In the final months of 1975, Friedman, mere months away from winning the Nobel Prize, wrote a column denouncing busing and another that labeled affirmative action as "reverse discrimination." In the October 1975 column titled "Whose Intolerance?," Friedman condemned busing, asking, "Can enforced confrontation of race with race produce racial harmony?" He ultimately blames the racial violence surrounding busing not on white intolerance to integration but on "liberals" who were "intolerant" of whites who opposed integration and proceeded to "force" integration on them.[95] Two months later, Friedman combined his hatred of government with his disdain for affirmative action in the column titled "Bureaucracy Scorned": "The affirmative-action program is one of those bureaucratic monstrosities that have become all too familiar: noble objectives, ignoble results. The objective is to eliminate discrimination on the basis of sex or race; the results are mountains of paper, hiring criteria that are irrelevant to the mission of institutions of higher learning and, frequently, the substitution of reverse discrimination for no discrimination."[96] He concludes the piece, "Freedom is for everyone or no one. . . . Government controls destroy freedom for everyone." Together, Friedman and Sowell posit a direct relationship between the market and racial equality. Racial discrimination is entirely the product of government interventions in the market mechanism. Eliminating racial inequality, therefore, is simple: Keep the government out of matters of racial equality by eliminating busing mandates, affirmative action orders, and so on, and allow the free market to do its work. Doing so will magically eliminate all racial discrimination by imposing intolerable costs on those who discriminate. For Friedman and Sowell, the market's "invisible hand" is also a colorblind hand.

Friedman's opposition to busing and affirmative action was typical of the mid- to late-1970s white backlash. What is important here is not simply the emphasis on the supremacy of the free market as the arbiter of racial equality but the manner in which Friedman and Sowell not only privilege freedom over equality but frame freedom at strictly the level of the *individual*. Group rights of, say, blacks, women, or workers have no legitimacy under neoliberal thought. According to Harvey, "The founding figures of neoliberal thought took political ideas of human dignity and *individual freedom* as fundamental, as 'the central values of civilization [emphasis added].'"[97] Under this neoliberal taxonomy, racism is therefore limited to interpersonal interactions. Any effort to treat racial inequality as affecting entire groups only enhances discrimination, in the neoliberal view. Government legislation addressing group inequality wrongly, as the logic goes, prioritizes equality over freedom and, more importantly, treats citizens as groups, not individuals. Again, for Friedman, all roads lead back to the free market. Political freedom is insignificant; the freedom of the market is the only freedom that matters because it guarantees all other freedoms. It is important to note that personal freedom was a key feature of the rights revolutions across the globe in the late 1960s. Yet those movements were ultimately motivated by a moral commitment to social justice for all persons. Neoliberalism, on the other hand, possessed no such morality. Instead, it captured the notion of individual freedom and turned it against the "interventionist and regulatory" efforts of the state.[98] This logic, moreover, was embedded into whites' complaints of reverse discrimination.

The neoliberal commitment to the supremacy of the freedom of the individual over the equality of a group, and to the idea that a strictly colorblind approach to the law was a way to ensure individual freedom, became an increasingly common feature of civil rights opposition in the late 1970s in both implicit and explicit ways. Consider the two major affirmative action Supreme Court cases of the decade—*DeFunis v. Odegaard* (1974) and *Regents of the University of California v. Bakke* (1978). Lawyers for DeFunis and Bakke argued that individual rights and personal freedom superseded the right of underrepresented minorities as a group to equality. In essence, they argued that the equality of people of color was subordinate to the freedom of an individual white male. Ironically, the legal standard of individualism that informed anti–civil rights court cases like *Bakke* was established by perhaps the most iconic pro–civil rights decision—*Brown v. Board of Education* (1954). As legal scholar Lani Guinier argues, in subsequent decades the court used the *Brown* ruling (falsely, perhaps) to justify a view of racism limited to individual prejudice.[99] Thus, the potential "reverse discrimination" or "unfair" treatment of one white male trumped the rights of underrepresented minorities as a group. Affirmative action opponents objected to the program because it treated people as groups, not individuals.[100] Group rights did not exist, affirmative action critics contended. This was despite the fact that the Constitution, like all other statutes of the early republic, is full of group references. Yet as historian Daniel T. Rodgers argues, "On the new constitutional plane [of the 1970s] . . . only individuals entered the law."[101] Moreover, the lawyers in both *Bakke* and *DeFunis* advocated a colorblind approach to the law in order to ensure individual freedoms and prevent the reverse discrimination of group rights. As Rodgers writes, "The affirmative action cases recast the forums of justice as a choice between two socially detached individuals' claims and merits. As the law recognized them, they resembled more and more closely individual consumers in a market: bidders for a medical school education or for a city contract."[102] In the anti–affirmative action Supreme Court cases of the 1970s, then, one begins to see the linkage of a neoliberal taxonomy of rights, wherein individual rights obliterate group rights, and colorblind free market logic.

More explicitly, among his frequent bellicose tirades against reverse discrimination policies like affirmative action, George Will linked colorblindness with the neoliberal conception of freedom as purely individualistic. Affirmative action, in Will's view, "is a stench in the nostrils of reasonable people, and not just because it repudiates the principle that government should be *color-blind*. It also repudiates the premise of our legal system and political order. That tenet is this: justice can only result from considering the rights and interests of *individuals*. The idea behind affirmative action programs is this: justice results from government's assigning rights and benefits to racial and ethnic *groups* [emphasis added]."[103] By the late 1970s, colorblindness was rhetorically positioned not merely as a discursively tactful revanchist discourse to civil rights programs in an economically slumped decade but as a fundamental reframing of freedom that subordinated group rights and racial equality to the freedom of the individual and the market.

Colorblindness and neoliberalism were natural bedfellows. They offered whites an attractive alternative to the race-conscious government actions—school integration and affirmative action—that sought to address racial inequality at the group level. The racial conflicts of the 1970s produced antistatist backlash that, cloaked in civil rights friendly colorblind rhetoric, demanded government divestment in matters of race. Moreover, the widespread antistatism of the early decade provided the foundation for the politics of colorblind neoliberalism to take root by the decade's end. Colorblindness and neoliberalism became mutually constitutive. Colorblindness is, in other words, the racial ideology of neoliberalism. Neoliberalism, in the American context, is just as much a racial project as it is an economic one. Its discourse offered free-market colorblind "solutions" to the civil rights battles of the 1970s just as it provided economic solutions to a sluggish economy.

"Contorted in Anger": *Blue Collar* and Hollywood Neoliberalism

Blue Collar, a film about the struggles of three Detroit autoworkers—two black, Zeke and Smokey (Richard Pryor and Yaphet Kotto), and one white, Jerry (Harvey Keitel)—and their corrupt union, premiered in the midst of the *Bakke* hearing, two years after Friedman's Nobel Prize, and two years before the 1980 election. As we have seen, by 1978 colorblind neoliberalism was becoming an increasingly influential discourse in civil rights and economic policy. *Blue Collar* marks the directorial debut of screenwriter and

Martin Scorsese–collaborator Paul Schrader. Confronted with financial hardship and fed up with the union brass, the three men devise a plan to rob their local union headquarters. Inside the safe, the men find only $600; however, they also obtain a notebook documenting illegal union lending. Unsatisfied with their monetary take, Zeke, Jerry, and Smokey decide to use the ledger to blackmail their union, a process that eventually leads to the murder of Smokey, the buying off of Zeke with a promotion, and Jerry turning state's witness in an FBI investigation in exchange for police protection.

Organized labor lost its status as a major influence in America's social and political fabric in the first half of the 1970s.[104] Many Americans blamed unions, specifically their negotiated high wages and diminished productivity, for the stagnated economy and high inflation of the 1970s. As a result, states across the country passed right-to-work laws limiting union power. Unions took another hit with the migration of the U.S. manufacturing industry from the Northeast to the Sunbelt, where right-to-work laws, free land, and state subsidies enticed business to relocate.[105] Unions had, over the previous decades, developed a stronghold in the manufacturing industries of the Frostbelt and wielded significant influence over the Democratic Party. This changed in the 1970s as the Democratic Party split over Vietnam and civil rights. The division between the pro- and antiwar factions of the Democratic Party ultimately led George Meany, head of the AFL-CIO, to refuse to endorse George McGovern, the Democratic nominee for president in 1972.[106] This marked the end of a decades-long marriage between Democrats and unions, and blue-collar whites increasingly fled to the Republican Party, which capitalized on the fractured Left and increasingly appealed to blue-collar social conservatism, particularly on issues of race.

As historian Dennis Deslippe notes, opposition to affirmative action originated as much in faculty clubs as it did on the assembly line, and among liberals and conservatives alike in the decade and a half between civil rights and *Bakke*. The conventional narrative of affirmative action opposition— that it came exclusively from white backlash "hard hats" fed up with civil rights programs—occludes the manner in which self-professed liberals who continued to support the Democrats dominated affirmative action opposition in its first decade.[107] Nonetheless, although opposition came from multiple sources, labor unions were a pillar of this movement from its inception. However, union opposition in the late 1960s lacked the rigidity it would acquire as the seventies unfolded. While some unions outright opposed equal opportunity and even resorted to violence to prevent implementation of affirmative action programs, the vast majority of unions supported "soft" affirmative action measures, which included recruiting and training programs for minority applicants in the program's early years. They did, however, oppose affirmative action policies that set aside a certain amount of jobs for minority candidates, especially when it challenged seniority laws of "last hired, first fired." It is important to note, however, that the exclusionary practices of unions left black workers without seniority, which then made them vulnerable to massive layoffs. Seniority, in other words, functioned in explicitly racist ways, which later inoculated unions from legal repercussions when they laid off large numbers of black workers who lacked it. Nevertheless, union opposition to affirmative action calloused as the seventies unfolded and the country slipped into recession, leaving an expanding workforce to compete for a dwindling number of jobs. As Deslippe notes, "If affirmative action in the 1960s focused on who should be hired, in the challenging economy of the 1970s it tended to deal with who should be fired."[108]

The men of *Blue Collar* find their financial stability, job security, and lives constantly threatened. Their corrupt union terrorizes their lives while the federal government undermines their union loyalty and nickel-and-dimes their shrinking wages with its punitive tax code. In one scene, an FBI official investigating corruption in the men's local, says, "Everybody knows your local is the most corrupt in the city," to which Jerry responds, "I also know you got your man inside the union, and the union's got its man inside the government, and if I farted upwind I would be out of a job in an hour, wouldn't I?" In an earlier scene, the same FBI official, masquerading as an instructor at a local college, infiltrates the workers' bar and, trying to obtain information about the union brass under the pretense of research for a doctoral thesis, says, "The thing I don't understand is why you let the union rip you off. . . . It's like you wanna get fucked over." In another, a Mr. Berg from the IRS visits the home of Zeke, investigating "discrepancies" in Zeke's tax returns. Two small errors along with the corresponding late penalty amount to $2,500 in back taxes. "It's not me, it's Uncle Sam," says Berg. After refusing Zeke's request for a "break," Zeke erupts, "Fuck Uncle Sam. They give the fuckin' politicians a break! Agnew and them don't pay shit! The workin' man's gotta pay every goddam thing!" These snapshots reveal the manner in which these men find their livelihoods and lives constantly threatened by their union and the federal government, two key components of the Keynesian welfare state. As Smokey says at one point, "The union ain't done shit for us, man." *Blue Collar* combines the antistatist components of 1970s discourse into one big indictment of government plan-

The men of *Blue Collar*: Smokey (Yaphet Kotto), Zeke (Richard Pryor), and Jerry (Harvey Keitel).

ning. Upon its release, the *Cleveland Plain Dealer* described the film as a "tale of blue collar blues." The film's script introduces the film as follows: "AUTO WORKERS: In the 1920's they came to Detroit like pretty girls to Hollywood. In the 1970's they are bored, brutalized, exhausted, angry. Most hate their jobs. Many hate their lives." The script's introduction succinctly captures the backlash and "malaise" of the late 1970s and directs its ire squarely at the feet of unions and big government.[109]

When *Blue Collar* premiered, there was nothing novel regarding antistatism in 1970s film. White backlash movies like *Dirty Harry* and *Joe* disparaged the legal system for its mollycoddling of blacks and so-called hippies in the decade's early years. Black independent cinema promoted black nationalism by taking on such issues as police brutality and welfare in films like *Sweet Sweetback's Baadasssss Song* and *Claudine*. And blaxploitation took up similar themes to those of black independent cinema, although in highly bastardized forms. What makes *Blue Collar* unique, then, is not its antistatism but the extension of that sentiment to an indictment of the entire Keynesian state, in which strong unions and a strong central government were key components. One reviewer noted the contrast of this film's depiction of union life with that of the glory days of the 1930s: "Unlike the radical plays of the Thirties, in which 'join the union' was always the pat solution, Schrader's film has no such affirmative to offer. The unions, he says, have become every bit as corrupt and divisive as the corporations. . . . Big government is also suspect."[110]

More importantly, not only does the film extend the antistatism of the 1970s to the entire Keynesian state, but it also warns its audience of the racial violence of the neoliberal order that will replace Keynesianism. After the union brass discover the men's involvement in the robbery, Zeke agrees to hand over the incriminating notebook in exchange for a promotion to shop steward and immunity from criminal prosecution. Zeke's self-serving betrayal shatters the steadfast loyalty between the three men exhibited throughout the first three-quarters of the film. His rhetoric changes from insisting "We are all in this thing together" in the aftermath of the robbery to "You got to take care of your own family" after the union's investigation zeroes in on the three men. From the point Zeke accepts the union deal, the brotherly triumvirate shatters and the men devolve into mercenary individualists, concerned only with protecting themselves and their families, even if it means betraying their union brothers and close friends. Ultimately, the union bosses murder Smokey, Zeke sells out Jerry, and Jerry is left with few options other than to turn state's witness in exchange for protection for him and his family against union repercussions.

These actions lead to the film's climactic confrontation and tragic conclusion on the shop floor, whereby the two friends exchange a series of racist slurs before lunging at each other, metal tools in hand raised as weapons. The film's ending in freeze-frame is all that spares the audience the horror of watching the bloodletting. As the frame freezes we hear Smokey's posthumous coda, "They put the lifers against the new boys, the young against the old, the black against the white. Everything they do is to keep us in our place." During their racist exchange in the seconds leading up to their physical confrontation, each man accuses the other of selling out. They are, in fact, both sellouts, but neither had a choice. Pinched by the government and betrayed by their union, these men have no option but to abandon social-democratic collective struggle in hopes that individuated neoliberal opportunism will pay off; it does not. As the former friends' anger turns to racist rage, the camera pans across a line of factory workers, blue-collar line workers and white-collar managers alike, who watch a damaged relationship descend into racial violence. As the men look on, they witness not only the destruction of a friendship but the annihilation of working-class power and interracial social-democratic struggle. The state has turned these men against each other and against their union, leaving them conscripted to avaricious self-interest. Zeke's corrupt deal with the union brass essentially transforms this main character from a social democrat into a neoliberal, which proves an equally helpless alternative. The cost of that transformation is not only union power but interracial collective action. In this, *Blue Collar* forebodes a neoliberal era rife with racial conflict as exploited workers, without collective-bargaining rights, struggle for ever-dwindling resources as wealth accumulates upward.

As *Blue Collar* prophesizes, the onset of neoliberalism can only lead to racial violence among the economically disadvantaged—even between friends. As the two men lunge at each other, cudgels in hand, right before the film's conclusion, a worker looks at Zeke and yells either "Get him!" or "Kill him!" It is difficult to tell if Zeke is the intended assailant or victim of this demand, a detail, like Smokey's diatribe, left deliberately vague. On the one hand, the obvious assumption is that the man commands Zeke to kill Jerry. Zeke is, after all, the man's boss, and it is Jerry, not Zeke, who betrayed the union. Yet the disparities between the film's script and the final edit suggest the opposite. While both end in freeze-frame along with Smokey's disembodied monologue, the film ends just as the two leads attack each other. The script, on the other hand, plays out their fight:

> Remaining close to him, Jerry knees Zeke in the groin. Zeke buckles over, then leans back and belts Jerry in the face. Blood streams from Jerry's nose. Jerry reaches down and picks up a wrench. Zeke hauls back and throws another punch. Jerry swings the wrench full force at Zeke's skull. The workers and FBI agents pull at the two men, trying to restrain them. An anonymous voice calls out:
> VOICE (O.S.)
> Kill 'im!
> Zeke and Jerry's eyes burn with hate. Their bodies lunge toward each other. FREEZE FRAME: Jerry's wrench is poised above Zeke's skull. Zeke's fist is frozen a bare two inches from Jerry's bloodied face. The workers' faces are frozen in contorted anger.

As with the film, only after the freeze-frame do we hear Smokey's prophetic words. Important here is not simply the fact that the two friends' rage plays out into a bloody melee but the off-screen demand for murder. As with the similar statement that actually appears in the film, it is unclear whether the off-screen voice directs the command at Zeke or Jerry. Yet given the

Blue Collar's freeze-frame ending: Zeke and Jerry lunge in anger at each other.

subsequent action described in the script, specifically that the film concludes with Jerry's wrench "poised above Zeke's skull," it appears that the demand is for Jerry to kill Zeke, not the other way around, as we might initially surmise from watching the scene. If we assume that the "Get him!" or "Kill him!" that appears in the film corresponds to the "Kill 'im!" that appears in the script, it is difficult to conclude that the intention of the film is the opposite of that of the script. If Zeke is thus the target of the command, the action presumably continues with Zeke's murder after the freeze-frame.

Read either way, the violent conclusion of this film makes clear the state's complicity in racial violence. Decreased productivity, foreign competition, and corruption have converted these factories' assembly lines from manufacturing automobiles to manufacturing racial conflict. The state's corruption and abandonment of the working class erodes interracial solidarity and, in so doing, forces former allies down a path of mercenary individualism and heightened racial antagonism that can only conclude with racial violence. Schrader's film reveals the neoliberal project for what it truly is—not merely the reestablishment of class power but the reassertion of white supremacy in the post–civil rights era.

Blue Collar's violent conclusion is not simply a tragedy but the revelation of the relationship between the neoliberal destruction of interracial collective action and racial violence. The film's conclusion predicts a colorblind neoliberal order in which working-class power, economic recession, and black mobility are extinguished. This is not to say that Paul Schrader endorses his film's premonition. Instead, the film, particularly through Smokey's final words from beyond the grave, offers one final warning against neoliberalism's inevitability and foreshadows the racial violence the political project will produce. While *Blue Collar* may not provide the happy ending typical of most Hollywood films, it nonetheless provides neoliberal resolutions—the destruction of interracial collective action and the welfare state—to all the "conflicts" of the 1970s. The film epitomizes what Tom Wolfe calls the "Me Decade" through the violent destruction of social democracy and interracial brotherhood.[111] The "problems" of unions, stagflation, and civil rights are solved by a neoliberal vision in which all three are destroyed.

With *Blue Collar*, Hollywood became integral in the cohering of neoliberal ideology and aesthetics. Hollywood is perhaps the most important mass culture industry in understanding the ascent of neoliberalism because of its inherent narrative structure, which typically revolves around an individual protagonist. With few exceptions, virtually the entire Hollywood canon depicts (often heroic) tales of individual heroism.[112] Hollywood is, as a medium, inherently individualistic. The logic of individualism, in other words, is built into Hollywood film. This feature of the industry is certainly not unique to the late 1970s. What made Hollywood particularly suited to neoliberal hegemony was the rise of the cult of individualism in the late 1970s. Historian Bruce Schulman states that the "prevailing concept" of the seventies is that of "an era of narcissism, selfishness, and personal rather than political awareness."[113] As the decade wound down, Norman Mailer looked back on the seventies as "the decade in which people put emphasis on the skin, on the surface, rather than on the root of things. . . . It was the decade in which image became preeminent because nothing deeper was going on."[114] As we have seen, the rise of the ethos of the individual was, in large part, a by-product of the white opposition to racial equality. Within this context, Hollywood's narratives of individual heroism take on new meaning and perform new work. These narratives transform from tales of protagonists whom viewers identify with as members of similar communities—who "represent" and "stand in for," as Stuart Hall argues, their racial, political, and class identities—to stories of characters whom viewers relate to but no longer as representatives of their social identities or the communities to which they belong but rather as individuals.[115]

The movement of Hollywood away from narratives of individual characters as representatives of particular identity groups toward narratives of individual characters as individuals mirrored a similar push among conservatives who sought to reframe civil rights as belonging to individuals, irrespective of race, in order to undercut the policies implemented in the 1960s to address racial equality. The rise of neoliberal discourse in the 1970s, and especially the usurpation of group identity by individualism, was shepherded in part by the work of Hollywood as a mass culture industry. In this, Hollywood was not only instrumental in framing neoliberal discourse but uniquely situated to aid its ascent.

Blue Collar's climax advances the argument that the state not only is incapable of alleviating racial inequality and the recession but manufactures racial violence. And while the film is equally cautious of the neoliberal alternative—one could even note that the violence occurs only when the men adopt a commitment to neoliberal individualism—it is still the inadequacies and corruption of the state that necessitate that shift. The state is ultimately the catalyst for the racial violence in the film. One cannot explain the rise of neoliberalism in the United States simply with the economic performance of the 1970s. Instead, more than anything else, neoliberal logic provided "solutions" to the government's "overreach" in civil rights that "subjected" whites to reverse discrimination. Whites adopted the discourse's market-centered approach, which treated everyone as individuals rather than members of particular groups—unions, racial groups, and so on—as a whole because it allied so well with their colorblind opposition to civil rights. We must understand neoliberalism, therefore, not merely as a class project but as a racial one. And colorblindness provided the racial politics of that project.

The second half of the 1970s marked the emergence of the racial project of colorblindness. The ideology cohered in the middle of the decade, as civil rights opposition united whites across political parties and as Hollywood began to master a colorblind aesthetics capable of drawing large audiences in the New Hollywood era. It was not just widespread opposition to school integration and affirmative action, or an increasingly supportive Supreme Court, that brought whites together in the late 1970s. Hollywood, through films like *Rocky*, proved fundamental to this unification. Movie screens offered heroic tales of whites facing reverse discrimination that decoded the colorblind dog whistles of white backlash. Hollywood films made it clear who benefited and who suffered under the "unfair" government overreach in civil rights matters in the 1970s. While whites professed a commitment to colorblindness, Hollywood provided the race-conscious visuality needed to fuel a white populist revolt against civil rights in the second half of the decade. Only a few years later, colorblindness would enter the Oval Office, and Hollywood would continue to prove fundamental to the rearticulation of white supremacy in the post–civil rights era under the alluring mantle of colorblindness.

4 I Can't Wear Your Colors

Rocky III and Reagan's War on Civil Rights

• •

There is a thesis, popular in conservative and neo-conservative circles, that there is no longer really a racial problem in the U.S. There is just the problem of individuals.

—Hodding Carter III, *Wall Street Journal*, April 26, 1984

Colorblindness entered the oval office with the election of Ronald Reagan in 1980, more than fifteen years after King's iconic speech and more than two decades after the *Brown* decision. Shortly after his inauguration, one of his staffers announced that the administration would be getting back to "color-blind" hiring laws. This meant fierce opposition to affirmative action and busing.[1] It is worth noting that Reagan and King understood colorblindness in profoundly different ways. For King, colorblind laws safeguarded people of color from the institutionalization of white supremacy in state and local governments under Jim Crow. For Reagan, colorblindness offered an effective ideology through which to roll back the victories of the civil rights movement. Reagan built his political career on a foundation of antiblack civil rights. He opposed the Civil Rights Act in 1964, calling it "a bad piece of legislation." A year later, he came out against the Voting Rights Act, which he deemed "humiliating to the South." During his 1966 California gubernatorial campaign, he defended the Golden State's Proposition 14, which passed in 1964 and nullified the state's fair housing law, effectively reinstating the right to discriminate in home sales and leases.

Reagan took office with the hope that he could ban affirmative action and stop school desegregation orders by reframing racial discrimination as an individual rather than a group issue. With this, Reagan's Justice Department developed a politics of colorblind neoliberalism. Unfortunately for the president and his anti–civil rights constituents, throughout his first term the Supreme Court routinely ruled against Reagan and in support of existing civil rights programs and existing law that treated racial discrimination as a group issue. Faced with uncooperative courts, Reagan took the long view in his first term. He restaffed federal courts and the U.S. Commission on

Civil Rights with people who shared his views in order to yield more favorable rulings down the line and ensure that his version of colorblind individualism informed the court long after his years in office. He also ordered the Justice Department to stop enforcing civil rights policies his administration disagreed with, thereby transforming the federal government's civil rights branch into one of civil rights' fiercest enemies.[2]

Midway through his first term, *Rocky III*—the third installment of the iconic pugilism franchise—debuted. The film pits Rocky Balboa, played once again by Sylvester Stallone, against Clubber Lang, the "South Side Slugger," played by Mr. T. Lang knocks Balboa out in the second round of their initial bout. The film concludes with a rematch between the current and former champions. In *Rocky III*, as in the original *Rocky* film, racial discourse is largely communicated through what Ian Haney López calls "coded racial appeals."[3] As we have seen, by the early 1980s the racial project of colorblindness had matured, become increasingly influential in popular discourse, and had begun to wield significant influence in the nation's courts and legislatures, as well as in the hearts and minds of white Americans. Hollywood was essential to this rise of colorblindness. Beginning in the mid-1970s, movies provided the racial visuality colorblind rhetoric elided. In other words, Hollywood offered the link between the coded dog whistle of colorblind language and the racialized bodies to which they referred. I begin with Reagan's war on civil rights via colorblind maneuverings to undermine existing civil rights law. I then examine *Rocky III* through the lens of Reagan's War on Drugs and colorblind neoliberalism. *Rocky III* reveals that although colorblindness in many ways represented a new racial discourse in America—one based in racially neutral language and neoliberal notions of individualism—beginning in the 1980s, colorblindness increasingly relied on very old tenets of antiblackness, namely the need for white masculinity to protect white femininity from the threat of a hypersexual predatory black masculinity.

Reagan and the Erosion of Civil Rights (1980–1983)

Criticism of Reagan's anti–civil rights position began soon after he took office. For example, in March 1981, after the administration had dragged its feet in providing federal aid to help the city of Atlanta investigate a large spike in unsolved child abductions and murders, the administration's listless response seemed too many to be due to the fact that all the victims were black. In response, Reagan immediately stated that his administration had moved as swiftly as possible and is "totally color-blind."[4] On the wrong side of civil rights for his entire political career and eager to embark on a protracted assault on existing civil rights programs, Reagan and his administration routinely invoked colorblind rhetoric to justify their efforts to undermine civil rights and defend themselves against the frequent criticisms they received from civil rights supporters. In this, colorblindness became both the rigid civil rights philosophy and the rhetorical broken record of the Reagan administration.

However, the Supreme Court proved uncooperative with the Reagan administration's opposition to civil rights programs and its insistence on a strictly colorblind approach to the law. Affirmative action held its ground in the Supreme Court as the 1980s dawned. In June 1979, the court upheld, in *United Steelworkers of America v. Weber*, Kaiser Aluminum and Chemical Corp's training program, which admitted blacks on a one-to-one basis with whites in order to improve the racial diversity of the higher-paying jobs in the company. And in *Fullilove v. Klutznick* (1980), the court affirmed, by a six-to-three margin, a federal law that set aside 10 percent of public works contracts for companies run by people of color.[5] Despite its growing influence on the American public, colorblindness, in the Reagan sense, struggled to wield much influence in the Supreme Court. Writing the majority opinion in *Fullilove*, Chief Justice Berger wrote that because of the "abundant evidence" that made it clear that "minority businesses have been denied effective participation in public contracting opportunities . . . we [the majority] reject the contention that in the remedial context the Congress must act in a wholly 'color-blind' fashion."[6] Even in *Bakke*, which ruled a medical school's affirmative action program unconstitutional a year before *Weber*, the court upheld the legality of racial considerations in college admissions.

Reagan's assault on civil rights, therefore, would require creativity in the absence of legal support. The president established a two-pronged approach to circumvent existing civil rights laws. First, his administration simply stopped enforcing civil rights laws he disapproved of. As Robert Detlefsen, a Reagan sympathizer, notes, Reagan and the Justice Department reversed course, rebuking the approach of all previous administrations since Johnson toward civil rights. Reagan "switched sides" to that of the "man on the street" in direct opposition to judges and the law.[7] According to Detlefsen, "Reagan spoke to what he believed was a growing sentiment among the electorate that government—especially the federal government in Washington—had become so large, unwieldy, and intrusive that its effect was often to undermine both economic efficiency and personal liberty."[8]

Second, Reagan fundamentally restructured the composition of the federal courts and the civil rights wing of the government, which included the Justice Department, the Labor Department, and the U.S. Commission on Civil Rights. This restructuring removed affirmative action supporters and restaffed these divisions with men and women—William Bradford Reynolds (assistant attorney general and head of the Justice Department's Civil Rights Division), Clarence Pendleton (chair of the U.S. Commission on Civil Rights), and, most notably, Clarence Thomas (chair of the Equal Employment Opportunity Commission)—who, like Reagan, opposed existing civil rights law.[9] This effectively turned the federal government entirely against the cause of civil rights.

Far larger in scope was Reagan's footprint on the benches of the lower federal courts. Reagan turned over nearly half of the judgeships in the lower federal courts, appointing nearly four hundred judges, the overwhelming majority of which were white male conservatives who shared Reagan's opposition to civil rights. Of these appointees, only seven black, fifteen Latino, and two Asian judges won federal judgeships.[10] The Reagan administration abandoned the long-held practice of using judicial nominations to reward patronage, replacing it with a review process that focused on the ideological stances of judicial candidates, particularly on issues like abortion and affirmative action.[11] Additionally, Reagan appointed three Supreme Court justices (his two predecessors appointed only one between them) and promoted William Rehnquist to chief justice.[12] Judicial appointments afforded Reagan an opportunity to impose his civil rights views more easily and more quickly. Outlawing affirmative action or changing the law more generally was a long, drawn out, and difficult process; appointing judges who shared his views, however, was not. Senate approvals for judicial appointments were far easier to come by than congressional approval of, say, a bill banning affirmative action. Additionally, judgeships were lifetime appointments, ensuring that Reagan's ideology would endure long after he left office. As Edwin Meese—a Reagan staffer since his gubernatorial days and attorney general during Reagan's second term—put it, the new judges could "'institutionalize the Reagan revolution so it can't be set aside no matter what happens in future presidential elections.'"[13]

Reagan's appointments both to the bench and to the civil rights division were part of a multifaceted process that fundamentally restructured the federal government's approach to civil rights. Upon taking office, Reagan aggressively tried to eliminate affirmative action and school integration. His Justice Department disagreed with the court's findings in *Weber* and *Fullilove* and proved determined to overturn those decisions. However, without the Supreme Court on his side, Reagan was unable to legally end affirmative action and busing programs. Instead, his administration took a different approach. If the Supreme Court would not eliminate affirmative action programs, Reagan would simply appoint new judges who eventually could, and in the interim, the federal agencies under his command would stop enforcing any civil rights law they took issue with. By Reagan's first summer in the White House, the secretary of labor had exempted 75 percent of companies contracting with the federal government from previously mandatory affirmative action programs.[14]

By the end of his first year, *New York Times* columnist Robert Pear explained, "The civil rights policy of the Reagan Administration is becoming clear, and it represents a profound change from past policies for eliminating job discrimination and school segregation."[15] This change extended beyond affirmative action to school integration. Regarding busing, William Bradford Reynolds outlined the administration's position in November 1981, stating, "'We are not going to compel children who don't choose to have an integrated education to have one.'"[16] The administration also stated it would "no longer seek to desegregate an entire school district on the basis of segregation found to exist in just part of it," despite the legal standards set by the Supreme Court beginning in 1973. Instead, the administration opposed busing, and segregation remedies would be applied to "only those schools in which racial imbalance is the product of intentionally segregative acts of state officials."[17] Within months of taking office, Reagan had completely reversed the position of the executive branch and Justice Department regarding affirmative action and busing in open opposition to the Supreme Court. Richard Nixon had implemented the first federal affirmative action plan over a decade earlier, Gerald Ford held the affirmative action line, and Jimmy Carter defended the program throughout his presidency, even going so far as to rebuke the ruling in the *Bakke* decision. And while the previous three presidents were less supportive of busing, especially Nixon, none were willing to defy the law when it came to affirmative action.

Less than one year into his presidency, Reagan was actively undermining civil rights and reconstituting how the executive branch approached and conceived of civil rights and discrimination. He took the white backlash invention of reverse discrimination out of localized struggles over busing and affirmative action and gave it the credibility of the White House. At the close of Reagan's first year, two members of the U.S. Commission on Civil Rights—an independent and bipartisan federal agency tasked with protecting and furthering civil rights—characterized the administration's civil rights position and its directives to the commission as "wholly inconsistent with established civil rights law." Robert Pear, in explaining the discrepancy between the agency and the administration, notes, "The rights commission and the Administration start from different premises. The commission sees pervasive discrimination against women and minorities as the problem. Mr. Reagan's appointees see 'reverse discrimination' as an *equally serious* problem. Race and sex conscious preferences, they say, not only violate the rights of white men, but also violate the principle that Government action should be 'colorblind' [emphasis added]."[18]

By the start of 1982, Reagan had not only made his opposition to existing civil rights laws clear but had begun to use the power of the executive branch to make sure that the government agencies responsible for enforcing civil rights laws—beginning with the Justice Department—enforced his views on busing and affirmative action, despite the fact that the Supreme Court had maintained the legality of busing and affirmative action. Reagan disagreed and therefore recrafted the Justice Department to carry out his version of colorblind civil rights. As Pear notes, if there was a civil rights issue Reagan cared about, it was not school integration or affirmative action but rather reverse discrimination against white males.[19] Benjamin Hooks, executive director of the NAACP, noted this dynamic a year later. "The Reagan Administration," he contended, "acts as if the white male is the minority."[20] In fact, by May 1983, reverse discrimination against white males was the primary civil rights issue of Reynolds and the Justice Department.[21]

Reagan continued his assault on civil rights as year two kicked off. By the start of 1982, the *Los Angeles Times* was reporting, in a foreboding article titled, "Equality: A Chill in the Air," that "The Reagan Administration now speaks with one voice about affirmative-action. . . . It is not a voice raised to help minorities break out of the economic cellar."[22] In 1981, the Reagan administration stopped penalizing companies who refused to comply with mandated affirmative action programs. In 1982, Reagan took a similar approach to school integration. The Justice Department began advising the IRS to no longer deny tax-exempt status to religious schools, most famously Bob Jones University in Greenville, South Carolina, that openly discriminated against blacks. Taken together, the government's statements on civil rights and its efforts to reestablish the tax exemptions of segregated schools threw "a chill over hopes for racial progress," according to the *Times*.[23] There were other facets of this assault as well. For example, the Justice Department did not file a single case under the Fair Housing Act of 1968 in Reagan's first year in office. Previous administrations, including Nixon's, averaged thirty-two cases per year.[24]

Civil rights leaders did not stand idly by as Reagan attacked many of the gains of the civil rights movement. In a speech at the annual meeting of the Leadership Conference on Civil Rights, John Jacob, president of the National Urban League, criticized the civil rights policies of Reagan, stating, "We all know who our real enemies are. . . . We must all unite to defeat them and recapture the goals of the civil rights movement."[25] The subsequent study accused the Justice Department of attacking the country's civil rights laws in an effort to curtail the opportunities of people of color. "The Justice Department has become a travesty," the study concluded.[26]

As Reagan continued to assert his agenda in the face of mounting criticism, colorblindness provided the oft-repeated defense of his actions. Reagan and his administration insisted they were pursuing a strictly colorblind approach to the law, as civil rights advocates had demanded a decade and a half prior. Civil rights leaders, on the other hand, understood the colorblind rhetoric as nothing more than a convenient cooptation of selective civil rights rhetoric used to undermine its very goals by conservatives who largely opposed the movement they now claimed to inherit. Benjamin Hooks bluntly stated that colorblindness is wrong "because it's stupid."[27] By March 1982, the *New York Times* noted that "a fundamental disagreement over whether the Constitution and civil rights laws are 'color-blind'" had intensified between the administration and civil rights groups.[28]

In the middle of 1982, the "chill" the *Los Angeles Times* had noted that January had cooled to an outright freeze. By July, the Justice Department had "discarded busing as a remedy for school segregation; has stopped using goals to pressure employers to hire and promote minorities; [and] has cut back on filing new school, housing, and voting-rights suits."[29] The administration also opposed the 1982 extension of the Voting Rights Acts of 1965.[30] Moreover, Reagan's judicial appointments reflected the white supremacy of his approach to civil rights. By July, only one out of Reagan's over sixty nominations for judgeships and zero of his over eighty nominations for U.S. attorneys was black.[31]

Midway through 1982, however, the administration began to take notice of the criticisms their civil rights actions were receiving. In response to the critics, Reynolds again reiterated in July that the administration was committed to the goal of a "colorblind" society.[32] Yet while colorblindness provided the broken record to play in response to civil rights critics, the administration understood that after a nearly eighteen-month relentless barrage on civil rights, the colorblind rhetorical defense could not camouflage the lengths the administration had gone to in attacking civil rights. With midterm elections approaching and Republicans down in the polls, Reagan and his team began to worry about the criticisms his civil rights actions were receiving. A White House political aide called the opinion of Reagan among blacks and the potential fallout in the 1982 elections "probably the area that causes us the most concern."[33] In response, Reagan went on the offensive to "seek better relations" with people of color. He began making more public appearances at events appealing to people of color and instructed the Justice Department to ease off exempting federal fund recipients who discriminated from disqualification, which it had done in earnest since Reagan entered office. "Now was not the time to press this issue," the White House informed the Justice Department.[34]

In the second half of 1982, government officials joined civil rights groups in criticizing Reagan's civil rights actions. In September, the annual meeting of state advisory committees of the U.S. Commission on Civil Rights sent a letter to the president asserting that he was responsible for a "dangerous deterioration in the Federal enforcement of civil rights."[35] At month's end, the *Wall Street Journal* was noting that the president was "coming under fire" for its handling of civil rights policy—bad news with the midterm elections only two months away. Referencing the state agencies' letter, it also said Reagan had made "severe reductions" in operating funds of civil rights agencies.[36] In response, white conservatives again came to Reagan's defense. The Washington Council of Lawyers dismissed the objections of the state committees on civil rights and issued a study of its own. "If the administration is to be criticized for its civil rights record," the article contends, "it should be for not moving more swiftly and forcefully toward a 'color-blind' approach to enforcement. . . . While the government has the responsibility to halt intentional racial discrimination that disrupts social and economic mobility, to overstep that responsibility itself *threatens civil liberties*." White male civil liberties, that is.[37]

Halfway through his first term, it was easy to understand why the *Los Angeles Times* would assert that Reagan has gone "farther than other recent administrations in advocating strict colorblindness."[38] As the second half of his first term began, the administration continued to aggressively pursue the elimination of affirmative action and mandatory school integration. At the end of April, speaking at Amherst College, William Bradford Reynolds insisted that racial preferences in hiring and promotion and mandatory busing to achieve racial balance were "morally wrong." "The use of race in the distribution of limited economic and educational resources in the past decade," Reynolds elaborated, "has regrettably led to the creation of a kind of racial spoils system in America."[39] He emphasized that the underlying goal of the administration's civil rights policy is to achieve a "color-blind" society. "If history has taught us any lesson at all," Reynolds insisted, "it is that the use of race to justify treating individuals differently—whether they be black or white—can never be legitimate. Racial classifications are wrong—morally wrong—and ought not to be tolerated in any form or for any reason." In place of busing, he advocated "voluntary desegregation" for segregated schools.[40]

As 1983 unfolded, Reagan began implementing phase two of his civil rights agenda—removing from the federal government's civil rights agencies those who opposed his positions on civil rights and replacing them with like-minded affirmative action and integration opponents. William Bradford Reynolds and Clarence Pendleton, the black conservative and civil rights foe whom Reagan had appointed chair of the U.S. Commission on Civil Rights, were, along with Clarence Thomas, the most high-profile examples of this. Nonetheless, this process extended far deeper than just the leadership of the Justice Department and the Commission on Civil Rights. Shortly after Reynolds's Amherst College speech, Reagan replaced three of the members of the U.S. Commission on Civil Rights. He had previously replaced two others, meaning that a total of five of the six members of the commission, designed as an independent and bipartisan federal agency tasked with protecting and furthering civil rights, were Reagan appointees whose views aligned with those of the president.[41]

Civil rights leaders were not optimistic about the forecast for civil rights under the stewardship of the new-look commission. Shortly after the commission was restaffed, Phyllis P. McClure, an NAACP lawyer, stated, "'I expect a 180-degree switch on every major position that the old commission took on such issues as affirmative action, school desegregation, and the nondiscrimination obligations of Federal aid recipients. I even anticipate a redefinition of what a civil rights issue is and what the legal precedents are.'"[42] A citizens' panel that included half a dozen former members of the commission characterized Reagan's reorganization of the commission as a "'concerted attack' on affirmative action programs and accused the administration of using colorblind rhetoric to advance its 'political and ideological goals.'"[43] The new commission members themselves explicitly confirmed McClure's fears. John H. Bunzel, one of Reagan's appointees, stated that there would indeed be "'a reassessment of past policies, approaches and viewpoints'" upon his confirmation.[44] The first action of staff director Linda Chavez, one of Reagan's appointees to the commission, was to issue a memorandum "urging the commission to reverse itself and support white Memphis, Tenn. firefighters in a Supreme Court case in which they are challenging the hiring of blacks under affirmative action." This prompted the state advisory committee to hold an emergency meeting to rebuke Chavez.[45] In response to Reagan's commission appointees, the state advisory committee chair characterized Reagan's restructuring of the commission as "a clear attempt to destroy the autonomy of the agency."[46] Reagan's efforts to shake up the members of the commission was "unprecedented and endangers the historic independence and integrity of the commission." He further argued that the Justice Department was "undermining judicial authority to eliminate the present effects of past discrimination."[47]

At the start of 1983, the conservative Heritage Foundation, which in 1982 issued a civil rights report calling for a strictly colorblind approach to civil rights, recommended that the administration "attack hundreds of existing affirmative action agreements as its top legal priority."[48] It did not realize that the process was already underway. By June 1983, journalist Hodding Carter III was asking in the *Wall Street Journal*, "When will Reagan do something for minorities?" "The president and his men," insisted Carter, "have repeatedly put themselves squarely at odds with mainstream thinking in the civil rights movement and with the policy decisions of every president since Eisenhower." In his rebuke, Carter also criticized the administration's use of colorblindness to defend its civil rights positions. "Rhetorical claims to belief in a colorblind society," he argued, "and repeated insistence that the goal of justice for all is near and dear to the president's heart cut little ice with people looking for concrete action."[49] Yet Carter's contention regarding the fallacy of colorblindness placed him in the minority, as Reagan's colorblind rhetoric continued to gain traction in the minds of whites. A September 1983 Anti-Defamation League study found that 73 percent of Americans "disapproved of giving members of minorities special advantages to rectify past discrimination," and 52 percent said that race should play no factor in hiring, and companies should not be required by law to hire a fixed percentage of minorities.[50]

By the end of 1983, the Reagan administration had directed its attention back to the Supreme Court in an effort to force the court to confront affirmative action yet again in hopes of eliminating the program entirely. In December, the Justice Department filed a Supreme Court brief arguing that the city of Detroit's affirmative action plan, which promoted black and white police officers in equal numbers, and a lower court ruling that mandated an affirmative action program in the Memphis firefighters union were unconstitutional.[51] While the court had defended the use of racial preference in hiring in order to undo past discrimination in both the *Weber* and *Fullilove* cases shortly before Reagan entered office, the administration hoped that those rulings, which dealt with affirmative action in the private sector, were unconstitutional when applied to the public sector. Moreover, the administration hoped that such a victory would open the door to banning affirmative action in other areas. Not surprisingly, Reynolds defended the administration's position as motivated entirely by a commitment to "colorblind law." The stance taken by the administration at the end of 1983 marked a wholesale reversal not just in position but in action of the previous administration. Carter disagreed with the *Bakke* decision, maintaining that race "was an appropriate criterion to use in remedying the effects of past discrimination."[52] Nixon disapproved of busing but did not use his Justice Department to stop it. Only five years later, the White House had reversed course entirely. It not only opposed affirmative action and school integration but had become the most active group trying to eliminate it. Colorblindness, and colorblindness alone, provided the justification. As the year closed, the editorial board of the *Los Angeles Times* published an article titled "Affirmative Action Is Under Fire."[53] The reason the Reagan administration so vigorously opposed affirmative action was simple to the board: it worked.[54]

The *Times* editorial had no effect on the civil rights course of the administration. As the final year of Reagan's first term unfolded, the administration continued its assault on civil rights programs. When the Supreme Court ruled that an employer could not lay off a senior ranking employee over a junior one in order to maintain a certain percentage of employees of color, Reynolds ordered all federal affirmative action plans reviewed to eliminate any "race-conscious provisions," a move the *Los Angeles Times* characterized as "an attack without foundation."[55] A month later, Reynolds made it clear that "there is nothing in the Fair Housing Act that requires any particular balance in a neighborhood." While he conceded that the administration would "stop practices that deny people opportunity," he nonetheless argued that "the natural consequences of people's choice of housing is not something the federal government ought to regulate, even if it results in buildings, neighborhoods or communities that are occupied entirely by persons of one race. There is nothing unlawful" about such a result and "nothing that would compel" the federal government to change it.[56] As with busing and affirmative action, the Reagan administration's position on civil rights marks not merely a reinterpretation of the law but a fundamental reversal of the federal government's approach to civil rights. As previously noted, Reagan's Justice Department did not file a single discrimination case under the Fair Housing Act during Reagan's first two years in office, compared to an average of over thirty per year in the previous two administrations. By the end of his first term, the Justice Department had filed only seventeen housing discrimination claims. This prompted the *Los Angeles Times* to report the Justice Department's approach to the Fair Housing Act under the title "The Undermining of Civil Rights."[57]

While historian Gil Troy insists that "the Reagan Administration's assault on civil rights was more rhetorical than real," one cannot minimize the effort Reagan and his Justice Department put in to make sure that their impact on civil rights was in fact real.[58] The restaffing of the federal government's civil rights division and the alterations to federal court benches were far more than rhetorical. More importantly, Troy underestimates the fundamental work such rhetoric played in building the ideology of colorblindness. The eliminations of civil rights programs Reagan sought in his first term might not have come to fruition, but their inevitability was sealed through the actions and colorblind rhetoric of Reagan and appointees like Reynolds. Throughout this drastic reframing of civil rights discourse and restructuring of civil rights organizations, Reagan repeatedly and exclusively turned to colorblind rhetoric to defend his positions. By the end of his first term, Diane Camper of the *New York Times* coined a phrase to refer to administration officials' habitual invocation of colorblindness to defend themselves against criticisms of their position on civil rights—"the Reagan race phonograph"—but also editorialized, "Playing the record is understandable; the content is not."[59] Colorblindness enabled Reagan to frame his relentless attacks on civil rights as motivated by a morally righteous and apolitical commitment to equality. This was not new, as white antibusers and affirmative action opponents used the same strategy at the grassroots level a half decade earlier, and people flocked to movie theaters to watch white supremacy reestablished through colorblind justice in a heavyweight prize fight. So while Reagan was certainly not the first person to deploy such a strategy, he was the first president to do so. As president, he was able to exert far more influence nationally through the use of colorblind rhetoric.

Rocky III and the War on Drugs

Rocky III sits at the intersection of colorblindness, deindustrialization, and Reagan's war on civil rights. Additionally, Reagan's first term saw the onset of his War on Drugs. Like *Rocky III*, Reagan's War on Drugs reveals the explicit antiblackness at the root of Reagan's social policies, obfuscated by a veneer of colorblind respectability. Moreover, television news played a fundamental role in racializing the visual politics of Reagan's drug war in the latter half of the 1980s. All of these larger political trends, however, are carefully outlined in *Rocky III*, years before television news and Reagan would adopt them as clichés.

During his presidential campaign, Ronald Reagan used racially coded dog whistles to appeal directly to disaffected whites by condemning lazy "welfare queens" and inner-city criminal "predators" for the rising rates of poverty in urban America in the early 1980s. The president spoke often of welfare cheats, including a fictitious one he repeatedly referenced who supposedly lived in Chicago with "eighty names, thirty addresses, [and] twelve social security cards [and who] is collecting social security benefits on four non-existing dead husbands. . . . Her tax-free income is over $150,000."[60] "As one political insider explained, Reagan's appeal derived [in large part] from . . . 'the emotional distress of those who fear or resent [blacks], and who expect Reagan somehow to keep [them] in [their] place.'"[61] And this appeal extended to whites beyond his own party. In 1980, 22 percent of all registered Democrats voted for Reagan. Among Democrats who believed civil rights leaders were "pushing too fast," 34 percent voted for Reagan. Even more, among Democrats who felt "the government should not make any special effort to help [blacks] because they should help themselves," 71 percent voted for Reagan. Reagan's appeal among Democrats, therefore, had less to do with his economic platform or fiscal policy than with their attraction to his racial politics of antiblackness.[62] Reagan's race-baiting, moreover, was easy to detect, but his avoidance of racially explicit language provided a bulwark from accusations of racial prejudice. As Michelle Alexander explains, Reagan's "'color-blind' rhetoric on crime, welfare, taxes, and states' rights was clearly understood by . . . voters as having a racial dimension," but it was difficult to prove without racially explicit language.[63]

Once in office, Reagan made good on his promise to get tough on crime and purge the welfare rolls of "lazy, undeserving, government moochers." In 1982, the president launched his War on Drugs, the same year *Rocky III* premiered. Immediately thereafter, Congress increased the FBI's antidrug funding twelve-fold. The Department of Defense and the Drug Enforcement Agency's antidrug budgets saw similar increases. Meanwhile, drug prevention programs saw significant cuts. Reagan, in other words, having helped construct and campaign against the boogeyman of the black, welfare-dependent, inner-city drug addict, used federal drug dollars that targeted and criminalized deindustrializing urban black communities. "In the era of colorblindness," Alexander writes, "it is no longer permissible to hate blacks, but we can hate criminals."[64]

Crack cocaine became the public face of Reagan's War on Drugs. Although media coverage of cocaine "rocks" did not appear until a year after *Rocky III*, and the "crack scare" would not become a staple of the evening news until 1986, "Crack attracted the attention of politicians and the media because of its downward mobility to and increased visibility in ghettos."[65] Crack users were predominantly poor, black, and urban, which politicians used to their advantage and the media capitalized on after nearly two decades of public demonization of the "culture of poverty" in low-income urban black neighborhoods. Clubber Lang's fight moniker, after all, is the "South Side Slugger," linking the fighter to the predominantly black inner-city neighborhood in Chicago, the nation's Second City, precisely the sort of community Reagan had helped to vilify. As drug scholars Craig Reinarman and Harry G. Levine note, the "drug war was not effective or wise policy. . . . Politicians promoted it nonetheless because . . . it provided a convenient scapegoat for enduring and ever growing urban poverty."[66]

As Jimmie L. Reeves and Richard Campbell note, television news was essential to framing the racial politics of Reagan's War on Drugs. "The journalistic recruitment in the anti-cocaine crusade," they explain, "was absolutely crucial in converting the war on drugs into a political spectacle that depicted social problems grounded on economic transformations as individual moral or behavioral problems that could be remedied by simply embracing family values, modifying bad habits, policing mean streets, and incarcerating the fiendish 'enemies within.'"[67] There were multiple stages of cocaine journalism in the 1980s. The first, from January 1981 through November 1985, characterized the "trickle down" of the "glamour" drug to the white middle class. Tackling this problem required nothing more than rehabilitation programs. Phases two and three, however—from December 1985 through December 1988—fetishized the new smokable and economical "rock" or "crack" version of the drug, and increasingly highlighted the racial and class profiles—black and poor—of crack cocaine abusers. Such coverage characterized crack users as an "enemy within" that required discipline and punishment, which culminated in the escalation of the War on Drugs and the rise of the modern prison-industrial complex. In fact, in 1990, the House of Representatives Committee on Ways and Means published a report titled *The Enemy Within: Crack-Cocaine and America's Families*.[68]

Contrasting the "black delinquents" who used crack cocaine with the "white offenders" of powder cocaine also relied on reanimating the Moynihan Report's discourse about black family structures.[69] As we saw in chapter 2, the fallout of the Moynihan Report affected federal policy and black civil rights organizing around racial inequality in the 1970s. In the 1980s, journalists across the political spectrum capitalized on notions of a "pathological" female-headed black family structure in order to occlude the economic underpinnings of the crack cocaine problem and belie the root causes of crack abuse as nothing more than personal moral failings. In January 1985, for example, CBS News aired a feature called "The Vanishing Family: Crisis in Black America," hosted by liberal journalist Bill Moyers. The piece contains the hallmarks of Moynihan discourse, blaming the "failures" of black family structures for the racial inequality black Americans face.[70] "The war on drugs was, at root," Reeves and Campbell conclude, "a Reaganite project that expressed the New Right's basic response to social problems grounded in economic distress. . . . That response [was] . . . to treat people *in* trouble as people who *make* trouble."[71]

Rocky III builds its drama around the "enemy within" discourse of the 1980s. Like the first two *Rocky* films, *Rocky III* is largely devoid of explicit verbal references to race, with one exception—Rocky's brother-in-law, Paulie. At one point in *Rocky III*, Paulie remarks that Balboa will never develop the footwork of Creed because he's "not a colored fighter." Yet as we saw in chapter 3, Paulie's racism works less to disrupt the colorblind politics of the film than it does to accentuate the modern colorblind white masculinity of Balboa, which stands in contrast to the antiquated backlash ideology of Paulie. Paulie, in other words, symbolizes the forgotten-man whiteness of George Wallace; Balboa, the colorblind whiteness of the Reagan era. Nonetheless, together they must now unite with Apollo Creed—who in this new context represents black bourgeois respectability—to defeat the new black urban threat embodied by Lang. Aside from Paulie, the film relies on the visuality of racialized bodies to dramatize the unification of the divergent versions of white and black masculinity to defeat Lang. However, unlike *Rocky I*, which steers clear of the most noxious elements of antiblackness, *Rocky III* places them at the film's center. *Rocky III* leans heavily on two very old elements of the black "buck" stereotype, specifically his superior physical prowess and his uncontrollable lust for white women, to dramatize the supposed need for the criminalization and punitive policing of urban black communities in the age of colorblindness.

The film begins with a short recap of *Rocky II* before shifting to a montage of a series of title defenses between Balboa and his unworthy challengers, interspersed with scenes from his idyllic life as a family man, in the time between the conclusion of the *Rocky* sequel and the beginning of the third film. As the audience watches Rocky dispatch his numerous challengers without breaking much of a sweat, one cannot help but notice that the overwhelming majority of Rocky's opponents are black. The opening montage, then, offers a sequence of images of white masculine physical supremacy. This culminates in a dramatic wide shot of Rocky walloping an unnamed black opponent with a left hook.

The aesthetics of resurgent white masculinity is followed by representations of its necessity in the deindustrialized Reagan years. The second half of the montage offers the latest "threat" confronting white masculinity—and, by extension, the nation. The film follows the aforementioned montage with one of the victories of Rocky's next, and most dangerous, challenger—Clubber Lang. Lang's knock-out punches contrast Balboa's physically dominant white masculinity with an equally potent black one as it defeats white challengers. Furthermore, Lang's fights highlight the "savagery" of Lang and his fighting style. A newspaper headline early in Lang's montage states that Clubber "mauled" his opponent and describes the challenger as "brutal." Paulie reinforces Lang's savagery later in the film, referring to the pugilist as an "ape." Shortly after the newspaper headlines, a split screen of a suited Balboa and a mohawked Lang precedes Lang beating up numerous white opponents. And whereas images of Balboa outside the ring as a doting and gentle husband and father, corporate spokesman, and charity volunteer soften those of his brutality between the ropes, the audience is offered no window into Lang's life outside the ring, leading us to believe that he doesn't have one. Instead, Lang appears to derive pleasure from fighting. He does it not for glory, money, fame, or fortune but because he enjoys it; it is engrained in his supposedly savage nature.

In the lead-up to the first fight, *Rocky III* repurposes but inverts the iconic training montage of *Rocky I*. In the first film, Balboa's relentless training contrasts with Apollo Creed's lack of preparation. In fact, we never see Creed throw a single punch, lift a weight, or elevate his heart rate before the bout. In *Rocky III*, Sylvester Stallone, the film's director and star, inverts that trope

Split-screen: Rocky the family man vs. the menacing Clubber Lang (Mr. T).

it is Clubber Lang who trains with rigor while Balboa's training sessions function largely as marketing ploys. However, the two training sequences work to different ends. In *Rocky*, Balboa's training and Creed's idleness contrasts the blue-collar work ethic of the *deserving* Balboa against the lazy and *undeserving* ethic of Creed, emblematic of white backlash politics of the 1970s. In *Rocky III*, however, Lang's training works less to establish his work ethic than it does to highlight his ferocity and the physical threat he presents to Balboa. Throughout Lang's training, he grunts and groans in an animalistic manner, like a predator on the hunt for prey. The Lang montage, then, repurposes the classical Hollywood "buck," representing Clubber as a remorseless killer with no moral compass who thrives on violence. This image of urban black masculinity became a justification for and target of Reagan's War on Drugs and anticipates many of the characteristics that would define "super-predators" in the Clinton years. Moreover, the space of the ghetto becomes the locus of black savagery. It is no accident, then, that while training for his rematch with Lang, Balboa visits Apollo Creed's former gym—a rundown, dimly lit facility in a blighted neighborhood in Los Angeles, full of exclusively black fighters. Balboa loses his first bout against Lang because fame and fortune had turned him "soft," according to his trainer, Mickey. Rocky's excursion to the urban ghetto of Los Angeles is necessary for him to reclaim the savagery required to defeat his most barbaric opponent to date. According to *Rocky III*, the urban ghetto functions as a crucible of black masculine brutality. It is the source of Lang's and, as we saw in chapter 3, Apollo Creed's savagery. Balboa, therefore, must travel to the source of Lang's savagery in order to develop a brutality of his own capable of defeating Lang. The rematch between Lang and Balboa therefore restages much of the drama and racial politics of the heavyweight title bout between Jack Johnson and Jim Jeffries more than seventy years prior. As Gale Bederman notes, public commentary for that fight, whereby Johnson easily defeated Jeffries to become the nation's first black heavyweight champion, insisted (erroneously) that the superior intellect of the white Jeffries would prevail over the brute physicality of the black Johnson.[72] In *Rocky III*, Balboa's defeat of Lang requires both his supposed superior intellect *and* his schooling in black brutality thanks to his best friend Apollo Creed and the other black fighters in the inner-city Los Angeles gym.

The image of the black "buck" is older than Hollywood itself. As movies like *Birth of a Nation* show, the function of the buck in film is to create a mandate for what Richard Slotkin and others refer to as "regeneration through violence"—the need of white masculinity to violently extinguish the threat of black masculinity in order to protect white womanhood and restore the racial order of white supremacy. In the lead-up to Lang and Balboa's first fight, the audience sees that the danger Clubber poses has nothing to do with a gold belt but rather the physical safety and security of white women. After avoiding Clubber and his requests for a title shot for the first half hour of the film, the "Southside Slugger" confronts Balboa at an event celebrating the unveiling of a statue commissioned in his honor in his home city of Philadelphia. After lobbing numerous insults that fail to provoke Balboa, Clubber turns his attention to Rocky's wife, Adrian, telling her to call him and come over if she ever wants to spend the night with a "real man." The sexual innuendo of Lang's comment launches Balboa into a rage. As the champ lunges at Lang, he angrily agrees to a fight. Importantly, none of Lang's previous comments phased Balboa, but the second he threatens Balboa's masculinity by challenging his sexual prowess and ability to "protect" his white wife from a black man, Balboa springs into aggression. Thus, the centuries-old racial discourse of white supremacy, and its triangulation of white and black masculinity with white femininity, serves as the underlying motivation of the entire *Rocky III* film. By extension, the sexual threat posed by Lang leverages historically rooted discourses of black masculinity to demonize black inner-city communities while also revealing that the anti-black urbanity of the Reagan years is rooted in much older tenets of white

Apollo Creed gifts his American flag boxing trunks, the same ones he used in *Rocky I*, to Balboa for his rematch against Lang.

supremacy. Reagan's efforts to eliminate civil rights programs foreclosed opportunities for black economic and educational advancement. His implementation of the draconian War on Drugs then criminalized urban black communities, further inhibiting their social mobility. Together, this comprises Reagan's dual-faceted antiblack political agenda in his first term. Moreover, what links these efforts is not only the targets of these policies— African Americans—but also how both projects were justified by the ideology of colorblindness.

These discursive threads all tie together in the moments before the film's climactic fight, a rematch between Lang and Balboa. Apollo Creed, Balboa's former nemesis turned best friend and trainer, brings Balboa a gift as he prepares in his dressing room. Creed opens the large white box and hands Rocky his American flag fight trunks, the "colors" he wore in his first fight against Balboa. As we saw in chapter 3, Creed's flag trunks from the first *Rocky* film are part of a collection of patriotic paraphernalia that personify the white backlash forgotten-man aesthetics of the mid-1970s, driven by widespread white opposition to affirmative action and school integration. By giving Balboa his flag trunks just minutes before watching his new best friend enter the ring for the toughest bout of his career, Creed offers Balboa not just his patriotic uniform but the support of the entire nation. *Rocky III* offers the unification of Creed and Balboa, the coming together of black bourgeois respectability (Creed) and white working-class determination (Balboa) against the common threat of urban black masculinity (Lang).

In the 1980s, white conservatives commonly cited the achievements of a handful of black stars—Bill Cosby, Whoopi Goldberg, Arsenio Hall, Michael Jackson, Michael Jordan—as proof that racism was dead. Neoconservative William F. Buckley Jr., for example, insisted that the *Cosby Show*'s ratings proved that America had moved to a colorblind reality. "A nation simply does not idolize members of a race which that nation despises," Buckley argued.[73] According to media scholar Herman Gray, the appropriation of black stars by white conservatives in order to substantiate claims of a colorblind racial America sought to justify "a middle-class utopian imagination of racial pluralism" based on "open class structure, economic mobility, the sanctity of individualism, and the availability of the American dream for black Americans."[74] As Gray elaborates, "In dominant media presentations, the figure of the model black citizen is often juxtaposed against poor and disenfranchised members of the black community, where it works to reinforce and reaffirm the openness and equality of contemporary American society." The unification of Creed and Balboa against the black "superpredators" of the urban ghetto that make up the "enemy within" marked a new phase of post–civil rights racial demagoguery.[75] Creed and Balboa's friendship counteracts the more explicit antiblackness of *Rocky III* and the Reagan administration. Moreover, such logic is rooted in colorblind individualism. In other words, individual black personas—Michael Jordan, Bill Cosby, or Apollo Creed—became the new fodder for the colorblind veneer that obfuscates the structural inequalities of the 1980s and the anti–civil rights policies of the Reagan administration.

Individual Rights Victorious by Knockout

As we saw earlier, Reagan's war on civil rights led to an outright reinterpretation of civil rights. Reagan's Justice Department, moreover, spent considerable effort trying to convince the Supreme Court to adopt its view. Prior to the Reagan presidency, civil rights programs were widely understood as addressing the inequalities and discrimination of people of color (and women), especially African Americans, experienced as a *group*. This was precisely the logic, for example, used in Supreme Court cases upholding affirmative action in the late 1970s. For example, Warren Burger's *Fullilove* opinion, handed down the year before Reagan's election, rejected color-blindness and defended the federal government's setting aside of 10 percent of funds for public works programs for minority-owned businesses in light of the fact that minorities had historically been excluded from participating in competition for public contracts as a group. The government was therefore perfectly within the law to implement a program that sought to rectify this issue by increasing the number of federal contracts administered to minority-owned businesses. The issue, then, was not whether or not an individual minority business owner was personally victimized by discrimination but the systematic exclusion of minorities from these opportunities collectively. Yet as Reagan critic Hodding Carter III noted near the end of Reagan's first term, "There is a thesis, popular in conservative and neo-conservative circles, that there is no longer really a racial problem in the U.S. There is just the problem of individuals."[76] The Justice Department was certainly one of the "circles" Carter referred to. In an address to the American Bar Association in August 1984, Carol Dinkins, the deputy attorney general, voiced her opposition to quotas: they "do not even focus on individual victims. They create new victims."[77] These new victims, it is worth noting, were white and often male. Only individual victims, she insisted, not groups, are entitled to legal relief.

William Bradford Reynolds, assistant attorney general, was the chief architect of the administration's doctrine of colorblind neoliberalism. As head of the Justice Department's Civil Rights Division, he used legally dubious methods and outright ignorance of the law to impose the doctrine of colorblind neoliberalism.[78] Reynolds made clear he was trying to get the Supreme Court to ban all preferential treatment for women and minorities in hiring, admissions, and promotion practices in both the public and private sectors. This was despite the fact that the court had upheld the constitutionality of such practices two years prior in the *Weber* ruling.[79] In the interim, the Justice Department promised to stop imposing numerical goals or timetables, which they slandered as "quotas," for the hiring of women and people of color on businesses and government agencies, as the Justice Department and Supreme Court had repeatedly done over the past decade and which remained legally mandated. Within a year of Reynolds's appointment to the Civil Rights Division, over half the lawyers working under Reynolds signed a petition protesting the hiring of Reynolds and his civil rights positions.[80] Under Reynolds, the Civil Rights Division and the Justice Department ignored violations of the Voting Rights Act and intervened to overturn and exempt affirmative action programs. Simultaneously, the Equal Employment Opportunity Commission (EEOC), established by the Civil Rights Act of 1964 to enforce civil rights laws against workplace discrimination, stopped using class action suits to enforce affirmative action hiring programs.[81]

It is therefore not surprising that in May 1984, with Reagan's first term nearly complete, Reynolds published an article in the *Yale Law Review* titled "Individualism vs. Group Rights: The Legacy of *Brown*," outlining the administration's commitment to colorblind neoliberalism. In the article, Reynolds repeatedly insists that throughout American history, civil rights have always belonged to individuals, not groups, despite the fact that the Constitution is full of references to the rights of groups.[82] Quoting the recent congressional testimony of a law professor, Reynolds insists that civil rights "inhere in individuals, not in groups."[83] In the 1970s, according to Reynolds, civil rights activism devolved into a misguided quest for equal results, resulting in a dilemma in which, he argues, sounding very much like Milton Friedman, "the individual-oriented concept of racial neutrality was blurred into the group-oriented concept of racial balance, on the representation that the former could not be fully realized unless the latter was achieved."[84] For Reynolds, the primary offender in this misguided strategy was busing. He contends, "Mandatory busing is an excellent example of the contemporary inclination to view a group-oriented social problem—racial stratification in public schools—as a civil rights issue and to seek to solve it with coercive judicial remedies. In the process, the social problem is generally worsened, and the real civil right—the individual student's right to be free from racial discrimination in assignment—is invariably sacrificed."[85] Like Friedman, Reynolds bases his argument on the assumption that government intervention in matters of racial equality not only is ineffective but actually infringes on individual freedom. "Indeed," Reynolds insists, "the more insistent government is on the use of racial preferences—whether in the form of quotas, goals, or any other numerical device—to correct what is perceived as an 'imbalance' in our schools, our neighborhoods, our work places, or our elected bodies, the more racially polarized society becomes." Again, like Friedman, Reynolds argues that government intervention actually increases racial antagonism. In its place, Reynolds advocates a strictly "colorblind" approach to the law, which treats people solely as individuals, as the only way to produce a more racially equitable society. He concludes, "We are all—each of us—a minority in this country: a minority of one. Our rights derive from the uniquely American belief in the primacy of the individual. And in no instance should an individual's rights rise any higher

Rocky Balboa vs. Clubber Lang, the rematch.

or fall any lower than the rights of others because of race, gender, or ethnic origin."[86]

Reynolds's article reveals the union of neoliberal philosophy and colorblind rhetoric. The colorblind neoliberal dogma of the Reagan administration prioritized the notion that individual freedom superseded group rights, championed the omnipotence of the free market, and linked both ideas to the rhetoric of colorblindness in order to cut the legs out from under civil rights legislation. In its strictly colorblind approach and refusal to consider group rights and discrimination, the Civil Rights Division of the Justice Department under Reagan became a tool to paralyze the federal government's ability to address racial discrimination.

To return to the locker room before the Balboa versus Lang rematch, the handing over of the nation's flag from Creed to Balboa via his trunks symbolizes not just the unification of the black middle class and the white working class but also the resurgence of white masculinity in the Reagan era. Whereas *Rocky I* mourns the abandonment of the white working class at the hands of the civil rights movement, *Rocky III* celebrates white working-class triumph over urban black communities. *Rocky III* illuminates that whatever elements of racial civility colorblindness insists on, the ideology is and has always been undergirded by very old notions of white supremacy and antiblackness. In his first term, Reagan launched his assault on civil rights programs. When courts handcuffed his ability to gut affirmative action and school integration orders, he changed course and ordered his Justice Department to stop enforcing civil rights laws he opposed. Simultaneously, his Justice Department sought to reframe civil rights in line with the idea of colorblind neoliberalism that privileged individual rights over group ones in order to reframe civil rights as a white male issue and undermine the federal government's ability to redress racial inequality. Reagan also launched his War on Drugs and ramped up his criminalization of urban black communities in his first four years, which proved fundamental to his larger social and economic agenda. In the years after *Rocky III*, Reagan and Hollywood would together reimagine black freedom struggles as driven by colorblind white heroes.

5 We Are What We Were

Imagining America's Colorblind Past

. . . .

> We want, we want what I think Martin Luther King asked for.
> We want a color-blind society.
>
> —Ronald Reagan, February 1986

While campaigning for Jimmy Carter on the eve of the 1980 presidential election, Coretta Scott King said she was "scared that if Ronald Reagan gets into office, we are going to see more of the Ku Klux Klan and a resurgence of the Nazi Party."[1] Reagan's anti–civil rights attitudes continued well into his time in the White House. In October 1983, Reagan admitted he sympathized with North Carolina Republican senator and staunch segregationist Jesse Helms's view that King was a communist. When asked if he agreed with Helms on the matter, Reagan refused to rebuke the senator's accusations, quipping, "We'll know in about 35 years, won't we?"[2] Yet three years to the day after Coretta Scott King voiced her concerns about a Reagan presidency, Reagan, sitting on the White House lawn, signed a bill, with King by his side, establishing a federal Martin Luther King Jr. holiday as a crowd of several hundred sang "We Shall Overcome."[3]

The victory of a federal King holiday was not easily won for its supporters. Civil rights leaders faced immense opposition from both Congress and the president in the years leading up to its passing. In October 1983, when the bill reached the Senate floor, Jesse Helms filibustered it, condemning King's "calculated use of nonviolence as a provocative act" and insisting there was "no doubt" he was a communist before finally relenting.[4] In the two years prior, as support for the holiday gained momentum, Reagan indicated that he was sympathetic to the sentiments of African Americans who sought the holiday but worried that such a tribute would cost the federal government too much money—an estimated $18 million per year—and that "we could have an awful lot of holidays if we start down that road."[5]

Reagan's support for the federal King holiday had nothing to do with his personal views of the civil rights leader. Instead, the holiday provided Reagan with political clout to silence the immense criticism of his positions on civil rights. After changing his mind late in 1983, Reagan wrote a letter to Republican governor Meldrim Thomson of New Hampshire, who had begged the president not to support the holiday, explaining his support for the bill and doubling down on his views of King. The president's new position on the holiday was based "on an image [of King], not reality," Reagan explained in the private letter.[6] As discussed in chapter 4, throughout his first term Reagan used the civil rights wing of the federal government to undercut existing civil rights programs. He also restaffed the federal courts and the U.S. Commission on Civil Rights with people who shared his opposition to civil rights, transforming the federal government into one of civil rights' fiercest enemies. This did not go unnoticed. By 1983, Reagan faced an onslaught of criticism on the issue of civil rights. He thus began, in the lead-up to his reelection, to make a more concerted effort to pacify his critics. The King holiday was the main component of this effort.

By supporting the holiday, Reagan not only addressed the criticism of his past actions but began to position himself as the inheritor of King's colorblind dream. By the end of 1983, Reagan's assistant attorney general, William Bradford Reynolds, frequently defended the president's positions on civil rights as akin to King's.[7] Throughout Reagan's second term, the president and Reynolds would routinely turn to the colorblind rhetoric of the civil rights movement to justify the president's continued assault on the movement's legal legacy. Administration officials actively sought to reimagine the black freedom struggles—civil rights and slavery—as motivated entirely by a commitment to colorblindness. In so doing, they strategically sought to position themselves, rather than the civil rights leaders who opposed the administration's position, as the true inheritors of the civil rights movement. Their opposition, they therefore insisted, was nothing more than the realization and implementation of Martin Luther King's colorblind dream. Moreover, it was not merely the legacy and memory of the civil rights movement the administration sought to remake during its second term. Buoyed by an increasingly sympathetic Supreme Court, the Reagan administration, although ultimately unsuccessful, mobilized to eliminate affirmative action entirely and reframe the manner in which racism was understood.

As Reagan left office, Hollywood took the lead in imagining a colorblind ethos at the center of the black freedom struggles. Beginning in the late 1980s, Hollywood rediscovered civil rights and slavery, making a number of films on the topics that insert a white hero at the narrative's center. Existing scholarship on these films note the neoconservative white-patriarchal rewriting of history in films like *Forrest Gump*, or the whitewashing of black freedom struggles.[8] Yet some scholars and critics frame these films as merely the latest iterations of Hollywood's whitewashing of American history. Other scholars, like Robyn Wiegman, are part of a scholarly tradition that has interrogated the manner in which the reimagining of America's racial past in Hollywood has served varying political interests at different historical moments. As Wiegman notes in her analysis of *Forrest Gump*, "'Liberal whiteness,'" defined as "a color-blind moral sameness whose reinvestment in 'America' rehabilitates the national narrative of democratic progress in the aftermath of social dissent and crisis," dominated the American popular imaginary beginning in the late 1980s. Hollywood representations of liberal whiteness, Wiegman continues, "put a seemingly benign touch on those material transformations that have accompanied the twentieth century's long and complicated transition from Jim Crow to official integration."[9]

Drawing on Wiegman's conception of "liberal whiteness," this chapter traces how the Reagan administration and Hollywood reframed the legacy of slavery and the civil rights movement. I argue that together, they imagined an abolitionist and civil rights movement led by whites determined to establish a colorblind society. By positioning himself not as an enemy of civil rights but as its staunchest ally, Reagan was able to relentlessly attack civil rights policies while shielding himself from charges of bigotry. Hollywood built on the success of this project to draw audiences into its theaters. In so doing, the movie industry played an indispensable role in shaping the manner in which civil rights and slavery were understood. The movies made about black freedom struggles in the late eighties and into the nineties fundamentally remade our historical memory of abolition and the civil rights movement.

I begin with an exploration of Reagan's continued incursion on civil rights during his second term—a siege that aimed to both eliminate civil rights laws and reframe the country's entire discussion on race. I then turn to the third component of Reagan's assault: reimagining and reframing the legacy of the civil rights movement. My analysis situates the reemergence of civil rights and slavery dramas alongside the Reagan administration's mobilization of colorblind rhetoric to build opposition to affirmative action in the late 1980s. I then turn to the manner in which Hollywood took over Reagan's colorblind racial project as he left the White House. Through close readings of the films *Glory* (1989) and *The Long Walk Home* (1990), I argue that civil rights and slavery dramas of the late eighties and early nineties have little to do with the past and instead speak far more to the civil rights curtailments of the post-Reagan years. These movies reimagine colorblind white heroism as the driving force behind black freedom struggles and ultimately reframe those battles as conflicts over competing notions of whiteness. They provide historical "evidence" of an enduring colorblind white ethos responsible for the abolition of slavery and the victories of the civil rights movement at precisely the moment in which white conservatives increasingly mobilized colorblind discourse to justify the elimination of many of the gains of the civil rights movement—most notably affirmative action—and defend themselves against charges of racism. This occurred not just in terms of narrative but, more importantly, at the level of aesthetics. In the late 1980s, Hollywood not only produced films that placed fictitious colorblind whites at the center of black freedom struggles but also developed a colorblind aesthetic that demanded audience identification with these films' colorblind heroes, regardless of an individual spectator's positioning. In so doing, movies played a fundamental role in shoring up the hegemony of colorblindness in the late 1980s and into the 1990s.

Civil Rights under Reagan, Term Two

Upon his reelection in 1984, Reagan wasted no time in continuing his civil rights offensive. He immediately appointed Edwin Meese III, a staunch opponent of affirmative action, busing, and other civil rights programs, to the position of attorney general, despite what the *Wall Street Journal* characterized as a "vicious fight" in the Senate to block his appointment because of his views on civil rights.[10] The president's defiant civil rights position via the Meese appointment was bolstered by a 1984 Supreme Court decision, *Firefighters Local Union No. 1784 v. Stotts*, which protected the Memphis Fire Department's seniority system, particularly its last-hired, first-fired policy, against affirmative action goals.[11] The Justice Department used the *Stotts* decision as justification to place all government affirmative action programs under review in hopes of eliminating or severely restricting them.[12]

One cannot understate the boost the *Stotts* decision gave the president. During his first term, the Reagan administration's ability to enact significant changes to civil rights policy proved difficult. The Supreme Court repeatedly came down on the side of affirmative action in cases like *Weber* and *Fullilove*. Regarding school desegregation, the court went so far as to step in and prevent Reagan's attempt to enable private universities to segregate without federal penalty. Moreover, the American public was still relatively sympathetic to affirmative action and school desegregation. With an uncooperative court and an unsympathetic public, the Reagan administration simply stopped enforcing those civil rights laws it disapproved of, replaced judges and civil rights officials who opposed Reagan's views with those who supported them, and tried to curry favor with the American republic through colorblind rhetoric. *Stotts* was the harbinger the Reagan administration needed to reboot its efforts to enact its colorblind civil rights vision at the level of policy.

Colorblindness continued to provide the philosophical underpinning of the administration's anti–civil rights position. In early February 1985, mere days into Reagan's second term, the president's chief civil rights enforcer, William Bradford Reynolds, proudly told the Florida Bar Association's labor and employment committees that America would soon "put behind us for good" court-ordered hiring goals regarding race and gender. Americans were ready, Reynolds claimed, for an approach to civil rights that was "blind to color differences." A colorblind approach, he insisted, "will help to bring an end to that stifling process by which government and society view citizens as possessors of racial characteristics, not as the unique individuals they are."[13] Reynolds's Florida speech embodied the neoliberal colorblind individualism he and the rest of the Reagan administration had carefully crafted during his first term and would aggressively try to implement during their second four years.

It was not only civil rights policy that the Reagan administration sought to shape as its second term got underway. The civil rights wing aimed to frame the entire conversation on race. In early March, Clarence Pendleton Jr., chair of the U.S. Commission on Civil Rights, accused civil rights leaders and supporters of practicing a "new racism" by defending affirmative action programs. "Our so-called black leaders are spending every moment peddling pain, complaining about budget cuts," instead of helping the president create, Pendleton argued, "a society that is truly color-blind."[14] When asked about the *Stotts* ruling, Pendleton replied, "I hope that [*Stotts*] will end what I call the new racism that confronts black people today."[15] The "new racism" that Pendleton referred to was not that of those in the administration, like himself, who sought to eliminate existing civil rights law. Instead, the "new racists," Pendleton argued, were those who supported supposedly reverse-discriminatory policies like affirmative action. Moreover, the "new racists" were mostly black. "Who are these new racists?" Pendleton asked himself. "They are typically supporters of civil rights. Many of them are media-designated black leaders. These new racists, many of them black, exhibit the classical behavior system of racism. They treat blacks differently than whites because of their race."[16]

The *Stotts* ruling was not the only court case involving fire departments that bolstered the administration's position. In April 1985, a federal district judge struck down an affirmative action hiring program in the nation's capital because the program crossed the nebulous legal boundary between "goals" and "quotas" that the court had established years prior.[17] For the first time, the Supreme Court and district courts had seemingly begun to waver on their support of race-conscious remedies to job and educational inequality. Before *Stotts*, the courts had, for much of the period since the late 1960s, defended the constitutionality of affirmative action plans, even if occasionally throwing out individual programs, as with *Bakke* in the late 1970s. The 1984 Memphis ruling, however, marks the moment in which this began to change. As *New York Times* columnist Robert Pear noted on April 14, 1985, "For more than three years, the Justice Department has been waging a campaign against the use of numerical goals and quotas by public employers"; by the start of Reagan's second term, as a critical mass of court cases moved through the courts, that campaign was beginning to produce results.[18]

With its position on civil rights cosigned by Supreme Court support for the first time, Reagan's Justice Department blitzed ahead to eliminate affirmative action programs across the country. In the wake of the Memphis and D.C. decisions, the administration sent letters to fifty-one local governments across the country, urging them to eliminate their affirmative action programs—which violated the administration's "color-blind" approach to civil rights—or face repercussions from the Justice Department.[19] Indianapolis received one of these letters. Carter's Justice Department had sued the city in 1978 because only 11 and 8 percent of its police officers and firemen, respectively, were black. The city then implemented an affirmative action program (under consent decree), and by 1985, 14 percent of its police officers and 13 percent of its firefighters were black. More importantly, because of the undeniable diversity gains, by the mid-1980s city officials overwhelmingly supported the program. Despite this, the Reagan Justice Department sued the city in order to eliminate the program.[20]

Indianapolis was one of several city governments asked to eliminate their affirmative action programs by the Justice Department in the wake of *Stotts*. Others were located in areas of the South, like Alabama, where the violent defense of Jim Crow segregation gave rise to the modern civil rights movement decades prior. Alabama had not one black state trooper until 1972. As a result, a judge ordered an affirmative action program to integrate the police force. By 1983, however, there were only four black corporals, and none at any superior ranks within the force, which prompted more ambitious hiring goals. The 1983 revision to the Alabama program became one of the many challenged by Reagan's Justice Department in 1985. Condemning the administration's appeal in Alabama, Anthony Lewis of the *New York Times* wrote,

> The U.S. Justice Department was an active party in the case for years, pushing for an end to racism in the Alabama force. But the Reagan Administration's Justice Department is now on the other side. It is fighting the latest court order on appeal, arguing that the numerical system of promotions is unlawful and unfair to whites— no matter what blacks suffered in the past. The Alabama case is an example of a policy that takes the Reagan Administration to its ideological extreme: the policy of undoing all past civil rights judgments that include affirmative action plans. History must be forgotten. The legacy of inequality must be overlooked. The realities faced by blacks seeking to enter forbidden quarters must be ignored.[21]

This marked a new phase in Reagan's assault on civil rights. During his first term, unable to make substantive legal changes, the administration simply refused to enforce civil rights laws with which Reagan disagreed. However, Reagan's ability to more aggressively attack affirmative action was held in check by the Supreme Court. *Stotts*, and to a lesser extent the D.C. decision, weakened the court's defense of affirmative action and provided the administration an opening to reactivate its legal challenges to affirmative action policies. The year 1985 marks the moment in which the Justice Department and the Supreme Court appeared to align just enough to drastically redefine civil rights, not just in rhetoric but in policy as primarily a white male issue. As Lewis's op-ed illustrates, the Justice Department under Reagan had "switched sides" in an attempt to undo previous civil rights gains, a process that required historical amnesia. The editorial board of the *Los Angeles Times* immediately picked up on this move as well, writing in an April op-ed titled "Backward Progress": "The Reagan Administration, pretending that it is colorblind, is systematically dismantling the affirmative-action programs that someday could allow the country to look beyond race, or sex, to genuine equal opportunity. Its meddling with plans already put into effect by public and private employers is at best an insensitive, legalistic interpretation of policy, and at worst a blatant attempt to undo more than a decade of civil-rights progress. . . . The Justice Department apparently has looked around the country and come to the ludicrous conclusion that the biggest civil-rights problem is that white males might be discriminated against."[22] A month later, the *New York Times* argued in a similar op-ed, titled "Affirmative Retreat," that Reagan was using the Justice Department to "[divert] precious resources from unfinished civil rights business and threatening to burden the courts with retrial of settled cases."[23]

While colorblindness provided the ideological foundation behind the administration's civil rights maneuvering, it was more specifically a credo of colorblind neoliberalism that more accurately describes Reagan's approach. It was not just that the Reagan administration prioritized the rights of whites over those of people of color. It was the fact that the administration, through its rhetoric and policy efforts, not only undermined and attacked race-conscious affirmative action policies through colorblind rhetoric but simultaneously sublimated group rights more broadly beneath those of the individual. As Anthony Lewis noted, "In the view of the present Justice Department, no member of a minority group may get special consideration in employment under a court order unless he or she was personally a victim of discrimination—and can prove it. Of course it is very hard to find such victims: an 'unfortunate' fact, as one brief put it."[24] In other words, the administration both challenged laws granting special accommodations to blacks as a group through colorblind discourse and also contested the legitimacy of group identity as a whole. Together, this two-pronged strategy made it nearly impossible to prove discriminatory intent—unless, of course, you were a white male "victim" of reverse discrimination, like Allan Bakke.

These actions set off a contentious public debate on the Reagan administration's position on civil rights. Predictably, William Bradford Reynolds responded to critics by invoking colorblind individualism. "Rather than weakening the civil rights law," Reynolds said, defending the administration in May 1985, "[it has] breathed new life and new meaning into the civil rights laws for every individual in this country."[25] Meanwhile, Benjamin Hooks, executive director of the NAACP, denounced the Justice Department. "They are catering to the worst instincts of the American public," Hooks insisted, "but they are hiding it behind mushy-mushy, goody-goody words: 'color-blind,' 'sex-blind,' 'equity, fairness and justice,' when in fact it is designed to perpetuate injustice and inequality."[26] Two months prior, *Los Angeles Times* writer Carl Rowan, in light of *Stotts*, penned an article titled "Abolish the Civil-Rights Panel—Pendleton Made It a Sham," arguing,

It makes no sense for American taxpayers to spend almost $13 Million this year on a commission that was created to promote racial harmony and justice but that has become the nation's single most effective perpetrator of racial polarization and its most ridiculous apologist for entrenched racial and sexual injustice. . . .

The Civil Rights Commission was meant by Congress to be an ally of the civil-rights movement. [Clarence] Pendleton, his deputy Morris Abrams and a majority of the commission are waging war on the civil-rights movement. They have turned the Civil-Rights Movement into nothing but a propaganda organ for far-right ideologues.

Pendleton labels the blacks of the NAACP, the Urban League and other groups—the people who endured cattle prods, fire hoses, police dogs, jail terms and more—as the "new racists." He has given great comfort to whites who recoil at any suggestion that white racism is still rampant in America. The head of the Civil Rights Commission has done what the Ku-Klux-Klan could never do: He has convinced white America that it can sleep better tonight after his declaration that Benjamin Hooks, John Jacob, Vernon Jordan, the black members of Congress, etc., are the "new racists" of America.

. . . Every major black organization in the civil rights field recently refused to testify before the Civil Rights Commission. I know what they perceive: that a black man, Pendleton, has turned an instrument of justice into an especially venal foe of the civil-rights movement.[27]

Reagan, however, was not without his supporters. Numerous letters were written to the *Times* after the publication of Rowan's article. One man responded that the commission was a sham from its inception because it sought "to overcome racism while at the same time focusing on race."[28] Pendleton had done more than any other member of the commission, he argued, because he stuck to a strictly colorblind approach to civil rights.[29] Another person wrote that the country needed more men like Pendleton and proceeded to identify herself as a "minority" and member of the "silent majority."[30]

The momentum the administration built during the first months of the year hit a roadblock in the second half of 1985. In June, the Senate denied William Bradford Reynolds, the chief architect of the Justice Department's civil rights maneuverings, a promotion to associate attorney general, primarily because of his views on civil rights. After his nomination, the *New York Times* editorial board published an op-ed stating that Reynolds did not deserve the promotion because of his determined effort "to reverse past progress" regarding civil rights.[31] Echoing the *Times*, Ralph G. Neas, executive director of the Leadership Conference on Civil Rights, mobilized civil rights groups against the nomination because of Reynolds's "repeated defiance of the courts, the Congress and even of the wishes of local governments and officials" in his approach to civil rights law enforcement.[32] Neas described Reynolds as a "rigid ideologue and an extremist who has done everything possible to weaken the civil rights laws of this country."[33] Civil rights groups even organized a picket line outside the Justice Department in May.[34] Ultimately, civil rights mobilization, combined with resistance from congressional Democrats led by Joe Biden of Delaware, derailed Reynolds's nomination. It marked a small victory in the middle of a large war civil rights activists were losing badly.[35] The president used the defeat of Reynolds to double down on his position on civil rights and make clear that he had no plans of easing off on his assault. Reagan released a statement that read, in part, "I am deeply disappointed by the action of the Senate Judiciary Committee this morning. That some members of the committee chose to use the confirmation process to conduct an ideological assault on so superbly qualified a candidate was unjust and deeply wrong. . . . Let me emphasize that Mr. Reynolds' civil rights views reflect my own. The policies he pursued are the policies of this Administration, and they will remain our policies as long as I am President. Mr. Reynolds retains my full faith and confidence."[36]

In August, the American public learned just how committed Reagan remained to a rigidly colorblind approach to civil rights. On the 16th of the month, the *Wall Street Journal* published a leaked memo given to them by members of the administration who disagreed with Reagan's civil rights position indicating that the president was in the process of trying to "rewrite" Executive Order 11246, a landmark piece of civil rights legislation issued by Lyndon Johnson in 1965 requiring nondiscrimination and goals in hiring and employment for women and minorities.[37] Eliminating the protections of the order would have repealed requirements of thousands of federal contractors to set goals to hire people of color and white women. Importantly, the businesses burdened by the requirement put no pressure on the administration to take such a drastic step; they overwhelmingly favored the use of numerical goals to diversify their workplaces.[38] Undoing Executive Order 11246 would eliminate the ability of future administrations to enforce federal affirmative action guidelines and penalize companies who refused to comply. Overturning the order, along with concerted efforts to prohibit affirmative action programs, were the two areas the Justice Department focused its efforts on during Reagan's second term.

Reimagining King in American Memory

The Reagan administration's efforts to eliminate affirmative action programs and Executive Order 11246 during its second term mark a significant escalation in its assault on civil rights. Whereas during Reagan's first term, an uncooperative Supreme Court relegated the administration's fight against affirmative action to public discourse, his second term brought the requisite court support to more explicitly attack civil rights laws. As in the early years of his presidency, colorblindness remained the Reagan "race phonograph" that his Justice Department regularly turned to in order to defend their positions on civil rights. However, during his second term, Reagan and his team escalated the stakes of their colorblind rhetoric, arguing not only that they were committed to a colorblind society but that colorblindness was the driving force of the civil rights movement, and they were the inheritors of the colorblind struggle for racial justice. While administration officials occasionally invoked the civil rights movement and leaders like Martin Luther King Jr. during the first term, this strategy increased significantly during the second as Reagan sought to eliminate affirmative action and the protections of Executive Order 11246.[39]

Aligning the Reagan administration with civil rights activists was a project that involved Reagan sympathizers on the editorial pages of some of the nation's leading newspapers. The *Wall Street Journal*'s editorial board published an article in March 1985 defending the president, contending that "a colorblind society was the goal of the founders of their own movement, including, of course, Martin Luther King Jr. After the Civil Rights Act of 1964, civil rightists made rapid progress toward equality under the law." "It was only in the 1970s," the editors continue, "that a new goal, 'affirmative action,' was introduced, putting the movement behind a new form of discrimination, racial quotas. Mr. Pendleton and the Reagan Justice Department are simply trying to return to the original track."[40] In response to the *Journal*'s op-ed, one man, Michael Kinsley, immediately noted the hypocritical alliance between Reagan and the *Journal* given their civil rights records. Reagan opposed both the Civil Rights Act of 1964 and the Voting Rights Act of 1965. The *Wall Street Journal* only "reluctant[ly] acquiesce[ed] to civil rights" after decrying black activists and defending white property rights for much of the movement. Most offensively, after three activists working for the Congress of Racial Equality during a voting rights drive disappeared in Mississippi in June 1964, the *Journal* commented, "Without condoning racist attitudes, we think it understandable if people in Mississippi should resent such an invasion. The outsiders are said to regard themselves as some sort of heroic freedom fighters, but in truth they are asking for trouble."[41] It appears, however, that few understood the irony of Reagan and the *Journal*'s insistence on colorblindness given their own opposition to it a decade and a half prior. The editorial board's column reveals the consistent support Reagan's anti–civil rights crusade received in the pages of the *Wall Street Journal*.

The *Journal* was not alone in its defense of Reagan. In response to articles in both the *New York Times* and the *Los Angeles Times* criticizing Reagan's civil rights views, Ken Masugi, a member of the California Advisory Committee to the U.S. Commission on Civil Rights, wrote letters to both newspapers proclaiming the defenders of affirmative action the true racists. Comparing the fight against affirmative action to those against slavery and Jim Crow, Masugi urged confidence among those who shared his opposition. "You should not have to be reminded," Masugi wrote to the *New York Times*, "that racial segregation and its predecessor, slavery, were far more established practices than affirmative action, and that the battle against those evils required perseverance."[42] He chastised the *Los Angeles Times* for completely ignoring the history of the Civil Rights Act of 1964. He concludes both letters by insisting that it is Reagan who is continuing the "noble struggle for the rule of law under a color-blind Constitution protecting individual rights."[43] The use of civil rights rhetoric to wage anti–civil rights political campaigns by Reagan and his surrogates was not a new strategy. As we saw in chapter 3, anti-integrationists throughout the country used the rhetoric of the civil rights movement to advance their cause. Furthermore, as political scientist Daniel HoSang details, Alan Robbins, "California's leading crusader against mandatory school desegregation" in the late 1970s, explicitly courted and displayed select black political and religious leaders who supported his cause (one of whom was allegedly acquainted with Martin Luther King) in an effort to give his anti–civil rights activism a pro–civil rights veneer.[44] Reagan and his supporters, however, took this strategy to the national stage with the intent to alter federal, rather than merely state, law.

By November, Reagan's civil rights officials began to interject in the public debate surrounding Executive Order 11246. Clarence Pendleton wrote to the *Wall Street Journal* to defend the administration's record on civil rights and to educate its readership about the history of civil rights. "The affirmative-action debate has recently focused on whether President Reagan ought to . . . prohibit racial goals, timetables, and quotas in federal contracting," Pendleton wrote. "Clearly, they were not contemplated at the time President Johnson issued the order. They arose gradually by means of an overzealous bureaucracy charged with the order's implementation."[45] In response to Pendleton's letter and the threat posed to Executive Order 11246, Benjamin Hooks wrote a letter to the *New York Times* stating that undoing the order would "negate one of the most important civil rights measures enacted since the Emancipation Proclamation."[46] He continued by rebuking the attempts of the administration to insert a colorblind ethos at the core of the Constitution and black freedom struggles. William Bradford Reynolds then wrote to the *Times*, reiterating what he felt was the colorblind history of the nation, stating, "To hear Benjamin Hooks explain it, there never was a Brown v. Board of Education." He continues, "It is, of course, that principle—the principle of colorblindness, of nondiscrimination—that has been wrenched from the executive order signed by President Johnson in 1965. As originally issued, the executive order in both its language and its application was blind to color."[47] Reynolds believed that civil rights laws and executive orders were limited exclusively to colorblind solutions. It was only in the early 1970s that regulations distorted this goal. Race-conscious remedies to racial discrimination, in Reynolds's view, were nothing more than misguided liberal policies enacted years after the modern civil rights movement concluded, which distorted its colorblind intent.

By the end of the first year of his second term, Ronald Reagan and his Justice Department publicly laid out their plans for civil rights. They developed a twofold strategy that sought to both implement their vision regarding affirmative action at the legal level and win the hearts and minds of Americans at the ideological level by positioning their actions as motivated by a commitment to colorblind justice—the same commitment at the heart of black freedom struggles throughout American history. They were not the enemies of civil rights; they were its staunchest defenders and the inheritors of King's legacy. Civil rights leaders, in their view, had strayed from the movement's colorblind intent and had become the enemy of racial progress. As we have seen, civil rights activists and their sympathizers tried to highlight the race-conscious nature of the Constitution and of black social movements. They cited Reagan and his sympathizers' long history of opposition to civil rights to debunk their pro–civil rights platitudes in the eighties. They fought to preserve a memory of the movement that foregrounded racial justice rather than colorblind dogma.

Not So Fast, Dutch (1986–1988)

Ultimately, 1986 slowed much of the momentum Reagan had built the previous year. However, the year began as 1985 had ended. On January 17, 1986, three days before the inaugural Martin Luther King Jr. holiday, Coretta Scott King unveiled a three-foot solid bronze bust of her slain husband in the Capitol Rotunda.[48] After the ceremony, Reagan met with King and other civil rights leaders and urged them to "never, never abandon the dream" of a colorblind United States.[49] On the eve of the observance, Reagan used his weekly radio address to defend his civil rights position and insist that blacks had benefited from his presidency. "We are committed to a society in which all men and women have equal opportunities to succeed, and so we oppose the use of quotas," Reagan said. "We want a color-blind society. A society, that in the words of Dr. King, judges people not by the color of their skin, but by the content of their character."[50] Yet as Pennsylvania Democratic congressman William H. Gray's rebuttal made clear, Reagan's claims to improving the lives of African Americans were simply untrue. Over Reagan's first term, black unemployment had risen from 12.3 percent to 15.6 percent, and the percentage of black families living in poverty grew from 32 percent in 1980 to 42 percent in 1986. Polls showed that African Americans' views of Reagan had diminished alongside their economic prospects. Over half of all blacks polled in January 1986 believed that Reagan was a racist.[51] Two days later, on the morning after the holiday, the *Los Angeles Times* published a column criticizing Reagan's "Distortion of History." "All last week President Reagan draped himself in the mantle of the late Dr. Martin Luther King, Jr.," the *Times* wrote. "He visited with youngsters at the southeast Washington school named after the slain civil-rights leader. He counseled with King's widow. . . . And he touted the progress that says blacks have made under his administration." In reality, the *Times* argued, Reagan had done nothing but "turn King's own words to uses that would subvert his goal of a truly open society." The main front of this attack had become, in 1986, Reagan's effort to undo Executive Order 11246, which makes no mention of quotas, yet Reagan insisted it was the legislation that legalized them.[52]

Like the *Times*, the National Urban League also did not buy Reagan's overtures. In the aftermath of the weeklong commemoration of King leading up to the first Martin Luther King Jr. holiday, the league released its annual *State of Black America* report. The report refers to Reagan as a "Rambo-like destroyer of civil rights," with "voodoo civil rights policies" that had left blacks in their worst economic shape in a decade.[53] Similarly, Roger Wilkins—civil rights leader, assistant attorney general under Lyndon Johnson, key contributor to the Kerner Report, nephew of NAACP executive secretary Roy Wilkins, and history professor—wrote an op-ed in the *Los Angeles Times* reminding Americans that "two men who lived in the same century could hardly have agreed on less" than King and Reagan. "In instance after instance," Wilkins continues, "this Administration has sought to narrow [King's] vision and constrict the pursuit of [King's] dream." Ultimately, Wilkins concludes, Reagan was praising one of their heroes and "pretending to adhere to ideals that his policies clearly indicate he opposes."[54] Two weeks later, a reporter asked Reagan, "Mr. President, in the '60's you opposed all the civil rights legislation. But more recently, you said that you were a part of the Martin Luther King revolution. . . . Why is your Administration so bent on wiping out the flexible hiring goals for blacks, minorities and women?" He responded, "We want, we want what I think Martin Luther King asked for. We want a color-blind society."[55]

The editorial board of the *Wall Street Journal* continued to provide support for Reagan's civil rights positions in the press, while the pages of the *Los Angeles Times* and the *New York Times* maintained their reluctant support of race-conscious remedies to discrimination broadly, and affirmative action more specifically.[56] In April 1986, the *Journal* published an article arguing that if Reagan had erred in civil rights, it was only because he was, as one headline read, "going colorblind too slowly." "We do wish," the *Journal* continued, "that President Reagan, who has often expressed his own wish for a colorblind society, would take stronger action to support it." The easiest way to do so, in the *Journal*'s opinion, was to rewrite Executive Order 11246.[57]

Many whites also vocalized their support of the president's civil rights maneuvers. On February 2, 1986, a white UC Irvine student named Brian C. Whitten, who qualified his op-ed by alleging that as a high schooler, he was moved to tears the first time he heard King's "I Have a Dream" speech, wrote to express the discomfort and outrage he felt after attending a rally on campus in honor of King. There, a black female speaker remarked that whites must accept responsibility for what their ancestors did to African Americans. In the column, Whitten argues that the woman feeds the fire of racism because she does not want America to be "unconcerned with skin color," as Dr. King did. "I thought about black fraternities and the Black

Student Union on my campus," Whitten concludes, "and I wondered if they really want to abolish discrimination as Dr. King did. Or do they really want to separate themselves from the mainstream to feel special?"[58]

One less frequently cited reason behind Reagan's and specifically the U.S. Commission on Civil Rights' opposition to affirmative action programs in the 1980s was that they did not work. In fact, this was not true. For example, over a ten-year period, a $2.2 billion federal works project was undertaken to expand the Amtrak rail line through the Northeast corridor. The federal government implemented an affirmative action program for those contracts, setting a goal that 15 percent of all businesses receiving contracts over the ten-year project would be minority owned. Ten years later, nearly 18 percent of all contracts went to minority-owned businesses.[59] So, in fact, the opposition from the Reagan administration to affirmative action programs was not because they were ineffective but because they worked. They repeatedly proved to grant employment and educational opportunities to qualified and deserving people of color.

In February, Reagan was still considering eliminating the protections of Executive Order 11246.[60] By July, Melanie Lomax, head of the Los Angeles Office of the NAACP, wrote in the *Los Angeles Times* that affirmative action was on "Death Row." "The attacks from the Reagan Administration," Lomax writes, "undoubtedly will continue and be intensified."[61] Yet the Supreme Court, which had begun to waiver in its support for affirmative action, halted the Justice Department's progress. Two decisions, one involving a sheet-metal workers union in New York (*Local 28 v. EEOC*) and the other a firefighters union in Cleveland (*Local 93 v. Cleveland*), solidified the legality of affirmative action programs, but only in cases that were "narrowly tailored," irrespective of previous discrimination."[62] Civil rights law "does not prohibit a court from ordering, in appropriate circumstances, affirmative race-conscious relief as a remedy for past discrimination," Justice Brennan wrote, rebuffing the president's colorblind doctrine.[63] Two additional rulings the following February (*U.S. v. Paradise* and *Johnson v. Transportation Agency*), involving the affirmative action hiring and promotion programs in Alabama and California, reinforced the court's view.[64]

These setbacks inhibited Reagan's efforts to eliminate affirmative action. With no legal ground or even ambiguity to stand on, the Justice Department began dropping its lawsuits against cities and states the following month, signaling the end of Reagan's assault on affirmative action.[65] The administration did not, however, go quietly. In September, an "unusually abrasive" William Bradford Reynolds, targeting Justice Brennan, the administration's nemesis when it came to affirmative action, accused the justice of misinterpreting the Fourteenth Amendment and imposing "a liberal social agenda" that "has no connection with the Constitution, The Bill of Rights or any subsequent Amendment." He continued, "The Constitution is and must be understood to be 'colorblind.'"[66]

That same month, Justice Thurgood Marshall, defending affirmative action in the aftermath of the two July rulings, stated, "The argument against affirmative action is an argument in favor of leaving that cost to lie where it falls." Affirmative action, Marshall continued, is "an instrument for sharing the burdens which our history imposes upon us all." "I too believe in the colorblind society," Marshall concluded, "but it has been and remains an aspiration. Given the position from which America began, we still have a very long way to go."[67] The data supported Marshall, not the president. In September, the United States Conference of Mayors concluded that affirmative action programs had improved the "efficiency and productivity" of city workforces: 90 percent of the 121 cities represented at the conference had voluntarily implemented affirmative action programs; 60 percent of these had fewer employee grievances, 40 percent had decreased absenteeism, and 45 percent had less employee turnover since implementing affirmative action. Most importantly, almost 40 percent of the cities credited affirmative action for contributing a "great deal to improved efficiency and productivity."[68]

With the wind taken from its sails, the Reagan administration was unable to make further changes in affirmative action policy. It did not, however, waver from its colorblind doctrine. In February 1987, EEOC chair Clarence Thomas responded to a *Wall Street Journal* columnist who accused him of not sharing the administration's strictly colorblind views. Thomas responded with a letter that was published in the *Journal* two weeks later, maintaining, "I firmly insist that the Constitution be interpreted in a colorblind fashion."[69] In his dissent to one of the pro–affirmative action rulings the same month, Justice Antonin Scalia wrote that the court had violated the colorblind foundation of the Constitution and had converted Title VII of the 1964 Civil Rights Act into an "engine of discrimination" against white men.[70] Moreover, by the end of 1987, William Bradford Reynolds had become the Justice Department's most important and powerful official, according to the *New York Times*.[71] In subsequent years, the triumvirate would complete the anti-civil rights crusade Reagan started. Two of them, moreover, would serve on the Supreme Court.

In August 1988, amid the rancor of the impending presidential election, a crowd marched to the Lincoln Memorial to commemorate the twenty-fifth anniversary of the 1963 March on Washington and Martin Luther King's "I Have a Dream" speech. Speakers exhorted the theme of "deferred dreams" to a crowd of roughly fifty-five thousand, roughly a quarter of the number who attended the 1963 march. Perhaps the number speaks to what Democratic presidential candidate Michael Dukakis called the "slow death of indifference," whereby twenty-five years had failed to yield the racial equality dreamed of two-and-a-half decades prior.[72] The smaller numbers may have had something to do with the co-optation of the civil rights movement, and King especially, by the Reagan administration over the previous eight years. The memory of the modern civil rights movement and its most celebrated leader were remade by the Reagan administration to hold up not as the dream of racial equality but as a cudgel to eliminate civil rights protections and exacerbate racial inequality. Surprisingly, or perhaps not, Vice President George Bush, the Republican candidate in 1988, did not attend the march, and the crowd was heard chanting "Where is George?" at various points in the rally. One speaker, disappointed in the turnout, remarked, "If Martin Luther King could get up from the grave he would see that he'd have to start all over again."[73] Civil rights leader Julian Bond offered his own explanation of the small crowd. To young people in attendance, "the 1963 march was ancient history," Bond argued.[74] By the end of the Reagan presidency, Bond would be right in more ways than he realized.

During its second term, the Reagan administration continued its attack on key civil rights programs that African Americans had won two decades prior. Whereas the Supreme Court handcuffed the administration's ability to make legislative changes during its first term, several key decisions at the end of the first term emboldened the president to more aggressively attack civil rights, namely affirmative action. Early in his second term, the Justice Department sought to eliminate federal affirmative action guidelines but was ultimately unsuccessful. Nonetheless, colorblind rhetoric and efforts to reimagine a civil rights movement driven by a colorblind doctrine were the two key strategies used by the administration to win public support for its anti-civil rights agenda. Their motivation, they insisted, was not white supremacy but a genuine commitment to King's colorblind dream. As I argued in chapter 4, scholars who minimize the damage Reagan did to civil rights by focusing solely on the inability of his administration to make significant changes to civil rights law miss the significance of the administration's reframing of the national discourse on civil rights. During Reagan's first term, his civil rights team positioned white males as the true victims of racial discrimination at the hands of affirmative action. In his second term, the Administration continued its rhetorical efforts by imagining an alternative civil rights history led not by black radicals but by colorblind white males. As Reagan left office, Hollywood took up the task of constructing a visual archive of a colorblind civil rights movement in order to reshape American memory. In the immediate aftermath of the Reagan presidency, the mass culture industry produced a number of films about slavery and civil rights that imagined white heroes and a colorblind ethos at the core of black freedom struggles. It is to those movies that I now turn.

Celluloid Slavery, Celluloid Civil Rights

Our collective historical memory performs crucial work in shaping the racial politics of the present. And film is a key medium through which to shape, contest, and reimagine our racial past. Collective memory is the product of a politicized process that, through representation, selects certain accounts of the past and silences others—real or imagined—in service of specific interests. Representations of the past "stand in for" rather than "represent" the event depicted.[75] Representations are not mere vehicles transmitting a preexisting meaning. Meaning is given to the event through the representations of the event itself, which continuously imbue it with new and changing meanings. Our collective memory is therefore not a record of historical fact but an inventory of, as Michel Foucault argues, "what [we] must remember having been" as determined by the interests of dominant ideologies and ruling discourses.[76] Moreover, emancipation and the civil rights movement are highly contested sites in American memory more generally, and groups spanning the gamut of American racial, social, and political life fight to shape the collective memory of these two events. Hollywood is crucial in this regard. Its popularity and consistent engagement with America's racial past reveal the central role the culture industry plays in our understanding of black liberation struggles.

As Reagan left office, Hollywood, for the first time, devoted considerable energy to dramatizing the civil rights movement. They also turned to slavery as part of a broader engagement with black freedom struggles. The cinematic iterations of emancipation and the civil rights movement in the 1990s differ significantly from those of previous eras. Hollywood's classical era generally depicted slavery as a benevolent institution that did not compromise the nation's immaculate moral character. Films like *Birth of a Nation* (1915) and *Gone with the Wind* (1939) offer representations of contented slaves and altruistic masters gone with the winds of northern aggression and industrialization.[77] Slavery dramas of the late 1980s and 1990s, on the other hand, depict a far more reprehensible institution. The horrors of human bondage, largely nonexistent in classical era treatments, are laid out more plainly in films like *Glory* (1989) and *Amistad* (1997). Indeed, late twentieth-century filmic portrayals of slavery rely on melodramatic depictions of the horror of the institution to elicit sympathy from audiences. Furthermore, in the classical era, abolition is depicted as either undesired (*Gone with the Wind*) by happy slaves or threatening the purity of white womanhood by unleashing rape-hungry black men to prey on chaste white women (*Birth of a Nation*). In slavery dramas of the 1990s, however, abolition became the central focus of slavery dramas.

A similar contrast characterizes civil rights dramas of the 1990s from those of the mid-century. The onset of the modern civil rights movement and the emergence of Sidney Poitier as the most popular black star of the civil rights era prompted Hollywood to begin regularly taking up the topic of racial equality with films like *No Way Out* (1950), *Blackboard Jungle* (1955), and *The Defiant Ones* (1958). The pace of these films only increased in the 1960s as both the movement and Poitier's fame grew. As film historian Donald Bogle explains, Poitier's immense talent, combined with the highly educated, mild-mannered, asexual characters he portrayed, satisfied both the standards of white audiences and middle-class black respectability in the civil rights era.[78] Racial melodramas of the mid-twentieth century use the debate over black equality to reform prejudiced white minds. Films from the classical era depict white bigots infected with the disease of racism in need of the tonic of racial equality. Viewers are therefore encouraged to sympathize with the infected white racists and root for their cure. Ultimately, these films are primarily concerned with portraying the triumph of the white psyche rather than with grassroots activism for black equality. Nevertheless, while heroic depictions of reformed white men lie at the center of mid-century civil rights dramas, it is nonetheless the black protagonist (typically played by Poitier) who serves as the catalyst of that transformation.[79]

Civil rights dramas of the late 1980s and 1990s are less often concerned with the reformation of white racists. More significantly, the transformation of white minds is not the primary function of these films. This is for two reasons. First, the white leads in films of the era are represented as already committed to racial equality. They are, in other words, colorblind, and have always been so. Their heroism, in fact, hinges on this quality. Second, while colorblind white heroes drive these films, unwavering white racists abound on the screen. Their resolute bigotry puts the colorblind heroism of our protagonist into sharp relief and frames black freedom struggles as conflicts over whiteness. The central work of civil rights dramas of the 1990s, then, is the representation of a triumphant colorblind whiteness as the driving force behind abolition and civil rights.

Glory

Edward Zwick's 1989 Academy Award–winning film *Glory* depicts the heroic efforts of the all-black Massachusetts Fifty-Fourth Regiment and their colonel, Robert Gould Shaw, in the Civil War. However, as Johari Jabir notes, the film's story also contains striking similarities to the memoir of Colonel Thomas Wentworth Higginson, who led the First South Carolina Volunteers, the first official black regiment in the Union army.[80] *Glory* received overwhelmingly positive reviews from critics, solid box-office receipts, and three Oscars, including Denzel Washington's win for Best Supporting Actor. Outside Hollywood, historians offered similar praise. Renowned historian Gerald Horne commended the film for "finally get[ting] this chapter in history right."[81] Noted historian Manning Marable was equally congratulatory, writing, "Freedom is only real when the oppressed themselves, through their own initiative and inner strength, shatter the chains of bondage. . . . This is the central message of *Glory*."[82] Yet like the civil rights dramas of the same era, the overwhelming evidence of the film suggests that it functions as a lionization of the regiment's white colonel rather than a long-overdue depiction of the efforts of black soldiers in the Civil War.[83]

The film's opening frame, a black screen with the text "ROBERT GOULD SHAW, THE SON OF WEALTHY Boston abolitionists, was 23 years old when he enlisted to fight in the War between the States," immediately centers the narrative on Shaw, challenging Horne's and Marable's characterizations of the film. Additionally, it is Shaw, through letters to his mother, who narrates the film. The bravery exhibited by the black soldiers in the film, while prevalent, is inspired by and filtered through the colorblind courage of Shaw. Historian Jim Cullen notes this dynamic, writing, "There is a patronizing subtext in *Glory* in that it is whites who make the most dramatic contributions to the black cause."[84] However, the content of Shaw's heroism and the representation of him as primarily responsible for gains won by African

Americans in the Civil War are not merely subtext but rather the central message of the film. As many scholars and critics note, historical inaccuracies abound in this film.[85] Be it the absence of representations of any of the actual black soldiers of the Fifty-Fourth Regiment, the erasure of the role of Frederick Douglass in assembling the regiment (which included two of his sons), or the fictional enthusiasm with which Shaw accepts his post, *Glory* makes no real effort to offer a historically accurate portrayal of the regiment. Moreover, historical accuracy is less significant than the manner in which the factual alterations made in the interest of entertainment work to magnify the colorblind heroism of Shaw while downplaying the bravery of the black soldiers.

The film's form, more importantly, performs the most substantive work in the manufacture of Shaw's colorblind heroism and a colorblind aesthetics more generally. In one scene, the regiment parades through a town of civilian supporters en route to the battlefield. As the black troops march down the street, they are filmed through wide shots that capture multiple members of the regiment. The wide shots make it difficult to distinguish the men from one another. Instead, the audience sees a homogeneous group of black bodies in blue uniforms wielding muskets. Shaw, on the other hand, is often shot with a low-angle close-up atop his horse, elevated above both his regiment and onlookers. This, along with the use of shallow focus, isolates Shaw and directs the spectator's gaze directly to him, creating an intimacy between Shaw and the spectator which further compels the audience to identify with his position. The low angle forces the audience to look up at Shaw, a classic cinematic device used to emphasize the heroism of a character. In the wide shots of Shaw and the black soldiers, Shaw rides on horseback against a backdrop of waving American flags, characterizing Shaw's heroism as quintessentially American. Furthermore, the depiction of Shaw riding alongside the marching Fifty-Fourth Regiment reproduces the visual imagery of the Robert Gould Shaw memorial in Boston, suggesting that the colorblind portrayal of Shaw is not the film's representation but a filmic *re*-presentation of a colorblind history already written.

The elevation of Shaw to visually render his heroic superiority occurs again, after the black soldiers learn of the salary discrepancy between them and their white counterparts. Private Trip (Denzel Washington), a black soldier in the regiment, orders his fellow corporals to refuse pay until it equals that of the white soldiers. Many black soldiers join in protest with Trip, and a raucous rally begins. In response, Shaw climbs atop a stage and proclaims that if black soldiers will not accept pay, then neither will the

In *Glory,* Robert Gould Shaw (Matthew Broderick) shot at a low angle against a blank backdrop.

white officers. Again, Shaw's movement to the stage literally elevates him above the group of black soldiers and enables Shaw's declaration to appear on-screen through a low-angle close-up, thereby magnifying the heroism of the act. Moreover, the blank blue sky that surrounds Shaw again isolates him in the frame, drawing the spectator's gaze directly to him. No such formal assistance is given to Trip, who, after all, came up with the idea.

The aesthetics of colorblind heroism reach their zenith during the final battle scene at Fort Wagner. Caught off guard and under attack without a strategy for counterattack, Shaw emerges from cover and charges the fort armed only with an American flag. As Shaw's body is riddled with gunfire, the film transitions into slow motion, and the diegesis is interrupted by the histrionic sounds of an orchestra and choir, maximizing the melodrama of our hero's death. As his limp body falls to the ground, real-time resumes and the black soldiers, shedding their fear and inspired by their lionhearted leader, emerge from cover and rush up the hill. Trip is killed, but slow motion does not capture his death. Instead, the film quickly cuts away as his body hits the sand. The modes of portrayal of the deaths of our two main characters reveal the value of white bodies in relation to black ones in *Glory.*

The dead body of Shaw cradles that of Trip (Denzel Washington).

The editing choices in the depiction of Trip's death suggest that his sacrifice for his own race is expected and therefore unheroic. Within this logic, the sacrifice of Shaw for a cause not his own—slavery—is the most heroic act of *Glory* because it marks the ultimate commitment to colorblind heroism; the melodrama in this sequence exaggerates this fact. Selfless white sacrifice for racial others is ultimately a narrative precondition on which the aesthetics of colorblind heroism are built.

Yet it is in the (in)famous flogging scene, in which Private Trip is punished for deserting camp in search of adequate shoes, that the true work of colorblind aesthetics is revealed. Jabir argues that the flogging scene functions as both a way to show a "black manhood that is largely unaffected by pain" and "a means to valorize black military masculinity."[86] While such a reading is certainly available, I argue that the depiction of black military masculinity is subordinate to the representation of white masculine benevolence. The scene uses a series of shot–reverse shot close-ups between Trip and Shaw. The audience watches the film cut back and forth between the pained face of Trip and the equally agonized Shaw. The use of the shot–reverse shot technique provides the audience with a mirroring of the tortured face of Trip as the lash tears his flesh with that of Shaw, who must bear witness to the savagery of his orders. In this sequence, the camera angle on the reverse shots of Trip align closely with the position and eyeline of Shaw; Trip's gaze points almost directly into the camera. The reverse shots of Shaw, however, are shot from an angle to the left of Trip's position. Shaw's eyeline, therefore, points markedly away from the camera toward

Trip. The spectator, then, is "sutured" into the position of Shaw, not Trip. In her analysis of "suture," film theorist Kaja Silverman writes, "The classic cinematic organization depends upon the subject's willingness to become absent to itself by permitting a fictional character to 'stand in' for it, or by allowing a particular point of view to define what it sees. The operation of suture is successful at the moment that the viewing subject says, 'Yes, that's me.'"[87] The sequence contains no point-of-view shots from Trip or any of the other black soldiers who look on in the background. This is not the only instance in which this formal strategy is used. In another scene, the regiment marches into Union training grounds and is greeted with a series of racist comments. Immediately after the slurs, the film cuts to a visibly anguished Shaw. The choice here to use a shot–reverse shot sequence to direct the spectator's attention to the effects of the antiblack slurs not on the targets of the slurs—the black soldiers—but on their white colonel suggests that it is Shaw, in fact, who suffers most from the bigotry of antebellum America. No matter the case, the viewer is given no option other than to identify with Shaw.

Moreover, in the flogging scene, cutting back and forth between Trip's lachrymose reaction and close-ups of a visibly troubled Shaw, who must at one point look away from the spectacle and from Trip, manufactures a sense of guilt in Shaw over his order and equates that guilt with the physical torture imposed on Trip. The production of guilt in this scene serves two functions. First, it preserves Shaw's heroism through what is perhaps his one immoral act in the film—punishing a man who left camp in search of adequate shoes. (It is worth noting that after the incident, Shaw demands that the men receive new shoes.) More importantly, as Judith Butler posits in her consideration of the racial implications of Freudian guilt, white guilt functions as "displaced satisfactions" that preserve desire; "the question is whether white guilt is itself the satisfaction of racist passion, whether the relieving of racism that white guilt constantly performs is not itself the very satisfaction of racism that white guilt ostensibly abhors. For white guilt— when it is not lost to self-pity—produces a paralytic moralizing that *requires* racism to sustain its own sanctimonious posturing . . . rooted in the desire to be exempted from white racism, to produce oneself as the exemption."[88] The manufacturing of white guilt in this scene of black trauma in order to represent Shaw as the colorblind exception to antebellum whiteness consolidates white privilege and reinforces white supremacy. Additionally, the absence of Trip's perspective—or that of any other black character, for that matter—eschews Trip's humanity. Trip's suffering is therefore intelligible

Juxtaposing point-of-view shots: Shaw looks slightly away from the camera, while Trip looks almost directly into it.

only through its equation to Shaw's guilt. As literary scholar Saidiya Hartman argues, in requiring "that the white body be positioned in the place of the black body in order to make this suffering visible and intelligible . . . in making others' suffering one's own, this suffering is occluded by the other's obliteration."[89] The formal elements of this sequence force the spectator to identify with the white gaze of Shaw and see the black body in suffering as a point of alterity. Most importantly, this is accomplished in this sequence at the level of form and aesthetics, revealing colorblindness for what it really is: the glorification of white privilege in the post–civil rights era camouflaged by stories of colorblind heroism.

In his review of the film, Roger Ebert wrote, "Watching 'Glory,' I had one recurring problem. I didn't understand why it had to be told so often from the point of view of the 54th's white commanding officer. Why did we see the black troops through his eyes—instead of seeing him through theirs? To put it another way, why does the top billing in this movie go to a white actor?"[90] In an interview, Edward Zwick, the film's director, claimed, "It is hugely difficult in any society, black or white, to come up with legitimate heroes."[91] Producer Freddie Fields's description of the film is also revealing. "In the form of an entertainment vehicle," Fields writes, "we tell a love story about the camaraderie between black and white men who learned and grew together."[92] These comments provide insight into what constitutes a Hollywood hero in the colorblind era. Neither the historic actions of Frederick Douglass and William Carney, the first black serviceman to receive the congressional Medal of Honor and a member of the Fifty-Fourth Regiment, nor a fictional account of black soldiers during the Civil War told through their own perspectives would be legible in an age in which whiteness was increasingly reconstituted as colorblind to justify an assault on civil rights.[93] *Glory* is not merely a film about interracial friendship, growth, and "bridge building." Rather, it is about the terms of those dynamics: the stipulation that the bridges of racial progress be built through the leadership and benevolence of a colorblind white hero, whose colorblindness is the basis of his heroism. This was Hollywood's version of historic American heroism in the political context of colorblindness in the 1990s.

The Long Walk Home

Unlike *Glory*, which is at least based on true events, *The Long Walk Home* is an entirely fictitious story of white female leadership in the civil rights movement. Nonetheless, it similarly dramatizes a triumphant moment in the struggle for black equality in order to credit the victory to a colorblind white heroine. In many ways, 2011's *The Help* is a remake of *The Long Walk Home*. *The Long Walk Home* depicts the story of a white housewife, Miriam (Sissy Spacek); her black maid, Odessa (Whoopi Goldberg); and their families in Montgomery, Alabama, at the onset of the Montgomery bus boycott. In solidarity with the boycott, Odessa begins walking several miles to work each day. In response, Miriam offers Odessa rides twice a week and then daily before eventually driving for the boycott's carpools five to six days a week. Rosa Parks, the woman whose refusal to give up her seat on a Montgomery bus ignited the boycott, said of the film, "To my knowledge, there were no white women who actually drove in the carpools."[94] *The Long Walk Home* provides a far more flagrant reimagining of American history than does *Glory*; the film is not unique in this regard in the late 1980s and 1990s. *Mississippi Burning* (1988), loosely based on the FBI investigation into the murder of three civil rights workers in Mississippi in 1964, transforms the bureau from one of the movement's fiercest opponents to its staunchest defender.[95] *Ghosts of Mississippi* (1996), on the other hand, is a true story that dramatizes only a select period of a much longer civil rights battle in order to maximize its portrayal of colorblind white heroism. *Ghosts of Mississippi* takes up the murder of civil rights leader Medgar Evers in 1963 to dramatize not his work or his wife's decades-long effort to bring his killer to justice but the personal risks and sacrifices the white assistant district attorney, Bobby DeLaughter (Alec Baldwin), makes in the name of colorblind justice.

The Long Walk Home does make sincere attempts to depict the courage of African Americans in the boycott and the personal toll endured by Odessa's family. Yet these efforts are undermined in several ways. For example, while the film does allocate a significant amount of screen time to Odessa, her family, and the role of their church in the boycott, the film spends far longer inside Miriam's home, depicting the effects of the boycott on Miriam's household and her marriage. Additionally, Miriam's shuttling of Odessa to and from work indirectly involves her in the boycott from its onset. In fact, Odessa explains that she must quit when she learns Miriam can no longer give her rides to work. So although Miriam's initial reluctance to join the carpools limits her involvement, Odessa's participation in the boycott depends on Miriam's assistance from its inception. Furthermore, white female contribution is represented as a key feature of the carpools from its inception. In one scene, as Miriam and Odessa drive past a parking lot that serves as a meeting place for carpool riders and drivers, a point-of-view shot from Miriam's perspective in the driver seat of the moving car captures a white woman in the lot. The car, and therefore the camera, slow as the woman enters the center of the frame, and her blocking along with her white skin and blue coat distinguish her from the African Americans in the lot, who stand either off-center or in the background dressed in brown, tan, or gray coats that blend in with the background. Further, the blue coat the white woman in the lot wears matches that of Miriam in this scene, foreshadowing her inevitable participation in the carpools. The sight of the white woman in the lot prompts Miriam to ask Odessa about white involvement in the carpools, and Odessa tells her of the several white women from a nearby air force base who are driving for the boycott. Be it Miriam's indirect but integral assistance or the significant white presence in the carpools, the film makes clear that white women played an indispensable role in the success of the boycott from its inception.

That Miriam's discovery of white participation in the boycott occurs outside the home speaks to the spatial and gender politics of the film's representation of white women's participation in the civil rights struggle. David Ansen argues that the film portrays the "genesis of the link between feminism and civil rights."[96] Indeed, Miriam's increasing participation in the boycott coincides with her increasing defiance of her husband's explicit orders not to drive Odessa. Miriam ultimately tells her husband that she will drive Odessa whenever she pleases, run her household how she sees fit, and get a job of her own and donate every penny to the boycott if he objects. Her defiance destroys her marriage. Further, it is only after this confrontation that Miriam joins the carpools, explaining, "I want to do this. I want to help." When Odessa explains that there are other ways to help, including monetary donation, Miriam replies, "If I wrote you a check it would be Norman's money. This is something I can do." The key here is not simply the film's depiction of the link between civil rights and feminism but the temporal relationship between the two. In *The Long Walk Home*, it is not the civil rights movement and its legislative victories that inspire and open the door for second-wave feminism; rather, it is the opposite. The boycott's success depends on Miriam's participation, and her participation depends on her feminist awakening. This inversion of the relationship between the two social movements implicitly credits not only Miriam but an entire generation of feminist white women for the victories of the Montgomery bus boycott. The civil rights movement becomes, in *The Long Walk Home*, a struggle between white patriarchy and white feminism. As a result, the film is ultimately not a celebration of black equality or even white contributions to civil rights. Instead, it extolls a colorblind whiteness capable of vanquishing sexism and racism in one fell swoop.

That the recounting of the Montgomery bus boycott on-screen must center on an invented white presence is perhaps the most blatant evidence that Hollywood's rediscovery of the Civil War and civil rights movement in the 1990s had little to do with the past and was instead part of a larger racial project that sought to redefine whiteness. Yet the film's invention of white participation in the boycott carpools was not the only trope employed in using the civil rights movement as a platform to imagine white colorblind heroism. Like *Glory*, the narrative and form of the film place Miriam and her actions at the center of the boycott and its success. As with *Glory*, this supposed representation of the tireless efforts and sacrifices of blacks to integrate the public buses is narrated by a white character—Miriam's daughter Mary Catherine, who, although only a child in the film, narrates her recollection of her mother's activism years later as an adult. While the film received widespread critical praise, its choice of narrator did not go uncriticized. In his otherwise approving review of the film, Roger Ebert nonetheless questioned why a black character like Odessa's daughter, who is much older during the boycott and "probably has more interesting memories" than Mary Catherine, did not narrate the film.[97]

As with *Glory*, the form of *The Long Walk Home* forces spectators to identify with white characters, revealing again the manner in which the colorblind actions of these films' white heroes belie the glorification of white privilege inherent in the aesthetics of colorblindness. In the film's conclusion, a rabble of 150 White Citizens' Council members, including Miriam's husband and brother-in-law, descend on the carpool meeting lot in order to "get these niggers out of here." Eventually the white men form a wall, lining up several feet in front of the black women and chanting, "Walk, nigger! Walk!" Odessa then walks toward the crowd, pausing stoically as she reaches the mob. The rest of the black women join her, forming a line of their own a few yards in front of the white men, and sing the gospel song "I'm Going Through." As their voices drown out and silence the white men, a black woman from the line offers her hand to Miriam, pulling her and her daughter (the narrator) across the divide between the black women and the white men, including her husband. The physical gap between the black women and the white men through the blocking of the actors, as well as the contrast of the racist chants of the men and the gospel singing of the women, create a physical and auditory metaphor for the philosophical distance that Miriam travels in the film. It also literally distances her and her colorblindness from the segregationist attitudes of the Jim Crow South and aligns her with those of the civil rights movement. It is important to note that the only point-of-view shots in this sequence are from Miriam's perspective. After Miriam joins the line of black women, the film cuts to a point-of-view shot from Miriam's perspective as she looks at Odessa, who turns her gaze to Miriam and stares at her approvingly, directly addressing the camera. The reverse shot of Miriam is not a point-of-view shot from Odessa's perspective, however. As with the reverse shots of Shaw in the flogging scene in *Glory*, the reverse shot of the white character is not from the perspective of the black character, forcing the spectator to identify with the white woman in this scene and rendering the black women as a point of alterity. Moreover, Odessa's approving gaze into the camera validates not only the colorblindness of Miriam but that of the entire audience sutured into Miriam's perspective.

Furthermore, the presence of Mary Catherine, who hardly appears in the rest of the film, at her mother's side indicates that she, along with the rest of the white children of the civil rights era, inherited the colorblindness of her mother, not the segregationist attitudes of her father and uncle. The tearful glance exchanged between father and daughter dramatizes a generational conflict of whiteness. As a sobbing Mary Catherine looks into and then away from the eyes of her father, the adult Mary Catherine's voice-over states, "It would be years before I understood what standing in that line meant to my mother, and as I grew older, to me." Mary Catherine's concluding narration combines the essential role of a white woman in the civil rights movement and the lasting effect that involvement had on notions of whiteness. The immense sacrifice of colorblind white heroes is a key feature of all slavery and civil rights dramas of the 1990s. In *The Long Walk Home*, Miriam sacrifices her marriage and risks her life for colorblind justice. In *Glory*, Shaw gives his life for abolition. In fact, the white heroes in all these films, from the FBI officers in *Mississippi Burning* to the white lawyers in *Ghosts of Mississippi* and *Amistad*, risk or sacrifice their lives, marriages, familial relationships, friendships, and careers for the cause of colorblind justice. Similar black sacrifice is understood as expected and therefore either not shown or relegated the film's background. The interplay between selfless colorblind white heroes who propel racial justice and formal choices that glorify white privilege through editing, camera angle, and melodrama are the essence of the colorblind aesthetics that emerged in the 1990s.

Lastly, white bigots are a central feature of and serve several functions in films like *The Long Walk Home*. First, they provide a culprit for the racism the black characters experience. In other words, if whites in these films were all colorblind, there would be no slavery and no Jim Crow. These films rely on white bigots—like Mulcahy in *Glory* and Miriam's brother-in-law, Tunker, in *The Long Walk Home*—to serve as a source of blame for past racial sins that does not implicate the colorblind hero. Second, actually representing the white racists, rather than keeping them off-screen, is a powerful cinematic device through which to display the heroism of the colorblind protagonist. In his article on *Glory*, Martin H. Blatt defends the film's racial politics because "the film quite openly and directly confronts the racism in American culture by characterizing many Union Army commanders as deeply prejudiced."[98] While there are, as mentioned earlier, numerous examples of racist Union commanders, the important point is that Shaw is not one of them. The racists, therefore, become the benchmark on which the heroism of the colorblind protagonist is measured. To see, in other words, how far removed Shaw is from his racial brethren only amplifies his heroism. Finally, the representation of white racists provides a tomb in which whites can bury their racist past. The bigots represent the antebellum (*Glory*) or Jim Crow (in *The Long Walk Home*) editions of whiteness. Those identities, these films would have us believe, died with slavery or the civil rights movement. What persists and always existed in opposition to explicit white supremacy is a colorblind white heroism that spectators are invited to imagine they inherit. Ultimately, then, the characters in these civil rights dramas depict white bigotry as specific to and trapped in a particular moment in our nation's history. Colorblind heroism, on the other hand, is transhistorical: it conquered slavery and Jim Crow, and it endures to this day.

Lies Agreed Upon

African Americans were relieved to see the Reagan presidency end. Whatever prosperity the Reagan revolution had brought, the vast majority of African Americans were excluded from it. Moreover, throughout his time in office, Reagan aggressively sought to eliminate or undermine civil rights policies that most civil rights leaders supported. Yet as he left the White House, Reagan acted surprised on the popular television news program *60 Minutes* when informed of blacks' negative attitudes toward him. In fact, he took the opportunity to launch one last salvo at the group he had so thoroughly battered throughout his years in office. When asked why the vast majority of African Americans felt so negatively toward him, Reagan suggested that he was, perhaps, a victim of a massive conspiracy concocted by black civil rights leaders hell-bent on keeping the belief of racism alive for their own personal profit. "Sometimes I wonder," queried Reagan, "if [black leaders] really want what they say they want because some of those leaders are doing very well leading organizations based on keeping alive the feeling that they're the victims of prejudice."[99]

Reagan's *60 Minutes* remarks so dumbfounded the editorial board of the *Los Angeles Times* that the column they published in response to the interview—cleverly titled "Colorblind," which punned Reagan's civil rights ideology and his "blindness" to the racial animosities and inequities those policies wrought—asked, "Where has the President been these past eight years that he can be so detached from the brutal reality of the effect of his policies and his programs and his leadership on black Americans?"[100] Blacks throughout the county held similar views as Reagan's time in the White House ended. Walter Malone, a construction worker from Arlington, Virginia, told the *Los Angeles Times* that the Reagan presidency "has set a bad tone for white people. . . . [Reagan] wants to keep the black man down."[101] Norman Amaker, a law professor at Loyola University in Chicago, echoed the blue-collar Malone. Reagan has done "a disservice to the American people," Amaker began, "He has sent signals to the community at large that the civil rights laws will not be taken seriously."[102] The evidence in 1989 substantiated these sentiments. According to a nationwide survey conducted by the NAACP, by the end of his tenure, 80 percent of blacks considered the Reagan presidency not only unfriendly to African Americans but "oppressive." A similar poll found that only 29 percent of whites concurred.[103]

The Reagan years fundamentally altered the role of the federal government regarding civil rights. Prior to the Reagan presidency, the federal government served as the chief protector and enforcer of civil rights law; Ronald Reagan transformed the federal government into the primary aggressor *against* civil rights policy. Even worse, many of the affirmative action hiring and admissions programs the Justice Department sought to eliminate were programs that employers and universities found effective and even supported.

Reagan's jab at his African American detractors during his *60 Minutes* interview highlights the civil rights discourse the president had established by the end of his two terms: a hostile environment for civil rights activists in which even suggesting the persistence of racial inequality was received with derision and charges of reverse discrimination. On the other hand, by the time he left office, a majority of whites had bought into the idea that anything but a colorblind approach to the law amounted to reverse discrimination. As Reagan's insult makes clear, in his view, as the 1980s closed, the only explanation for someone who believes in persistent racism against African Americans was a massive conspiracy. Reagan's comments also speak to the rhetoric of white victimhood that he and his supporters so effectively used in advancing their colorblind agenda—both in thought and in practice.

Reagan's assault on civil rights did far more than change the discourse and national attitudes about race. Reagan left behind a country far more divided not only in terms of attitude but in material reality. The results of the Reagan years were massive reductions in social programs, including employment training, community health centers, legal assistance, housing, block grants for antipoverty programs, and compensatory education.[104] Moreover, the cuts to these programs, which impoverished communities relied on, affected blacks most significantly, as the black poverty rate rose to 33.1 percent during Reagan's presidency. White poverty, meanwhile, remained roughly the same. Thus, the Census Bureau estimated that although blacks made up 11 percent of the population in the late 1980s, they received as much as 40 percent of the benefits of the social programs Reagan cut. Furthermore, during the 1980s, as black poverty rose, Food Stamp benefits fell by 15 percent, and over 400,000 families lost their AFDC (Aid to Families with Dependent Children) benefits entirely.[105] By 1987, median black family income was $300 *less* than its 1970 level and $900 less than in 1978. Meanwhile, the white–black income gap had increased, with black median family income constituting only 56.1 percent that of whites, compared to 61.3 percent in 1970.[106]

The Reagan years were marked, then, by an assault on blacks across class lines. Although the black middle class expanded during the 1980s, it appeared to occur in large part despite Reagan's efforts, not because of them. College-bound blacks saw programs designed to make sure they received equal consideration in the application process attacked; working- and middle-class blacks witnessed agreements to ensure fairness in hiring thrown out; and the black poor saw the safety net programs they depended on slashed. All this was accomplished under the logic, or shadow, of a colorblind ideology that Reagan and his supporters aligned with 1960s civil rights leaders like Martin Luther King Jr. Perhaps most importantly, by appointing 384 federal judges, the most by any president, virtually all of which were vetted to ensure that their politics aligned with Reagan and of which only seven were black, Reagan ensured that his colorblind anti–civil rights agenda would endure for decades.[107]

A detailed report released in July 1989 by the National Research Council further attested to the widening, rather than the closing, of the racial gap between whites and blacks. The study's author, Gerald D. Jaynes, concluded, "The major fraction of this improvement [in black equality] was in place by 1970. Since then, material measures of status relative to whites have not improved and many have deteriorated."[108] The full integration of blacks into a "color blind society is unlikely in any foreseeable future," the study found.[109] The report also found that the gains made by African Americans "in the 1940s, 1950s, and 1960s were attributable largely to a growing economy and social policies such as the passage of civil rights and equal opportunity employment legislation."[110] Reagan's colorblind crusade masked the manner in which his policies had undone much of the progress toward racial equality won in the decade and a half between the civil rights legislation of the mid-1960s and his presidency.

Reimagining the civil rights movement in public memory was an essential part of the growing influence of colorblindness in the 1980s. Hollywood's heroic depictions of colorblind whites tirelessly risking their lives to combat racial discrimination were essential to this project. The representation in films depicting black freedom struggles constitute what Friedrich Nietzsche defines as "monumental history." "The great moments in the individual battle form a chain," Nietzsche writes, "a highroad for humanity through the ages, and the highest points of those vanished moments are yet great and living for men; and this is the fundamental idea of the belief in humanity that finds a voice in the demand for a 'monumental' history."[111] For Nietzsche, this history is never and can never be entirely factual. Instead, it "will always bring together things that are incompatible and generalize them into compatibility, will always weaken the differences of motive and occasion. . . . As long as the past is principally used as a model for imitation, it is always in danger of being a little altered and touched up and brought nearer to fiction. Sometimes there is no possible distinction between a 'monumental' past and a mythic romance."[112]

Elaborating on these ideas, W. E. B. Du Bois, in the final chapter of his canonical *Black Reconstruction in America, 1860–1880*, distinguishes the "scientific" from the "propagandist" uses of history:

If history is going to be scientific, if the record of human action is going to be set down with that accuracy and faithfulness of detail which will allow its use as a measuring rod and guidepost for the future of nations, there must be set some standards of ethics in research and interpretation.

If, on the other hand, we are going to use history for our pleasure and amusement, for inflating our national ego, and giving us a false but pleasurable sense of accomplishment, then we must give up the idea of history either as a science or as an art using the results of science, and admit frankly that we are using a version of historic fact in order to influence and educate the new generation along the way we wish.

It is propaganda like this that has led men in the past to insist that history is "lies agreed upon"; and to point out the danger in such misinformation. It is indeed extremely doubtful if any permanent benefit comes to the world through such action. Nations reel and stagger on their way; they make hideous mistakes; they commit frightful wrongs; they do great and beautiful things. And shall we not best guide humanity by telling the truth about all this, so far as the truth is ascertainable?[113]

As Ronald Reagan left office, Hollywood began to demonstrate a similar inability to distinguish the past from mythic romance. The "will" to remember black freedom struggles on-screen has foregrounded an enduring colorblind past that no historical record supports. Hollywood's take in the 1990s on America's racial past illustrates how memory can just as easily accommodate or "nourish" fiction as it can disregard facts, particularly in regard to slavery and civil rights.

Films like *Glory* and *The Long Walk Home* position colorblindness as an uncommon feature of American history yet an omnipresent characteristic of white heroism responsible for the triumphs of abolition and civil rights. The combination of this narrative structure, along with formal elements that suture the audience into white perspectives, produced a uniquely colorblind aesthetics by the 1990s that, like the political work of the discourse, seeks to disguise white privilege as racial justice. This was a project begun during the Reagan presidency and taken over by Hollywood in its immediate aftermath. The movies reimagined America's two most significant struggles for racial equality as driven by colorblind white heroes at the precise moment in which conservatives were using the rhetoric of King's colorblind dream to attack civil rights programs like affirmative action. As one ad for *The Long Walk Home* read, "At a time in America when everyone else did what was expected, they had the courage to do what was right."[114]

Beginning in the late 1980s, American audiences found fictional representations of colorblind white heroism more entertaining than historically-accurate representations of black heroism, bravery, and political agency. The latter, which far more faithfully reflects the historical record, is illegible in the colorblind era. This process of imagination and memory is not merely a question of "entertainment." Colorblindness served as a cudgel, wielded by Reagan against critics of his civil rights policies to justify the rearticulation of white supremacy. Concurrently, film in the late 1980s developed a colorblind aesthetics that performed indispensable work in building colorblind hegemony. The false historical imagination and memory of colorblind black freedom struggles, constructed by the Reagan administration and Hollywood, became a key site, perhaps the only one, for finding evidence of a colorblind society. Beginning in the late 1980s, film was the primary medium through which to construct our alleged colorblind past. As John Quincy Adams (Anthony Hopkins) states as he lobbies the Supreme Court to free captive African slaves in *Amistad* (1997)—a film about the zealous efforts of two white lawyers to free African slaves—"We are what we were." With no colorblind past to look back on, Hollywood helped reinvent what we were.

6 Lord, How Dare We Celebrate

Colorblind Hegemony and Genre in the 1990s

∙∙∙

I think we've won.

—William Bradford Reynolds, June 1989

Less than a week before he left office, Reagan publicly promised "that bigotry and indifference to disadvantage will find no safe home on our shores." As chapters 4 and 5 illustrate, the Reagan administration consistently used colorblind rhetoric to justify its assault on existing civil rights law and the legacy of the civil rights movement. The end of the Reagan presidency did little to slow the ascent of colorblindness. Gentler rhetoric and a less aggressive executive branch characterized the George H. W. Bush years, on the one hand. On the other, the Supreme Court continued Reagan's colorblind crusade. The subsequent Clinton years saw much of the same—public support for affirmative action, appointment of people of color in high-profile cabinet positions, but the inability and lack of desire to stop the momentum Reagan built.

In 1996, colorblindness achieved its most significant victory: California voters passed Proposition 209, the California Civil Rights Initiative, which banned considerations of race in college admissions and hiring. This marked the culmination of colorblind hegemony. While the ideology had won several important legal victories over the previous two decades, it was with Proposition 209 that a ballot initiative, passed by popular vote, used the language of the civil rights movement to eliminate its own legal legacy. Reagan's colorblind agenda—to use the colorblind rhetoric of the civil rights movement to combat civil rights policy—was no longer taken up *only* by groups of white suburbanites resisting school integration and supported in the editorial pages of the *Wall Street Journal,* nor was it merely the ideology of the Reagan Justice Department and the Supreme Court. Colorblindness had, by the mid-1990s, won the hearts and minds of a majority of voters in the country's most populous state. And it did so not in the cradle of the Confederacy or in a blue state like Massachusetts, which had experienced nasty antibusing battles, but in California, a state often characterized as the country's most progressive yet one that was essential to the rise of modern conservatism.[1]

Just as California voters turned to race and schools in the mid-1990s, so too did Hollywood. By then, the politics of colorblind neoliberalism had matured. Its effects were felt not only in the realms of fiscal and civil rights policy but in education as well. Hollywood produced a series of films about disadvantaged urban pupils in the 1990s. While numerous other scholars have criticized the racial politics of films like *Lean on Me*, *Stand and Deliver*, and *Dangerous Minds*, my aim is to frame these films collectively as a new colorblind genre.[2] Just as the passing of ballot initiatives marks the sociopolitical culmination of the racial project of colorblindness, so too does the emergence of generic conventions in mass culture, particularly Hollywood. The hegemonic moment of colorblindness in the mid-1990s, then, was one in which colorblindness became "common sense" in law, policy, attitude, and Hollywood aesthetics.

This chapter analyzes the nature of "teacher films" as a colorblind genre. To do so requires that I first trace the social history of colorblindness during the Bush years and Clinton's first term. While neither president ascribed to the colorblind literalism of Reagan, colorblind logic, as a result of Reagan's legacy, dominated civil rights policy in the federal courts, which continued to overturn race-conscious programs designed to redress racial inequality. I then provide an overview of neoliberal education reform to illustrate the implementation of colorblindness in areas far beyond college admissions and hiring procedures. From there I offer an analysis of teacher films themselves. Focusing on *Dangerous Minds* (1996), *Stand and Deliver* (1988), and *Freedom Writers* (2007), I argue that teacher films rely heavily on old tropes of Hollywood melodrama, like the home and the victim-hero, as well as racialized discourses about black and Latinx families from the post-Moynihan and Reagan years, which had moved to the center of national discourses on race and education. Colorblindness, therefore, offers the neoliberal colorblind solution to the problems of urban America in the 1990s.

Civil Rights under George H. W. Bush

As the George H. W. Bush presidency began, many African Americans were both deeply concerned and cautiously optimistic about the future prospects of racial justice. During the 1988 campaign, Bush ran a now infamous attack ad on his opponent, Michael Dukakis. The ad featured William Horton, a black murder convict whom the ad referred to as "Willie" despite the fact that he did not use that name. Two years prior, Horton was granted a weekend release as part of Massachusetts's furlough program. Horton fled and almost a year later raped a Maryland woman and assaulted her fiancé. The ad painted Dukakis, who was the governor of Massachusetts at the time of Horton's furlough, as soft on crime. More importantly, the image of a black murderer and rapist, whose skin the Bush campaign deliberately darkened in the ad, resonated with white voters who, in the aftermath of the Reagan presidency, felt fed up with the federal government's supposed coddling of undeserving minorities. The ad's architect was Lee Atwater, Bush's campaign adviser and the man who designed the strategy of framing conservative ideology as protecting states' rights, and leveraged school integration and affirmative action backlash to attract voters who could no longer broadcast their racial bigotry. As the Horton ad illustrates, Atwater continued to build a Republican coalition grounded in white supremacy and antiblack racism well into the 1990s. However, despite deliberately fanning the flames of antiblack bigotry to attract white voters, Bush, once elected, made concerted efforts to distance himself from Reagan's hostile opposition to civil rights, promising a "gentler" approach in the months leading up to his inauguration. Throughout his presidency, in fact, Bush insisted that he supported affirmative action, so long as it did not come in the form of quotas.

Scholar Imani Perry writes extensively on the ways in which "media generally provide a powerfully influential narrative about race."[3] Pointing specifically to the immediate post-Reagan years, she notes the hypervisibility of people of color on network news, overwhelmingly in stories of crime. She, along with Ian Haney López and others, also points to the rise of what she calls "racial coding," in which terms like "welfare queen," "law and order," "inner city," "fatherlessness," and "crack baby" were successfully used to speak about race without explicitly stating so. These code words established further protection against claims of racism when understood purely in terms of intentionality. The Willie Horton ad was paramount in this regard. According to Perry, the ad "did not simply say that Democrats can't protect you; it said something about how to expect Dukakis to act if he were to be elected; that is, he would advocate furlough programs that let rapists and murderers come to communities like yours to commit violent crimes."[4] Similarly, Howard Winant noted that "the 1988 Bush presidential campaign's incessant hammering on the theme of law and order and its scurrilous use of the image of the black rapist to mobilize white voters exemplifies the ongoing efficacy of racial coding in the mainstream political process."[5]

Yet while Bush may have offered a softer approach to civil rights in rhetoric, the reality was that even if he wanted to curtail some of the previous administration's attacks on civil rights, the legacy Reagan left on the benches of the nation's courts ensured an enduring civil rights legacy. In June 1989, the *Chicago Tribune* denounced the Supreme Court's "'retreat' on civil rights" as a result of three rulings against affirmative action.[6] The *Los Angeles Times* warned, "The Supreme Court has handed Congress its civil rights agenda for the 1990s. In three out of four decisions just handed down, the court weakened the rights for minorities and women. It is now up to Congress to reaffirm the nation's commitment to stamp out discrimination based on race or sex."[7] In 1989, the Supreme Court, in *City of Richmond v. James A. Croson Company*, eliminated a set-aside plan for minority hires. A "noose" was forming around the neck of affirmative action, hailed one conservative columnist.[8] Several other cases resulted in similar rulings. It was apparent that racial and gender discrimination now required far more proof than data reflecting underrepresentation.[9]

Bush's supporters, meanwhile, basked in their victory. George Will wrote proudly in 1989 that "the court Reagan built" was doing "much to roll back the racial spoils system."[10] In the wake of the anti–affirmative action *Richmond* decision, Will gloated, "Government may allocate benefits on the basis of race only to compensate identified individual victims of the government's own past system of racial classification."[11] He concluded the piece as he did many others dealing with civil rights: "Rights belong to individuals, not groups, and least of all, races."[12] In June, William Bradford Reynolds, no longer serving as the country's chief civil rights enforcer, told *Wall Street Journal* columnist Paul Gigot, "I think we've won. . . . We wanted to get rid of group entitlements and equal results and move toward equal opportunity. . . . I think that has been accomplished."[13] He also voiced frustration with the Supreme Court's inability to go further in outlawing race-conscious affirmative action policy. "We're in [Justice Antonin] Scalia's camp," by which he meant a rigid colorblind interpretation of the constitution. As Gigot argues, "The Supreme Court is shattering, in short, the pre-Reynolds orthodoxy that coercive racial preference is required to make amends for past racism. Mr. Reynolds came into office arguing that two creations of the 1970s—involuntary 'affirmative action' and forced busing—distorted the meaning of the civil rights movement led by Martin Luther King Jr."[14]

Reynolds wrote a column in June celebrating his legal legacy of color-blind anti–civil rights: "The Supreme Court is closing the 1988 term with a ringing reaffirmation of America's unyielding commitment to civil rights for all its citizens, whatever their race, gender, religious, or ethnic background. The principle of nondiscrimination, for which so many marched in the 1960s, has at last been stripped of the quota barnacles that became an encrusted feature in the 1970s."[15] Praising the Supreme Court and the growing number of Americans who shared his civil rights views, Reynolds continues, "A solid and reliable majority has emerged to provide the kind of clarity of thinking and purpose needed to fulfill Dr. Martin Luther King Jr.'s dream."[16] The court "has recognized—as should we all—that the principle of nondiscrimination is indeed colorblind."[17] More importantly, not only had Reynolds's hostile stance toward civil rights entered the mainstream, becoming the party line of the Supreme Court, but people like Gigot were beginning to lionize the most influential man in the fight against civil rights in the previous eight years. "Because Mr. Reynolds took the spears in the chest," wrote Gigot, "[George H. W.] Bush can aim to consolidate a new, less divisive civil rights consensus based on colorblindness."[18]

Yet the elder Bush's "softer" stance on civil rights alienated him from the colorblind literalists of the Reagan years. The congressional struggle over the 1990 Civil Rights Bill highlighted this divide.[19] The Democrat-led Congress sought to reinstate some of the "burden of proof" protections in employment discrimination the Supreme Court had eliminated in the preceding years. Although he eventually vetoed the bill, Bush's reluctance to come out publicly against a civil rights bill angered the Reagan loyalists. George Will used his column to criticize not only the bill's supporters but the president's hesitance to veto it. The bill "mocks the core tenet of what was once the civil rights movement. That tenet is: rights inhere in individuals and do not derive from membership in government-favored minority groups," wrote Will, and the president's hesitance was unacceptable because it demonstrated his "minimal" interest in "achieving a colorblind society."[20]

The debates around the 1990 and 1991 Civil Rights Acts, the former of which was vetoed and the latter of which established relatively little, revealed two key issues in the area of civil rights and of colorblindness more specifically.[21] The first of these was the divide among Republicans over the *colorblind literalists* and the *colorblind pragmatists* in the party. The literalists were the Reagan loyalists who advocated a rigid colorblind approach to civil rights in all instances. As a result, their philosophy produced a far more hostile approach to civil rights issues like affirmative action than their more pragmatic counterparts. The pragmatists, like Bush, supported the larger politics of colorblindness but were willing to make concessions in certain instances. Put another way, the literalists saw no difference between goals and quotas when it came to hiring or admissions, whereas the pragmatists believed, however messy, that the two could be distinguished to some extent.

The issue of race-based college scholarships became another battleground issue where this distinction among conservatives played out. In December 1990, the Department of Education banned racially restricted scholarships on the basis that they violated the colorblind principle.[22] The context for this was actually a college football game—the upcoming 1991 Fiesta Bowl. The organizers of the event received a significant amount of backlash for the game's location: Arizona. The state had repeatedly rejected the establishment of the Martin Luther King Jr. holiday. As a result, supporters of civil rights did not think it an appropriate venue for a major football game played largely by black athletes. In response, the Fiesta Bowl's organizers donated $200,000 for college scholarships for African Americans to honor Dr. King. That donation in turn angered many whites, who felt earmarking that money for blacks was reverse discrimination.[23]

Days after the Department of Education's ruling, Bush, unaware of the department's plans until they were announced publicly, delayed the scholarship ruling, promising that no scholarships would be affected for the next four years. Bush saw no issue with the scholarships; "I've long been committed to affirmative action," the president said.[24] For Bush, these scholarships, though not technically colorblind, helped improve diversity on college campuses without the "reverse discrimination" of quotas. Sorting this out turned into a mess for administration officials, especially the secretary of education, Michael Williams. The Bush administration believed it was illegal for universities to finance such scholarships but legal for private entities to do so. Bush thought this was a reasonable compromise that prevented the government from using tax revenue to dole out race-conscious scholarships, which conservatives liked, but also left room for such efforts in the private sector, which he hoped would satisfy civil rights activists without offending conservatives.

The colorblind literalists disagreed.[25] At the end of 1990, George Will published another op-ed titled "Racial Spoils System." Will lambasted the organizers of the Fiesta Bowl for their donation. "This is a perverse homage to King," Will fumed, "whose dream was an America where people 'would not be judged by the color of their skin, but by the content of their character.'" "The country really does honor King," Will continued, because it "really does aspire to colorblindness. Conservatives believe colorblindness is not just one among many competing values, it is a constitutional imperative." The refusal of Bush to fully endorse colorblindness made his administration a "donut," in Will's view, with fine material in the outer circle—conservatives who supported strict colorblindness—"but a hole at the center."[26]

It was also during the Bush years that a more vocal contingent of the American public in support of colorblind literalism emerged. This group popularized the idea that merely speaking about race amounted to racism. By the 1990s, white affirmative action opponents frequently wrote letters to the editors of the country's major newspapers, insisting that not only the Supreme Court but the news media itself adopt a strictly colorblind approach to reportage. These affirmative action opponents derided journalists not only for writing about racial issues but for noting a subject's race in their columns. For example, in April 1989, a reader of the *Chicago Tribune* wrote to the editors in protest of race-conscious affirmative action plans and organizations like Jesse Jackson's Rainbow Coalition that supported such programs. "If we want to be non-discriminatory, we should just not refer to skin color when describing a person. . . . What we need in Chicago now is not a rainbow coalition, but a color-blind coalition."[27] Another angry reader wrote the *Washington Post* in September, "Why do you encourage racism and sexism by asking the people you poll if color and gender enter into their political choices? . . . Stop asking race and gender-related questions in your polls. Be colorblind."[28] By the end of 1991, Tom Wicker of the *New York Times* noted that many Americans had bought into the existence of "a level, colorblind, playing field."[29]

The battles over Supreme Court nominations during Bush's tenure illuminate the growing influence of colorblindness in the future of the judiciary. Upon the nomination of David Souter to the Supreme Court, George Will criticized the overwhelming support the nomination received in Congress and in the press and criticized the lack of interrogation of Souter's views. In a September 1990 column, Will posed a number of constitutional questions to the nominee pertaining to the First and Second Amendments, *Miranda* rights, the death penalty, and abortion. Included in that list was the following: "Does the 'equal protection' clause require that government action be colorblind? If so, can 'affirmative action,' granting preferential treatment to individuals on the basis of race, be constitutional?"[30] By including this question, Will demonstrated that he viewed Souter's stances on colorblindness to be just as important as those pertaining to the most pressing issues of the court. In Will's view, the civil rights legacy of the Reagan years should not merely end with the colorblind efforts of the courts during the 1980s but continue with colorblind hegemony on the Supreme Court in perpetuity.

Will found a much more favorable candidate in Clarence Thomas in 1991. While the Thomas nomination hearings, specifically the testimony regarding his relationship with Anita Hill, proved to be major theater, they also reiterated the centrality of colorblind philosophy in a Supreme Court justice.[31] Bush nominated Thomas as the successor to Thurgood Marshall, the civil rights titan and first black Supreme Court justice. Yet Thomas's similarities to Marshall began and ended with their race. Politically, Thomas could not be further from Marshall, who supported affirmative action consistently throughout his time on the bench. As his time as head of the EEOC under Reagan proved, Thomas was an outspoken opponent of affirmative action and advocated a strictly colorblind approach to the law. In 1987, Thomas wrote in a letter to the *Wall Street Journal*, "I firmly insist that the Constitution be interpreted in a colorblind fashion. It is futile to talk of a colorblind society unless this constitutional principle is first established. Here, I emphasize black self-help, as opposed to racial quotas and other race-conscious legal devices that only further and deepen the original problem."[32] That same year he wrote, "The Constitution, by protecting the rights of individuals, is colorblind."[33] In hindsight, Thomas's ardent defense of colorblind literalism read like campaign ads to replace Thurgood Marshall on the Supreme Court. The Thomas nomination revealed the central paradox of the colorblind literalists; it was entirely a race-conscious decision. Thomas was chosen because he both supported colorblind literalism *and* he was black. His race, therefore, exculpated his civil rights views from charges of racism. The *Wall Street Journal*, a steadfast supporter of Reagan's civil rights views, called the nomination a "deft political choice."[34]

On Martin Luther King Jr. day in 1992, the president—who, like his predecessor, opposed the 1964 Civil Rights Act and was vice president when Reagan reluctantly approved the King holiday—spoke at a celebration held at the Martin Luther King Jr. Center for Nonviolent Social Change in Atlanta. Like Reagan before him, Bush used the occasion to emphasize King's commitment to colorblindness, and only colorblindness, as if the civil rights leader had said only a few sentences in his entire life. Bush praised King for his role in a "battery of laws dedicated to a colorblind society."[35] King's daughter Bernice found no reason to celebrate, only cause to mourn: "Lord have mercy on us, for how dare we celebrate when the bank of justice has been robbed, the storehouse of knowledge has been contaminated and the citadel of truth has been raped and violated." "How dare we celebrate," the Reverend Bernice King rebuked, "when the ugly face of racism still peers at us." "Lord, how dare we celebrate," she repeated. The *New York Times* reported that Bernice's ire seemed squarely directed at the president, who sat mere feet from the podium.[36]

Bush's inability to win reelection reveals, in part, how unpopular his "softer" view on civil rights had become within the Republican Party. The racial demographics of the GOP's leadership highlight this divide. On the eve of the 1992 Republican National Convention, the 165-member national committee had only three blacks, all of whom were representatives from the Virgin Islands.[37] It appeared that the GOP, and much of the country, had fallen in line with Reagan in adopting a literalist approach to colorblind civil rights policy, despite the unanimity of evidence to the contrary. In 1991, *Rethinking the American Race Problem*—a book written by Roy L. Brooks, a law professor at the University of Minnesota—examined how civil rights reforms under Reagan and Bush required plaintiffs to show incredibly stringent proof of discrimination in education, employment, and housing in order to win a legal ruling.[38] The discriminatory intent and effects of zoning laws become nearly impossible to prove in court.[39]

Colorblindness under Clinton

Bill Clinton went even further than Bush to appear far more supportive of civil rights than his Republican predecessors, but appearances were all he offered. Unlike for Reagan and Bush, blacks and Latinx folks voted overwhelmingly for Clinton; 83 percent and 61 percent, respectively.[40] Clinton appointed several people of color to high-ranking cabinet positions, whereas Reagan had appointed only one. His nominations, however, were not without protest from the Right. Most offensive, in conservatives' view, was Clinton's nomination of Lani Guinier, a black law professor at the University of Pennsylvania, for assistant attorney general for civil rights. While none of Guinier's published writings dealt with affirmative action, her advocacy of increasing minority political power led Republicans to slander her as the "quota queen."[41] As a result, Clinton ultimately withdrew Guinier's nomination in order to continue to court support from white bigots, as he had previously done by publicly disparaging Sister Souljah and executing Ricky Ray Rector. The backlash to Guinier reveals the manner in which support for affirmative action, even if only perceived, had become not just a polarizing issue but a death sentence for political ambitions. In 1993, at the time of Guinier's nomination, affirmative action was increasingly under attack, as conservatives tried to ban it entirely and the Supreme Court continued to restrict its use. It was, in fact, still the law, yet support of the law in the case of this civil rights issue at this time in history was unacceptable for someone seeking to enforce that very law.[42]

Despite the racial diversity of his political appointments, Clinton enacted few policies to redress racial equality. This was due in large part to the fact that although blacks and Latinx folks constituted key segments of Clinton's base, so too did whites. In 1990, one sociologist noted an emerging population of working- and middle-class white males who were fed up with affirmative action and felt they were discriminated against. By 1993, almost 60 percent of white men felt that affirmative action had resulted in "less opportunity for white men." In 1987, only 16 percent of white men felt that equal rights had gone too far. By 1994, half did. During his campaign, Clinton's staff's polling data showed that a significant number of white Democrats believed their party was doing too much for people of color at the expense of white men. Clinton's approach to civil rights, then, was an attempt to satisfy both white and nonwhite factions of his base. Clinton's tightrope walk marks one of the most significant features of Ronald Reagan's legacy. Reagan's relentless attacks on civil rights may not have eliminated policies like affirmative action like he had hoped, but they nonetheless turned (white) public opinion against the civil rights laws he opposed, laying the groundwork for the realization of his civil rights agenda less than a decade after leaving office under a Democratic president.

Even though a member of the opposing political party now occupied the Oval Office, Reagan's colorblind legal philosophy continued to inform the Supreme Court's rulings on matters of racial inequity. This influence pushed the court away from prioritizing group rights, as it had in the years since *Brown*, and toward an approach of colorblind individualism.[43] As historian Terry H. Anderson argues, the "protector role" of the court was replaced by "a more color-blind approach."[44] Colorblindness provided the impetus for this shift. Throughout the Bush and Clinton years, the Supreme Court continued to throw out existing affirmative action programs and put greater restrictions on what constituted "narrowly tailored" considerations of race in hiring and college admissions. In 1995, the court issued a ruling that, while not banning affirmative action entirely, illustrated that race-conscious hiring and admissions policies were on their deathbed. In *Adarand Constructors v. Peña* (1995), the court upheld a ruling banning a program that established set-asides for highway construction contracts in Colorado. The court made other conservative rulings in the spring of 1995 that prompted the *Washington Post* to remark that the court had finally become what Reagan wanted it to be.[45] In the wake of *Adarand*, Clinton signed an executive order that mandated the review of all federal affirmative action programs. In order to continue, affirmative policies were required to meet four criteria: the programs could not require quotas, result in reverse discrimination, grant preferences for unqualified individuals, or continue after equal opportunity was established. The executive order, in other words, highlighted the synergy between Clinton, Reagan, and the Supreme Court's civil rights philosophy of colorblind neoliberalism.

The White House was not the only government body that was taking cues from the Supreme Court in considering the elimination of affirmative action entirely. White backlash throughout the country led in large part to the GOP takeover of Congress in 1994, the first time Republicans controlled Congress since 1952. Almost two-thirds of white men voted for the GOP in 1994. With the GOP takeover in 1994, Republicans revealed they would review whether all federal affirmative action programs should be ended entirely. Additionally, individual Republicans announced hearings to prove that Clinton's civil rights agenda, which did nothing to substantively address racial inequality, had gone beyond the original intent of the 1964 Civil Rights Act. One congressman announced his intention to conduct hearings regarding the overhauling of the EEOC and possibly the elimination of the 1964 Civil Rights Act.[46] The GOP takeover in 1994 also resulted in a new chair of the Senate Judiciary Committee: Orrin Hatch. Upon appointment, Hatch announced a review of Clinton's entire civil rights agenda. In the 1970s, Hatch was one of the leaders of the opposition to affirmative action and school integration in the Senate. Now he was head of the judiciary committee charged with rooting out alleged race-conscious policies of reverse discrimination. The appointment of Hatch mirrored Reagan's judicial appointments and his restaffing of the U.S. Commission on Civil Rights. The Clinton years, like the Reagan presidency before them, saw opponents of civil rights being tasked with its enforcement, a situation that proved fundamental to the reinforcement of white supremacy in the final decades of the twentieth century.[47]

The Colorblind Ballot: California Proposition 209

As the newly elected GOP congressional representatives took office, California laid the groundwork for its first colorblind ballot initiative—California Proposition 209. Named the California Civil Rights Initiative, it proposed the prohibition of all considerations of race in public employment, contracting, and education. Early in 1996, the initiative had received 700,000 signatures, enough to put it on the November ballot. Proposition 209 was not the genesis of California's dismantling of affirmative action. Governor Pete Wilson began that process earlier in the year, when he signed an executive order repealing previous orders that merely *encouraged* voluntary affirmative action programs. It also dismantled boards designed to support agencies that needed help establishing and implementing an affirmative action program, and cut the amount of money set aside for minority-owned contracts by half. At a July 1996 meeting of the University of California regents, Ward Connerly announced, "Affirmative action is dead," months before the vote on Proposition 209 even occurred. At this meeting, the regents voted to end affirmative action in employment and contracting at the University of California.[48] Taking their cue from the Golden State, in the fall of 1996, a dozen other state legislatures across the country submitted proposals for similar bills to ban affirmative action.[49]

In November, Proposition 209 passed with 55 percent of the vote. Two-thirds of white men and almost 60 percent of white women favored it. Moreover, only seven of the state's fifty-eight counties voted against it, and three of those did so by only a single point.[50] Those seven counties represented the major Bay Area counties and Los Angeles County. In other words, both suburban and rural constituencies voted in favor of Proposition 209. The suburban opposition to affirmative action in California in the 1990s mirrored the suburban opposition to school integration in the 1970s, which gave birth to modern colorblind politics. The life of colorblindness was thus proved cyclical; it was born and reached maturity in large part due to the activism of suburbanites in blue states.

The Supreme Court refused to consider the constitutionality of Proposition 209, thereby permitting other states to ban affirmative action through their own ballot measures. The effects of Proposition 209 were immediate and severe. In 1996, blacks, Latinx and Native Americans made up more than 23 percent of UC Berkeley's incoming class; the year after, when Proposition 209 went into effect, that number fell to 10 percent. UCLA witnessed similar results. The number of blacks admitted to the law schools at UC

Berkeley and UCLA fell by 80 percent in the first year, 50 percent for Latinx folks. The University of Texas Law School had similar results in the aftermath of *Hopwood v. Texas*, which banned the law school's affirmative action program.[51]

As historian George Derek Musgrove argues, "The key to the anti-affirmative action movement's victory in California was its strategic use of the discourse of a 'colorblind society' and 'equal opportunity' to appropriate the historical memory of the Civil Right Movement."[52] The architects of the California Civil Rights Initiative took cues from the Reagan administration and successfully aligned their language with the supposed colorblind ethos of the civil rights movement. By naming an anti–affirmative action initiative a "civil rights initiative," the backers of Proposition 209 took a page directly out of Reagan's playbook. Moreover, the initiative itself was misleading; it read as though it had been cut and pasted from the 1964 Civil Rights Act. "The state shall not discriminate against," it began, "or grant preferential treatment to, any individual or group on the basis of race, sex, color, ethnicity, or national origin in the operation of public employment, public education, or public contracting."[53] However, it was not simply the initiative's title or language that borrowed from Reagan's civil rights playbook. In the months leading up to the vote, supporters of Proposition 209 redefined, appropriated, and decontextualized the civil rights movement to advance their anti–civil rights agenda.[54] Ward Connerly, one of the initiative's authors, insisted he was "acting on the basis of what [Martin Luther King] said and giving literal meaning to his words."[55] Ads promoting the initiative, paid for by the California GOP, featured actual footage of King's "I Have a Dream" speech. In reality, the supporters of Proposition 209 consisted of some of the most strident opponents of King, including outspoken white supremacist and Louisiana Senate candidate David Duke, who came to California to speak at a state college in support of the proposition. Moreover, at least one of the major financial backers of Proposition 209 was also a donor to Duke's campaign.[56] In fact, in the months leading up to the vote, groups on both sides ran television ads that tried to align their position on the initiative with that of the civil rights movement. Supporters like Connerly borrowed King's colorblind rhetoric to position themselves as inheritors of his dream. Opponents tried to highlight the fact that many of Proposition 209's high-profile supporters had, at the very least, opposed civil rights in the 1960s and that some, in the case of David Duke, even had white supremacist ties to groups like the Ku Klux Klan. On the other hand, organizations like the NAACP, which were largely responsible for the victories of the civil rights movement in the 1960s, opposed the proposition.[57] In either case, the fact that the fight to win votes for or against Proposition 209 centered largely around which side could more convincingly lay claim to the legacy of the modern civil rights movement highlights the weight of colorblind rhetoric by the 1990s. Moreover, the sophisticated colorblind strategy of Proposition 209 proponents was not new. Rather, it drew on over two decades of civil rights opposition via colorblindness. Proposition 209 supporters combined the rhetorical strategies of the school integration opponents of the 1970s with the legal strategy of the Reagan administration in the 1980s to pass anti–civil rights legislation in the 1990s.

California became the first of what would be a series of states that outlawed affirmative action entirely through ballot initiatives. The Supreme Court would continue to assist this cause by further restricting or banning affirmative action in college admissions in places like the University of Michigan and the University of Texas.[58] In 2000, the most definitive study of affirmative action to date was released, titled *Assessing Affirmative Action*. The authors, Harry Holzer and David Neumark, detail how affirmative action programs had significant "tangible benefits" for women, minority business owners, students of color, and the economy writ large. They estimate that affirmative action programs alone boosted the numbers of women and minorities working in those companies by 10–15 percent. The virtually all-white labor unions of the 1960s were 15 percent black by the mid-1990s; the number of black police officers and electricians tripled between 1970 and 1990. The percentage of Latinx college graduates doubled between 1970 and 1990, and more than tripled for blacks. Black enrollment in professional schools rose from 1 to 7 percent, and the number of black medical school students rose from 2 to 8 percent.[59] However, the two authors found zero evidence that these programs had any detrimental impact on the job prospects and wages of white males. Instead, affirmative action recipients received only a greater and more equitable share of new jobs added to the economy. In fact, although sizable gains were made in many areas as a result of affirmative action programs, it is important to emphasize that white males maintained the lion's share of the country's economic largesse. Nearly 96 percent of all federal contract money went to white-owned businesses in the first half of the 1990s as affirmative action collapsed.[60] In other words, affirmative action worked, which is why it had to go.

As affirmative action became moribund in the Bush and Clinton years, Hollywood turned their cameras toward the K–12 classroom, in teacher films including *Lean on Me* (1989), *Stand and Deliver* (1988), and *Dangerous*

Minds (1996). The appeal of these films to Hollywood audiences was two-fold: first, the subject matter was directly linked to the national political debates surrounding affirmative action that had persisted since the 1970s, specifically who "deserved" to be admitted to the country's elite universities; second, the declining performance of American public schools, particular in the inner cities, garnered increasing attention as the 1980s progressed. The erosion of America's secondary education system was the result of neoliberal education reform that coincided with colorblind neoliberalism. Like colorblind neoliberal civil rights policy, neoliberal school reform wielded increasing influence beginning in the 1980s, but its roots ran much deeper.

Neoliberal Education Reform: A Historical Overview

For most of our nation's history, the federal government played only a small role in the education of our children. School legislation—curriculum, class size, and so on—was left, for the most part, to the states. The primary and secondary public school system was understood as more or less functional, and states were tasked with addressing any structural issues. This changed, however, with Lyndon Johnson's Great Society programs in the mid-1960s. Johnson's War on Poverty brought to light gross inequities in numerous segments of American life, including education. In 1965, Congress passed the Elementary and Secondary Education Act (ESEA), which established an active role for the federal government in the nation's education system. ESEA programs provided temporary measures to address the vastly inferior educations many students—the poor and people of color chiefly among them—received. Primarily, this entailed supplemental support for impoverished school districts in order to close the gap between wealthy and poor school districts. The ESEA was built on a model that sought to achieve equity across the nation. As a result, ESEA programs were popular for much of the 1960s and 1970s.[61]

This began to change, however, in the late 1970s and 1980s alongside the larger revolt against Johnson's Great Society programs. As we saw in chapters 1 and 3, busing, affirmative action, and stagflation turned large segments of the country against Johnson's Great Society—its civil rights programs in particular. Education was no different. By the end of the 1970s, voters that would constitute Reagan's base were fed up with what they felt was a massive overreach of federal power. The 1980 GOP platform called not just for a rolling back of federal power in education but for the elimination of the Department of Education altogether.[62] In 1981, as part of Reagan's

New Federalism program, Congress passed the Education Consolidation and Improvement Act (ECIA), which modified many provisions of the ESEA. These included reducing the amount of federal funding for education by nearly 20 percent, and increasing flexibility for states on how to use those funds. Some estimate that as many as 85 percent of federal education mandates were nullified during the Reagan presidency. As political scientist Patrick McGuinn explains, "Reagan hoped either to eliminate the federal role in schools or to redefine the nature of the federal education policy regime by making privatization, choice, and competition—rather than equity—its guiding principles."[63]

The important point here is not simply Reagan's rolling back of Johnson's Great Society programs. Rather, as with civil rights, it is the manner in which he did so and the alternatives he offered to those programs that are worth highlighting. In education, Reagan replaced federal programs—in which the government took an active role in eliminating racial and economic equality—with neoliberal alternatives that prioritized the supposedly small government and free market over government intervention. As I argued in chapters 3 and 4, the election of Ronald Reagan marked the rise not just of neoliberal economic policy but of neoliberal governance. In the area of civil rights, this meant strictly colorblind approaches to racial inequality; in education, this meant charter schools, an ever-increasing reliance on standardized testing, and privatization. By neoliberal education reform, I refer to the ways in which the federal government introduced school reforms "which commodify public education by reducing learning to bits of information and skill to be taught and tested and marketize education through programs that promote privatization and user fees in place of free, public education."[64] More specifically, as education scholars E. Wayne Ross and Rich Gibson argue, these reforms "emphasize opening up the educational services market to for-profit educational management organizations" and "focus on creation of curriculum standards (where the state defines the knowledge to be taught) and 'accountability.' The specification of curriculum standards is nearly always accompanied by accountability strategies."[65] Under neoliberal reform, schools do not need more money; they just need to become more efficient through market competition with other private, public, and charter schools.

As with his fiscal policy, Reagan's education policy drew heavily on neoliberal forefather Milton Friedman. Friedman advocated for neoliberal education reforms long before Reagan entered office. In his 1962 manifesto, *Capitalism and Freedom*, he devotes an entire chapter to "the role of government in education." For Friedman, a key flaw in the public education system of the 1960s was the lack of distinction between which elements of education the government should finance and those it should administer. The purpose of education, in Friedman's view, is to develop "citizenship," "leadership," and "greater economic productivity." He insists that reform "center attention on the person rather than the institution." The primary way to do this is through school choice, vouchers, charter schools, and privatization. "Governments could require a minimum level of school financing," he advocates, "by giving parents vouchers redeemable for a specified maximum sum per child per year if spent on 'approved' educational services. . . . The educational services could be rendered by private enterprises operated for profit, or by non-profit institutions. The role of government would be limited to insuring that the schools met certain minimum standards."[66] If properly implemented, he concludes, "The development of arrangements such as those outlined above (e.g., vouchers, privatization, market-based education models) would make capital more widely available and would thereby do much to make equality of opportunity a reality, to diminish inequalities of income and wealth, and to promote the full use of our human resources. And it would do so not by impeding competition, destroying incentive, and dealing with symptoms . . . but by strengthening competition, making incentives effective, and *eliminating the causes of inequality*."[67] Friedman's neoliberal reforms replace the state with the private sector. According to the economist, by privatizing education and thus implementing a competition for profit, private enterprises would have no choice but to offer the best education possible at the lowest cost in order to remain economically viable. Students would therefore get a better, and cheaper, education, and economic productivity would increase; everyone wins.

The president was unable, however, to realize his party's goal of eliminating the Department of Education altogether. Early in his presidency, a disagreement between Reagan and his secretary of education, Terrell Bell, over the effectiveness of the nation's public school system prompted the president to commission a study of the country's education system. The resulting report, *A Nation at Risk: The Imperative for Education Reform*, released in 1983, depicted a public education system in crisis, plagued by declining test scores and graduation rates, and a student body that was performing at levels behind those of many other countries.[68] As education scholar David Hursh argues, "*A Nation at Risk* explicitly blamed schools for the Reagan-induced economic recession of the early 1980s and the perceived failure of the United States to compete internationally."[69] To that point, education was hardly a major national issue. That changed with *A Nation at Risk*. The report moved education—and specifically the need for the federal government to intervene in (or divest from) it—to the forefront of the domestic agenda. Interestingly, although the report made no recommendation as to vouchers, tuition tax credits for private schools, or school prayer, the president used the press conference announcing the release of the report to praise its call for all those things. The report did not recommend the explicit neoliberal remedies championed by Friedman and Reagan, but the president insisted they did.[70] As education scholar Pauline Lipman argues, "Beginning with *A Nation at Risk* . . . there has been a steady push for standards, accountability, and regulation of schools, teachers and students."[71]

Although ultimately unsuccessful, Reagan tried throughout his time in the White House to eliminate the Department of Education and to convert federal spending in education to vouchers. Though his efforts were unsuccessful, his attempts to make neoliberal reforms to education did succeed in substantially limiting the personnel, budget, and regulatory authority of public education, thereby undermining its ability to improve student achievement, which would set the stage for further neoliberal reform in the future, as public school performance continued to decline. Reagan cut the Department of Education budget by 11 percent during his time in office, and the National Institute of Education lost 70 percent of its funding.[72]

Reagan's successor, George H. W. Bush, continued the neoliberal education reform revolution when he took over the Oval Office. His America 2000 plan, introduced in the spring of 1991, called for more stringent academic standards in core subjects in order to move the country toward national education goals. It also included a panel to create "American Achievement Tests" for all fourth, eighth, and twelfth graders, as well as many other goals that placed a greater emphasis on testing and the privatization of public education. While the bill that ultimately passed did not contain many of Bush's proposals, it did implement national academic standards that directed the country down a path of increasing importance on standardized testing. Bush also favored vouchers. Despite fierce opposition by Democrats and teachers unions, he put forward an aggressive voucher plan in 1992—the GI Bill for Children—which sought to divert $500 million in federal education funds to vouchers for public or private education.[73] "Choice can open up opportunity," Bush argued. "For too long, we've shielded our schools from competition. . . . It is time we began thinking of a system of public education in which many providers offer a marketplace of opportunity."[74]

Bush's maneuverings for more federal control over education through vouchers, standardized tests, and merit pay rather than increased spending on public education represented a compromise between Republicans and Democrats, who had been battling over federal intervention in education since the 1960s. Conservatives, like those who supported Reagan's New Federalism, wanted less federal oversight of schools and more state power and flexibility to address sluggish school performance. Democrats, on the other hand, sought a more active federal intervention and expansion of funding for education. What occurred under Reagan and Bush, then, was actually a compromise—federal oversight, but with a neoliberal ideology. Ultimately, America 2000 centered on three issues—national standardized tests, school choice, and federal funding. As McGuinn states, "The Bush administration represented the first concerted attempt to fundamentally shift the Republican Party's approach to federal education policy and to create a new policy regime based on federal support for standards-based school reform."[75]

Yet while Reagan laid the foundation and Bush began implementing neoliberal reform, the neoliberal restructuring of American public schooling was a bipartisan effort. During the presidency of Bill Clinton, Bush's education vision was more fully realized. Clinton's legislative contributions to education centered around two bills: Goals 2000 and the reauthorization, but amending, of the ESEA. Each of these bills placed a greater emphasis on testing and opened up further opportunities for privatization. More importantly, they completed the reversal of the federal government's role in education begun under Reagan. With Goals 2000 and the reauthorized ESEA, the federal government's education policy had wholly shifted from targeted educational inequality to addressing the needs of each student as individuals. And while the full neoliberal revolution in American education would finish with the 2002 passage of No Child Left Behind (NCLB), under George W. Bush, the central tenets of NCLB were first legislated with Goals 2000 and the ESEA reauthorization and reflected contributions from both Republican and Democratic presidents, highlighting the increasing hegemony of neoliberalism.[76]

Education scholars have documented the detrimental effects of neoliberal education reform on large segments of the nation's public school populace, particularly poor students and students of color. As David Hursh argues, the changes made in education over the last several decades "reflect policymakers' greater faith in markets and competition than in teachers and students."[77] The net result of this approach, according to Hursh, is not only increased inequality across schools but rising inequality *within* schools. The ever-greater emphasis placed on standardized testing forces teachers to teach to the tests in order to ensure that the highest number of students will pass them. This often leads teachers to devote more attention to those students thought to be most able to pass the tests and obtain grades of C or higher. This practice has had serious racial implications, as persons of color and ESL learners are already located toward the bottom of performance indicators.[78] Hursh concludes,

> Since [the 1980s], we have witnessed in the United States, England, and elsewhere the increasing transformation of schools into institutions governed by market principles of accountability, choice, and efficiency. . . . Neoliberal policies promote corporate growth through increased trade and decreased taxation and regulation, and decreased public support for or even the privatization of public services such as health, transportation, and education. Furthermore, the shift toward promoting corporate over social welfare redefines the relationship between the individual and society. Because governments are less responsible for the welfare of the individual, the individual becomes responsible for him or herself.

Hursh's analysis points to a broader process of neoliberalization in the post-Reagan years that extends beyond fiscal policy. As Carolyn Hardin illustrates, this process has not simply meant the dismantling of the welfare state; it has instead led to the corporatization of the welfare state and the decline of government's ability to protect its citizens.[79]

Teacher Films

Education reform explains only part of the appeal of school dramas to Hollywood in the last decade of the twentieth century. As we have seen, the racial and cultural politics of the 1970s and 1980s played an integral role in growing the popularity of notions of colorblind neoliberalism that led to neoliberal education reforms. Therefore, the appeal of school dramas to Hollywood filmmakers in the 1990s was likewise informed by the centrality of racial melodrama in the formal aesthetics of the American popular culture canon. As film scholar Linda Williams notes, citing texts across diverse media forms, from *Uncle Tom's Cabin* to the double-murder trial of O.J. Simpson, "it may not be accidental that the most innovative, form-breaking works of American mass culture have been what I call melodramas of black and white. Every time we are ready to bury the supposedly archaic mode of melodrama it has a way of rising from the ashes."[80] As Williams elaborates, melodrama lends itself to racially charged narratives because it "is not a static, archaic, stereotyping and non-realist form, but a tremendously protean, evolving, and modernizing form that continually uncovers new realistic material for its melodramatic project."[81] For Williams, racial melodramas fall primarily within two traditions—"Tom" and "Anti-Tom." The former, taking its name from Harriet Beecher Stowe's novel *Uncle Tom's Cabin*, uses the suffering and inhumane treatment of the enslaved African to write an abolitionist novel. The latter, mobilized most notably by D. W. Griffith's *Birth of a Nation*, portrays the savage black male as a constant threat to white womanhood in order to present a narrative of white victimization that justifies brutality toward African Americans. It is no coincidence, in Williams's view, that the "Tom" tradition paralleled the growing abolitionist movement of the mid-nineteenth century, or that the "Anti-Tom" tradition coincided with increased white backlash, most notably through the resurgence of the Ku Klux Klan, against blacks in the early twentieth century. Similarly, Lee Grieveson has noted how "White Slavery" films arose alongside the anxieties surrounding the increased presence of white immigrants.[82] In other words, throughout twentieth-century film, racial melodrama provided a key site to represent, shape, and contest the racial anxieties of the historical moment. The 1980s, and specifically the emergence of colorblindness, necessitated yet another new form—nonetheless steeped in previous melodramatic modes. This new narrative is what I call the "teacher film." Tara J. Yosso and David G. Garcia have written extensively on the "formulaic" nature of teacher films. "This formula tends to focus," explain Yosso and Garcia,

> on an optimistic (White) novice teacher struggling to inspire urban (Black and/or Latina/o) youth. Often, in the introductory classroom scene students shoot spit wads and dance on the desks, fight with one another, ignore, or otherwise completely disrespect the new teacher. A student usually brutalizes and/or sexually threatens a female teacher in the first act. Having lost their belief in the sense of service or mission, deflated faculty work in misery to collect a paycheck and seek refuge from students in the teachers' lounge. The protagonist teacher distinguishes him/herself from these pessimists, determined to make a difference. . . . Delinquent and

remedial students eventually become inspired to learn academic basics, build up self-respect, and to pursue their education.[83]

It was, I contend, the combination of growing national concern over the state of public schools, Reagan-era fears of urban black and brown youth, the ever-present allure of melodramatic renditions of social causes, and colorblind hegemony that proved irresistible for Hollywood.[84] It is important to distinguish here the difference between the racially melodramatic teacher films of the 1990s and the slavery and civil rights dramas of the same era. In other words, one may wonder what distinguishes the teacher films of the 1990s from the historical dramas of the same period when analyzed within Williams's framework of "melodramas in black and white." The historical dramas of the 1990s fit neatly within Williams's taxonomy of melodrama. Teacher films, however, require a more critical analysis of racial melodrama precisely because they illustrate what I believe to be the key *evolution* of the melodramatic form in the context of neoliberalism, colorblindness, and education reform. The conflation of these three issues in the post-Reagan era not only produced the latest evolution of the "protean" melodramatic form in American mass culture but marked the emergence of a genre in which neoliberal colorblindness is inherently embedded into the logic of the narrative and form itself. In other words, if Rocky Balboa was the first colorblind hero, *Blue Collar* marked the emergence of neoliberalism on-screen, and *Glory* and *The Long Walk Home* marked a colorblind revision of black freedom struggles, teacher films constituted the first colorblind *genre*.

What follows is an analysis of the generic conventions of teacher films, highlighting the manner in which colorblindness and neoliberalism function as genre in these films. Teacher films consistently use the tropes of the welfare-dependent pathological home, the white teacher as savior, and the militarization of the inner-city classroom to position race consciousness as the symptom of black and Latinx pathology and colorblindness as the cure for dysfunctional family life and the only path toward racial, social, and economic inequality. The liberal state in teacher films is not only incapable of solving the problems of urban poverty—it is the actual cause of those problems. This notion harkens back to the 1970s antistatism covered in chapters 1 and 2. However, what distinguished the 1990s version of antistatism is the maturation of colorblind neoliberalism and widespread faith in its ability to address racial inequality.

Teacher films' neoliberal politics are grounded in part in the Reagan-era narrative that Great Society programs aimed at eliminating poverty and racial inequality had actually made them worse.[85] Moreover, as Roopali Mukherjee argues, the individual "savior," whose salvation comes through her own individual determination rather than through state action, is a key feature of neoliberal narratives. The savior functions contradictorily, according to Mukherjee, to "deracialize subjectivities" through "logics of race and racial differentiation."[86] My interest here, unlike in previous chapters, is less about close readings of the texts—in this case, *Dangerous Minds*, *Freedom Writers*, and *Stand and Deliver*. Instead, I will focus on how these three films function generically—that is, how their key themes and tropes work to impregnate an inherently colorblind neoliberal logic into each film. Teacher films rely heavily on deeply rooted tropes of Hollywood melodrama, like the home and the "victim-hero," and racialized discourses about black and Latinx families and intellect from throughout the twentieth century in order to position colorblindness as the solution to the problems of urban America in the 1990s.

It is important to note that teacher films in the late 1980s and 1990s differ significantly from those made prior to the colorblind era, most notably *Blackboard Jungle* (1955).[87] *Blackboard Jungle* is a prototypical social problem film. As the opening titles of the film state, "Today we are concerned with juvenile delinquency—its causes—and its effects. We are especially concerned when this delinquency boils over into our schools. . . . We believe that public awareness is a first step toward a remedy for any problem. It is in this spirit and with this faith that BLACKBOARD JUNGLE was produced." The film was made to bring awareness to an increasing social problem of urban education in the 1950s. Teacher films of the 1990s, on the other hand, are colorblind neoliberalism disguised as social problem films. Put another way, teacher films are only interested in urban education to the extent that they provide an important issue through which to illustrate the "reality" of colorblindness and the "necessity" of colorblind neoliberalism. For example, whereas the heroic teachers of teacher films of the 1990s are entirely colorblind, *Blackboard Jungle*'s teacher Richard Dadier (Glenn Ford), at one point in the film, nearly uses a racial slur in reference to a black student, Gregory Miller (Sidney Poitier). In other words, *Blackboard Jungle* subtly depicts that even those dedicated to alleviating the social problem of urban education in the 1950s may harbor racial prejudice. The later iterations of this genre lack this distinction. The heroic teacher-saviors of the 1990s cannot be racist, as such a character trait would undermine the credit colorblindness is afforded in these films for "saving" students of color.

The Pathological Home

Teacher films borrow significantly from racial melodrama's previous incarnations, relying on several of its tropes, including the home. For Williams, "One of the key ways of constructing moral power is the icon of the good home. The icon of home helps establish the 'space of innocence' of its virtuous victims."[88] Thus, from the cabin of Uncle Tom to the southern plantation of *Birth of a Nation*, the home is "essential to establish the virtue of racially beset victims."[89] The importance of the home is no less prominent in teacher films. However, the space of the home in the teacher film is not an actual home but the classroom. The need for a surrogate home results primarily from the absence of a "good home" in the familial life of the students. Delinquent home life is part of a larger trope within teacher films—pathological black and Latinx families. As we have seen, the "culture of pathology" thesis emerged in the 1960s as, according to Robin D. G. Kelley, social scientists studying urban poverty concluded "that a common, debased culture is what defined the 'underclass.'"[90] These projects, most prominently the Moynihan Report, popularized notions of cultural pathology among African Americans—specifically in the ability of black women to raise children. Tracing this discourse back further, Hazel Carby explains, "As early as 1905 the major discursive elements were already in place that would define black female urban behavior throughout the teens and twenties as pathological."[91] And as we saw in previous chapters, the delinquent black household headed by the welfare queen became the boogeyman of the Reagan presidency. Moreover, as Yosso and Garcia insist, the roots of teacher films run much deeper than the post-Moynihan discourse of black families and the neoliberal education reforms of the Reagan era. Instead, these films resurrect "racialized allegations similar to those found in early 1900's biological determinist theories."[92]

Each of these films relies on the supposed cultural pathology of African Americans and Latinx communities to create the need for surrogacy, which the teacher and classroom then fulfills. In *Dangerous Minds* and *Stand and Deliver*, the families of the students are unsupportive of their children's education. In fact, in each film, parents actually force their children to drop out of school. In *Dangerous Minds*, after two of her students, brothers Lionell and Durell, miss several consecutive days of class, a concerned LouAnne Johnson decides to visit the home of the brothers. Johnson arrives at the home to find the two young men on the front porch. After saying hello, the boys' mother emerges from the house, instructs her sons to go inside, and has the following conversation with Johnson:

Johnson: Hi. I'm LouAnne Johnson.

Mother: I know who you are. You're that white-bread bitch messing with my babies' minds.

Johnson: I beg your pardon?

Mother: My boys don't go to your school anymore, and that's gonna be it.

Johnson: You took them out of school?

Mother: You're damn right I did. I saw what they were bringing home, poetry and shit. A waste of time. They got more important things to worry about.

Johnson: Don't you think that finishing high school will be valuable to their future?

Mother: That's not in their future. I ain't raising no doctors and lawyers here. They got bills to pay. Why don't you just get on out of here. Find yourself some other poor boys to save.

This is not the only instance in which Johnson attempts to convince the parents of her students of the value of education. After Johnson's smartest student, Callie, becomes pregnant and leaves school in order to transfer to a school that has a "mother-to-be" program, Johnson visits her home to try to convince her to stay in Johnson's class. Although Callie does eventually return, after the visit the audience assumes she will not return because her mother, ailed by the supposed cultural pathology of Latina motherhood, prefers the mother-to-be program, which stresses practical training in motherhood over a formal education.

Two similar scenes occur in *Stand and Deliver*. The first occurs after one of Jaime Escalante's students announces she has to drop out of school to work full time. Escalante visits her family's restaurant hoping to persuade her father to allow his daughter to stay in school. The tense and unsuccessful discussion concludes with the girl's father insisting that earning money is more important than school. In the second instance, concerned that her daughter is spending too much time studying, a mother warns her daughter about becoming too intelligent: "Boys don't like it if you're too smart," she says.

The dysfunctional homes in these films necessitate a surrogate, one from outside the racialized "ghettos" and therefore immune to the "pathology" of

The mother of two students of LouAnne Johnson (Michelle Pfeiffer) scolds Johnson for teaching her sons "poetry and shit."

the communities of their students. The classroom in teacher films serves this function. In fact, in *Freedom Writers*, one student even calls the classroom his home. However, while the space of the home in teacher films operates similarly to that in racial melodrama in general, the narrative of the home is reversed. As Williams explains, in racial melodrama, "The narrative proper usually begins when the villain intrudes upon the idyllic space" of the home.[93] In the teacher film, the narrative begins with the idyllic hero entering the villainous space of the inner city. The struggle becomes, then, not over the external threat to the harmonious home but of the seemingly insurmountable task of remaking the urban home and the inner city more generally.

Beyond simply identifying the inner-city home—specifically the student's parents—as the site where education is devalued, the cause of this feeble commitment to their child's education takes on specifically colorblind rhetoric. During Johnson's visit to the home of the two brothers in *Dangerous Minds*, their mother calls Johnson a "white-bread bitch." Her racially explicit language suggests that race consciousness factors into the overall failure of the black family. Like many of the colorblind crusaders of the Reagan era, the film here alleges that it is race consciousness itself that limits the opportunities of people of color. Colorblindness is, therefore, implied as the solution to their "pathology." During one scene in *Freedom Writers*, a girl's father instructs her to lie to the police about the identity of a person she saw murder another man. He explains to his daughter that the two of them are engaged in a "racial war." In fact, all the students of Erin Gruwell (Hilary Swank), the white teacher and "savior" in *Freedom Writers*, are initially members of racially exclusive gangs (black, Latinx, Asian) that outwardly hate all other racial gangs—called "tribes" in the disc menu. The father insists that it does not matter what actually happened because "in war you got to take your victories when you can." For the girl's father, having an African American take the fall for a Latino's crime equates to a victory in the greater race war. In both instances, race-conscious politics are cited as a source, if not the primary driver, of the poverty and lack of social mobility that plagues these communities.

If race consciousness is the cause of social, economic, and educational inequality in these films, colorblindness offers the solution. Erin Gruwell is routinely portrayed as a colorblind individual, and convincing her students of the colorblind "reality" of the world in which they live is essential to her pedagogy. Gruwell puts significant effort into facilitating her students' transformation from "misguided" race consciousness to colorblindness. In one instance, after several of her students fling racial slurs at her—saying, among other things, "I hate white people!" Gruwell responds by insisting, "It doesn't matter what color I am." In another case, Gruwell extends a strip of red tape from one end of her classroom to another and forces her students to play the "line game," whereby Gruwell asks a series of questions, and students, standing on either side of the line, step up to the line if the question applies to them. The questions include basic ones, like "How many of you have the latest Snoop Dogg album?" to more serious and personal questions, like "Stand on the line if you have lost a friend to gang violence." As a result of the game, the students realize that their obsession with racial difference inhibits their ability to find common interests and shared struggles. The exercise reveals the foolishness of their belief, as one student puts it, that "it is all about color." Ultimately, the line game acts as a pedagogical tool for Gruwell to demonstrate the "reality" of colorblindness.

The Victim-Hero

In both *Freedom Writers* and *Dangerous Minds*, as the students begin to buy into the colorblind discourse their teacher preaches and begin to shed their "pathological" race consciousness and allegiances, they begin to succeed academically. The solution to the problems of inner-city schooling in teacher films, then, is not increased funds, smaller class sizes, or changes to standardized tests or curriculum, but a change in attitude. The solution, in other words, is neoliberal and colorblind. No government action is required; instead, a mere adjustment in racial attitudes will enable these students to succeed. In addition, the catalyst of this change is not structural but individual: the teacher.

Equally important to the racial melodrama is the victim-hero. As Williams describes, "Melodrama focuses on victim-heroes and on recognizing their virtue."[94] Indeed, the heroes of teacher films are constantly victimized—or, perhaps more specifically, suffer as a result of their relentless moral action. For example, the white teachers in these films are subjected to frequent racist and sexist slurs. Slurs like "white-bread bitch," "I hate white people!" and a number of inappropriate sexual innuendos are directed at the white female teachers in these films. Further, the teachers' personal relationships are damaged, in some cases beyond repair, as a result of the amount of attention their students require for "saving." In *Dangerous Minds*, LouAnne Johnson has no social life because teaching requires all her time. In *Stand and Deliver*, Jaime Escalante's wife grows increasingly hostile as a result of his neglect of his family. At one point she even points out that Escalante's own son is struggling with math because his father, a math teacher, is never around to help him. In *Freedom Writers*, Erin Gruwell becomes estranged from her husband, and the two eventually divorce. In addition, she takes on two extra jobs to buy books for her students. Finally, even Gruwell's father, who was active in the civil rights movement, disapproves of her teaching in the inner city. This sets up an important distinction between the leaders of the civil rights era and those of the decades afterward. As we have seen, throughout the twenty-plus years between the busing battles of the mid-1970s and the culmination of colorblind hegemony in the mid-1990s with the passage of California Proposition 209, white opponents of civil rights and school integration used colorblind language to position themselves as the inheritors of the civil rights movement. They also successfully labeled defenders of these civil rights programs as opponents of the movement's supposed core ideology of colorblindness. Gruwell's father's disapproval of her actions personifies that division.

While the teachers in these films suffer in their quest to educate their students, in the end they heroically save their students, convincing them of the value of education and accomplishing whatever academic goal the film sets out to achieve. Jaime Escalante's students all pass the AP Calculus exam, LouAnne Johnson's students strengthen their commitment to academic success, and Erin Gruwell's students graduate high school and live to see their eighteenth birthdays (which, according to the film, is a statistical anomaly in inner-city Los Angeles). The heroism of the teachers in these films becomes recognizable through their determination to "save" their students and the sacrifice of their personal happiness to lead others—specifically those who have no other hope because of their pathological mothers—to salvation. Further, the savior role the teachers perform provides surrogate parenting for the students. Just as the classroom serves as the surrogate home, the teacher serves as a surrogate parent to those students who lack proper parental figures as a result of their supposedly debased cultural values. In addition to the obvious parental nature of the salvation mission, in each of these films, students visit their teacher outside class, seeking guidance for nonacademic issues.

Militarizing the Classroom

As the aforementioned discussion illustrates, teacher films are deeply indebted to modes of racial melodrama. However, they updated these modes in several key ways, which enable them to more directly speak to white anxieties around black and brown urban communities and the rising influence of neoliberal colorblindness. While there is much that is new with these films, teacher films also engage in the far older binary of the civilized white settler–colonizer and the black savage–colonized, whereby the inner city becomes the unsettled jungle. Interpreted within this colonial dichotomy, the ghetto "savages" can only become civilized with the aid and instruction of the "civilized" white outsider-teacher. For example, in *Dangerous Minds*, the ability of Johnson's students to learn to sit properly in their seats serves as a metaphor for their broader civilization. In addition, in both *Dangerous Minds* and *Freedom Writers*, the teachers are English teachers. In each of these classes, the teachers conduct basic grammar exercises with their students in order to teach them "proper" English. Sentences like "Odysseus didn't have no since [*sic*] of direction," "We ___ green beans today," and "Never shoot a homeboy" are examples of sentences Gruwell and Johnson write on the board to use as tools to teach their high school students proper English. Setting aside the exaggerated elementary nature of these sentences, language, under colonial discourse, is often seen as the first step in curbing the savagery of the colonized. In fact, forcing the colonizer's language on the colonized was one of the primary tools of subjection and domination during colonialism.[95]

Johnson's "uncivilized" students do not sit "properly" at their desks.

Johnson attempts to teach her students grammar by using sentences she thinks relate to their lives, incentivizing their participation with candy.

However, as cultural studies scholar John D. Márquez argues, the work of representing the "savagery" of inner-city students of color does more than enable the heroism of the white savior.[96] Rather than offer hope for and solutions to the problems of poor language, a proclivity for violence, loose sexual mores, and a lack of interest in their education, the representation of the colonizing process reinforces the alleged natural savagery of inner-city communities of color. In popular imagination, the ghetto, for Márquez, is like the jungle for the African savage: it signifies the "state of nature" in which poor communities of color exist. Therefore, "because it is inhabited by the racial 'other' whose existence enacts its own *expendability*, this literal and figurative place is in need of conquest and violent control by the state, to allow for the construction of a rational and morally sound civil society, inhabited by the 'middle-class' family, the one to which a few *exceptional* blacks and Latinx folks are also welcome, in the postracial United States."[97] As Márquez elaborates, "Because this space/condition [the inner city] is natural—those who live there cannot change it at will—there is the need of persistent and vigilant policing by the state's law enforcement and military apparatuses. The scene of nature grants those apparatuses their moral/ethical/legal legitimacy, which is drawn out discursively."[98]

The militarization of the students in teacher films is another key trope of the teacher film genre. This militarization is necessitated by the inherently "savage" nature of the black and Latino men, in particular. For example, in *Dangerous Minds*, as Johnson enters her classroom for the first time she is greeted with the shrill clamor of black and Latinx students rapping and beatboxing at the front of the class, others listening to music, and finally others simply speaking boisterously. When Johnson asks about her predecessor, Ms. Shepard, the class responds as follows:

Black Female: Hey everybody, White-Bread wants to know about Ms. Shepard.
Latino Male: We killed the bitch! (The class erupts in cheers.)
Raul: Emilio ate her!
Emilio: That's Bullshit! That bitch was too ugly to eat. I fed her to my dog (laughter). But I'll eat you.

Johnson's first interaction with the class reveals their savage nature. The clever use of pun—"I'll eat you"—illustrates the murderous, cannibalistic, and libidinous impulses of these students.

Combating this savagery requires a highly militarized approach. LouAnne Johnson is an ex-marine. Similarly, in one scene in *Stand and Deliver*, Jaime

Escalante lines up his students and walks down the line like a drill sergeant, asking each student a mathematical question. This militarism of the teachers, specifically through the discipline and pedagogical nuances it affords, is presented as integral to their teaching success. The best example of the militarization of students in the teacher film occurs in the 1989 film *Lean on Me*. The film takes place in Paterson, New Jersey's Eastside High School and centers on its bat-wielding black principal, Joe Clark (Morgan Freeman). George Lipsitz explains that like other teacher films, the film portrays the predominantly black student body as "lazy, licentious, boisterous, and brutal," and suggests that schools "can succeed by becoming prisons—or more precisely that prisons are more important to society than schools. . . . Clark brings the model of the military and the penitentiary to urban education. It does not matter that such behavior cannot develop the intellectual and personal resources necessary for a lifetime of citizenship and work; what does matter is that it imposes a dictatorial and authoritarian model on the poor and presents people who have problems *as* problems."[99] Ultimately, what these films seek more than educational success is the disciplining of these uncivilized bodies. Consistent with colonialism, these films work toward the eradication of the savagery of these students.

In teacher films, discipline is more important than education. In *Freedom Writers*, the head of Gruwell's department makes the following statement regarding how Gruwell should approach teaching: "You can't make someone want an education. The best you can do is try to get them to obey, to learn discipline. That would be a tremendous accomplishment for them." While Gruwell's commitment to educating her students distinguishes her from her superior to some degree, in both cases the acculturation of these students is reliant on white educators. In either case, one finds a neoliberal and colorblind solution to the problems of the inner city. The highly militarized response is in line with neoliberalism's tolerance of a large state military apparatus. Furthermore, as we have seen, the state—through welfare, along with the race-conscious attitudes of its inhabitants—is implicated in the production of inner-city pathology. As Márquez concludes, "Postracial discourse *naturalizes* ghetto violence, rendering it, once again, an expression of the intrinsic racial and cultural attributes of working-class and Latinx communities."[100] In other words, the project of a teacher film is to ultimately use the conventions of racial melodrama to offer hope to inner-city communities of color through heroic, based-on-a-true-story tales of white women "saving" a few young blacks or Latinx youths. This project, moreover, is built on the "natural" pathology of these communities, and the exceptions do little but reinforce the norm.

Finally, further compounding the neocolonial undertone of these films is the "tourist" nature of these protagonists. The teachers in these films are not from the community in which they teach, and in each film, with the exception of *Stand and Deliver*, they leave as soon as they complete their saving mission. As in colonial discourse, the necessity of the outsider results from the plague of wretchedness in the communities of these students. An outsider becomes the only possible savior because the degeneracy of the urban community in which they teach is contagious. The savior must therefore leave as soon as possible in order to avoid becoming infected by the "ghetto." The other white teachers in these films, who have taught at their respective schools for many years, exemplify this. Most of them make racist comments at some point in the film. The most illuminative of these racist comments occurs in a scene in *Freedom Writers*, in which a white male teacher has the following conversation with Gruwell in response to her optimism about teaching *The Diary of Anne Frank* in her class because she believes it to be a story to which her students can relate:

> *Teacher*: How dare you compare [these kids] to Anne Frank? They don't hide. They drive around in the open with automatic weapons. I'm the one living in fear. I can't walk out my door at night.
> *Gruwell*: And you blame these kids?
> *Teacher*: This was an A-list school before they came here. And look what *they* turned it into. Does it make sense that kids who want an education should suffer because their high school gets turned into a reform school? Because kids who don't want to be here and shouldn't be here are forced to be here by the geniuses running the school district? Integration's a lie. Yeah, we teachers, we can't say that or we lose our jobs for being racist. So, please, stop your cheerleading, Erin. You're ridiculous. You don't know the first thing about these kids.

In addition, other faculty members constantly try to undermine the work of the savior. Most importantly, all of them have thrown away their belief that the students are capable of salvation. They have, in other words, all "caught" the virus of the inner city. As Yosso and Garcia outline, this trope, of "deflated faculty" that have "lost their sense of service or mission," is central to the teacher film formula.

Writing in response to the anti–affirmative action and anti-immigrant ballot initiatives (Propositions 209 and 187, respectively), George Lipsitz labeled the Golden State "the Mississippi of the 1990s." He compares the leadership behind Proposition 209, which includes Governor Pete Wilson and UC regent Ward Connerly, to Ross Barnett and James Eastland, the Mississippi governor and senator who so ardently and violently defended Jim Crow segregation in the 1960s. Like Barnett and Eastland, California political leaders in the 1990s "deploy[ed] the same combination of racism and disavowal that proved so poisonous in Mississippi in the 1960s."[101] In his analysis of race-oriented ballot initiatives throughout California's history, Daniel HoSang concludes that "nearly every major civil rights and racial justice issue put before a vote of the people in California [in the postwar period] has failed."[102] HoSang notes that Californians voted against fair employment in the mid-1940s, repealed fair housing legislation in the 1960s, overturned school desegregation orders twice in the 1970s, enacted English-only school guidelines twice in the 1980s, passed a "three-strikes" law and banned undocumented immigrants from public services and benefits in the early 1990s, and ended affirmative action in 1996.[103] White California voters have consistently demonstrated what Lipsitz calls their "possessive investment in whiteness" and what HoSang terms "political whiteness." The latter works "as a kind of absent referent, hailing and interpolating particular subjects through various affective appeals witnessed in claims to protect 'our rights,' 'our jobs,' 'our homes,' 'our kids,' 'our streets,' and even 'our state' that never mention race but are addressed to racialized subjects."[104] Furthermore, as HoSang demonstrates, liberals, just as much as conservatives, have wielded the influence of "political whiteness" in California. Reaching a similar conclusion, Lipsitz argues that in California, as with Mississippi in the sixties, "elements of the state's past reappeared with a vengeance and undermined opportunities for peaceful, democratic, and egalitarian social change."[105]

Yet one cannot fully grasp the weight and influence of California's Mississippi-like actions in the 1990s without considering the substantive role Hollywood played in "hailing and interpolating particular subjects through various affective appeals" on-screen. It is the combination, then, of California Proposition 209 and the rise of the neoliberal colorblind genre of the teacher film that, in 1996, produced a hegemonic moment for colorblindness. Colorblind hegemony in the mid-1990s consisted of more than a ballot initiative in California; it wielded significant influence in the Supreme Court in the six years between the Reagan presidency and Proposition 209 despite two presidents who in no way supported the colorblind literalism of Reagan. Most importantly, it became the new "common sense" aesthetics of Hollywood social problem films. Hollywood had always been interested in the colorblind racial project. In fact, as chapter 1 illustrates, the reemergence of Hollywood as the center of American popular culture occurred in large part because of films like *Rocky*, which spoke to the anxieties of the larger racial project of colorblindness. By the 1990s, however, Hollywood's colorblind project had matured to an entire genre of films built on the racialized logic of neoliberal colorblindness.

Conclusion

• •

On January 21, 2019, President Donald Trump signed a proclamation elevating the existing Martin Luther King Jr. historic site to a national park. In his remarks about the slain civil rights leader, the president indulged in the colorblind claptrap that, as we have seen, has saturated public discourse around King and the movement he led since the 1970s. "Today," Trump tweeted, "we celebrate Dr. King for standing up for the self-evident truth Americans hold so dear: That no matter what the color of our skin, or the place of our birth, we are all created equal by God."[1] The image of King as a colorblind "prophet of U.S. progress and redemption,"[2] teeming with Christian symbolism, not only renders the civil rights icon and his politics wholly incommensurate with any serious consideration of his life, but seamlessly aligns with the historical "memory" of King as driven by a resolute commitment to colorblind ideology carefully constructed by white civil rights opponents in the decades since his death. Trump's speech, in this regard, mirrors those routinely given by Ronald Reagan three decades prior. As Brandon Terry wrote in the *Boston Review* four months before Trump's proclamation, "The King now enshrined in popular sensibilities is a mythic figure of consensus and conciliation, who sacrificed his life to defeat Jim Crow and place the United States on a path toward a 'more perfect union.' Such poetic renderings lead our political and moral judgment astray. Along with the conservative gaslighting that claims King's authority for 'colorblind' jurisprudence, they obscure King's persistent attempt to jar the United States out of its complacency and corruption. . . . He has become an icon to quote, not a thinker and public philosopher to engage."[3]

The election of Donald Trump to the nation's highest office raises the question as to whether Trump's election marks the death of colorblindness. Trump's efforts to align himself with King and his alleged commitment to colorblind justice came at an opportune moment for the president. Less than twenty-four hours prior, in a meeting in the Oval Office about immigration reform, Trump reportedly referred to Haiti, El Salvador, and African nations as "shithole countries." In response, many news anchors and columnists labeled Trump a "racist." "A Racist in the Oval Office," read a *New Yorker* headline the following morning; "No One Is Coming to Save Us from Trump's Racism," said another in the *New York Times*.[4]

The "shithole" incident was hardly the first, nor the last, time Trump broadcast his bigotry to the American public. In fact, white supremacy has proven the bedrock of his political philosophy. As real estate investors, Trump and his father were subjected to multiple discrimination lawsuits by black tenants. Furthermore, Trump's political career began as the leader of the "birther" movement. Sparked in 2008, the group insists Barack Obama's U.S. birth certificate is a forgery and that the former president was actually born in Kenya and therefore ineligible to serve as president of the United States. Trump kicked off his 2016 presidential bid by labeling Mexican immigrants as "rapists." He later questioned the objectivity of the federal judge hearing a lawsuit against the then candidate Trump because he is "a Mexican." In November 2017, during a ceremony honoring Navajo code talkers' contributions to U.S. military efforts in World War II, Trump referred, and not for the first time, to Senator Elizabeth Warren as "Pocahontas." He has also repeatedly made xenophobic claims about Muslims. Moreover, the "shithole" incident is not the first time Trump slandered Haitians and citizens of African nations. In June, he reportedly alleged that Haitians "all have AIDS," and groused that Nigerian immigrants would never "go back to their huts." In August 2017, after groups of neo-Nazis and other white supremacists rallied in Charlottesville, Virginia, and one man rammed a car into a crowd of counterprotesters in an act of terrorism that left one woman dead, the president refused to condemn the white nationalists, instead claiming that there was fault "on many sides" and insisting that there were "many fine people" among the white supremacists. And in July 2019, he told four Democratic congresswomen of color via Twitter to "go back" to the "totally broken and crime infested places from which they came."[5] "Trump moved racism," writes Ta-Nehisi Coates, "from the euphemistic and plausibly deniable to the overt and freely claimed."[6] The president's King proclamation, therefore, should be understood as little more than an effort to placate the most recent charges of bigotry. It is also not the first time a sitting president has used the King holiday to mollify accusations of prejudice. As this book has shown, since the 1980s, U.S. presidents have routinely invoked King's alleged colorblind dream to advocate a rigid colorblind approach to legislating matters of racial inequity.

Five days before Trump's King proclamation, Hollywood gathered at the Beverly Hilton Hotel in Los Angeles for the first major awards ceremony of 2018—the Golden Globes. Most actresses, and many actors, wore all black and pins that read "Time's Up" in protest of recent reports of rampant sexual harassment and assault by some of Hollywood's most influential men. That nineteen women, to date, have accused Trump of sexual misconduct was not lost on the Hollywood audience. The movie industry has, by and large, positioned itself strongly against the president—his enabling of white supremacists, his bigoted immigration policies, and his sexual assault allegations, in particular—since he took office. To that end, Meryl Streep devoted most of her Cecil B. DeMille Award speech in 2017 to the president's immigration policies. "Who are we?" Streep asked the audience, "and what is Hollywood anyway? . . . Hollywood is crawling with outsiders and foreigners, and if we kick them all out, you'll have nothing to watch but football and mixed martial arts, which are not the arts." The actress then expressed her disgust at Trump's mocking of a disabled reporter before concluding, "Tommy Lee Jones said to me, 'Isn't it such a privilege, Meryl, just to be an actor?' Yeah, it is, and we have to remind each other of the privilege and the responsibility of the act of empathy."[7]

Yet Hollywood's public disparaging of the president's racism rings hollow given the ongoing racial inequality within the industry itself. A 2017 analysis by Stacy L. Smith, Marc Choueiti, and Katherine Pieper of the top 100 grossing films of 2016 found that people of color constitute less than 30 percent of all roles, and only fourteen of the films have an actor of color in the lead role. In addition, twenty-five of the top 100 films have no black character, forty-four no Asian character, and a staggering fifty-four, more than half, no Latinx character—in a city that is nearly half Latinx.[8] The lack of representation of people of color on Hollywood movie screens extends beyond those films that perform well at the box office to those that compete for the industry's top awards. At the 2016 Academy Awards, there was, for the second year in a row, not a single actor of color *nominated* in an acting category, prompting the #OscarsSoWhite controversy. Given its continued racial trouble, one must question Hollywood's understanding and commitment to racial justice.

Looking even deeper into the history of race and Hollywood in recent years, one finds it even more difficult to place much faith in the antiracist politics Hollywood actors, directors, and producers claim to champion in the age of Trump. The colorblind aesthetics and genres Hollywood developed from the 1970s through the 1990s, which proved fundamental to the articulation and hegemonic rise of the racial ideology of colorblindness, remain essential elements of Hollywood's business model in the twenty-first century. The fictional boxing career of Sylvester Stallone's most successful character continues to find new audiences. *Rocky Balboa,* the sixth film in the *Rocky* franchise, premiered in 2006, and the spin-off franchise, *Creed,* based on the son of Apollo Creed, which, covertly fits into the *Rocky* franchise, debuted its sequel in 2018, three years after the premiere of the first *Creed* film. Moreover, sports movies like *Remember the Titans* (2000), *Coach Carter* (2005), *Glory Road* (2006), *The Express* (2008), *The Blind Side* (2009), *42* (2013), and *Race* (2015) continue to offer Hollywood audiences the sports field as a site for the production of colorblind racial unionism. Moreover, many of those films, like *Coach Carter* and *Glory Road,* combine the sports film genre with that of the teacher film. Others, like *42,* blend the sports genre with that of the historical colorblind genre, popularized in the 1980s in films like *Glory* and *The Long Walk Home.*

Historical colorblind dramas have also remained incredibly popular among Hollywood audiences and saw a resurgence during the Obama presidency. Movies like *The Help* (2011), *Lincoln* (2012), *Loving* (2016), and *Green Book* (2018) continue to restage black freedom struggles and to position colorblind white heroism as the driving force of black liberation. *Loving* depicts the story of Richard and Mildred Loving, whose interracial marriage eventually led to the dismantling of anti-miscegenation laws throughout the country. A film based on the true story of the Lovings makes sense within the contexts of Hollywood's enduring promotion of colorblindness and heterosexual marriage as reliable pathways to happiness and reconciliation, and the movie industry's much longer fascination with racial melodrama. Films like *Loving* continue to perform well at the box office and tend to make a splash at the big Hollywood awards shows, including the Oscars. Most recently, Peter Farrelly's *Green Book,* a colorblind civil rights drama about an interracial friendship, won the 2019 Academy Award for Best Picture.

Even as Hollywood directors have taken on more racially explicit subject matter in the twenty-first century, the results have proven underwhelming. While the 2004 film *Crash* gave audiences writer and director Paul Haggis's attempt to "bust liberals" and their naive proclamations of racial innocence, the movie ultimately removes all structural analysis from its interrogation of racism, thereby conflating prejudice with racism and leaving audiences with the notion that all people are both perpetrators and victims of racially bigoted language. Moreover, the film perpetuates Hollywood's and the nation's oldest stereotypes of black criminality.[9] In other words, the overwhelming evidence of Hollywood films in the years since the mid-1990s illuminates Hollywood's deep investment in the colorblind politics it helped to construct and that have been fundamental to the rearticulation of white supremacy in the post–civil rights era.

More recent efforts to explicitly address racial injustice have centered around the issue of police brutality and the #BlackLivesMatter movement. Films like *Blindspotting, Monsters and Men, The Hate U Give*, and *BlacKKKlansman*, all released in 2018, place white supremacy and police brutality at the center of the action. And yet as with *Crash*, the results underwhelm. As journalist Reggie Ugwu writes, *"The Hate U Give, Blindspotting, Monsters and Men* and *Black Panther* all answered the long-overdue demand for movies about the black experience by boldly grappling with one of its most pressing and painful dramas. But the films' common dependence on the tropes of superhero stories and revenge fantasies, whether explicit or in disguise, suggests the difficulty of making reality-based cinema out of the history we're currently living through."[10] While noble in intent, each of these films falls far short of the standard set by Spike Lee in his 1989 masterpiece, *Do the Right Thing*, which links Hollywood representations of blackness to the devaluation of black lives underlying the brutality poor black communities face at the hands of the police, and the state more generally.

There are, however, reasons for optimism. In the last several years, a number of black filmmakers have developed a new aesthetics of film that is deeply invested in contesting dehumanizing representations of blackness on popular movie screens while working within the aesthetic practices and generic expectations of Hollywood. I refer to this project as the "New Black Hollywood" school of filmmakers, which includes Ryan Coogler, Ava DuVernay, Steve McQueen, and Jordan Peele. Their films—which include *12 Years a Slave* (2012), *Selma* (2014), *Creed* (2015), *Get Out* (2017), *Black Panther* (2018), and *A Wrinkle in Time* (2018)—fundamentally disrupt Hollywood's essential function as a life source of white supremacy and aim to craft a new highly profitable and highly marketable black Hollywood aesthetics within the confines of established Hollywood genres: the historical drama, the superhero film, the horror film, and the sports film. Ava DuVernay's *Selma* dramatizes the civil rights struggle and violent resistance in Selma, Alabama, in 1964–65. Moreover, *Selma* offers the most significant representation of Martin Luther King Jr. on Hollywood movie screens to date. However, DuVernay's film makes a point to avoid images of the colorblind King. Instead, by setting the narrative *after* the "I Have a Dream" speech, DuVernay offers a representation of King and the civil rights movement that contests those presented by Hollywood over the past three decades. The King we see in *Selma* is not the one whose philosophy begins and ends on the steps of the Lincoln Memorial but one who tells a crowd, for example, "Who murdered Jimmy Lee Jackson? Every white lawman who abuses the law to terrorize. Who murdered Jimmy Lee Jackson? Every white politician who feeds on prejudice and hatred." *Selma* offers us not only a representation of King speaking to the needs of black communities in the age of mass incarceration but one that challenges the memory of King, and the civil rights movement more broadly, by acknowledging the essential role of Hollywood in its construction. In this regard, Steve McQueen's *12 Years a Slave* similarly uses the genre of the historical drama to rebuke Hollywood standards of slavery films by moving the white savior (played by Brad Pitt) to the margins and centering the physical, sexual, and psychological violence of the enslaved and the white supremacist ideology that informed the institution.

Even more promising, the films of Barry Jenkins distinguish him from the project of New Black Hollywood. Jenkins's movies mark a resurgence of black independent cinema that deliberately avoids Hollywood aesthetic practices and generic expectations and instead draws on the history of black independent filmmakers and artists who interrogate the category of blackness itself, and the essentialist notions that typically undergird it. As film scholar Michael Boyce Gillespie asks, "What if black film could be something other than embodied? What if black film was immaterial and bodiless? What if black film could be speculative or just ambivalent? What if film is ultimately the worst window imaginable and an even poorer mirror? What if black film is art and not the visual transcription of the black lifeworld?"[11] For Gillespie, black film is an art form, the assessment of which requires accounting for each film's "specific confluence of aesthetics of politics, history, and culture" in order to avoid the "paradigmatic crush of an essential blackness."[12] Jenkins's *Moonlight* won the 2017 Academy Award for Best Picture, only a year after the #OscarsSoWhite controversy. *Moonlight*, a film about a young black boy coming of age and coming to grips with his sexuality, is not only the most atypical, given the Academy's history, but the most racially significant film to ever win the Oscar for Best Picture.

While *Moonlight* took home the night's biggest award, albeit in shockingly dramatic fashion, the heavy favorite for Best Picture was *La La Land*, a nearly all-white classical Hollywood-style musical brimming with nostalgia. The *Moonlight* versus *La La Land* drama highlights the tension between competing impulses in contemporary Hollywood. *La La Land* overwhelms its audience with references to Hollywood classics like *Singin' in the Rain*, *Casablanca*, *An American in Paris*, and *Funny Face*. *La La Land*, like the films it references, "cheer[s] us up," as one reviewer put it.[13] In that sense, the film is not unlike the 1980s cover band featured in the pool party scene of the movie, indulging its audience with selections from a bygone era's greatest hits. *La La Land* incorporates all the tropes of classical Hollywood musicals—singing, dancing, stardom, love, heartbreak, and unapologetic white heteronormativity. *La La Land* shows contemporary audiences what nearly a century ago earned Hollywood the nickname "the Dream Factory."

Moonlight, on the other hand, explores the life of a young black boy living in the Liberty City neighborhood of Miami and wrestling with his sexuality. Adapted from a play by Tarell Alvin McCraney, the film challenges Hollywood notions of which identities and whose lives are worthy of the silver screen. The film's strengths abound. The virtual absence of white people, for example, enables the value of the black characters' lives to stand on their own, rather than be co-opted by colorblind white heroism (as Hollywood dramas about black struggle almost always do). Yet *Moonlight* is far more than just a movie about black people that does not rely on heroic white saviors; it's a work of heartbreaking beauty that evokes a long lineage of black independent filmmakers, including Julie Dash, Charles Burnett, Marlon Riggs, and Isaac Julien.

Moonlight is what scholar Robin D. G. Kelley might call a "freedom dream," the ethos at the center of "the black radical imagination," which, as he once explained, "refer[s] to the ways in which Black Leftists, some nationalists, feminists, surrealists, etc., envisioned collectively, in struggle, what a revolutionary future might look like and how we might bring this new world into being."[14] The masterpiece is a rare work of art that dreams boldly. By placing a narrative of black queerness at the center of the frame, Jenkins's sophisticated film imparts value in lives so thoroughly dehumanized in our society, thereby opening up space to dream of their liberation. Jenkins's project, therefore, which continues with his recent adaptation of James Baldwin's novel of the same name, *If Beale Street Could Talk*, is less interested in the racial politics of the New Black Hollywood and instead concerned with, as Stuart Hall writes, how "popular culture is not at all . . . the arena where we find who we really are, the truth of our experience. It is an arena that is *profoundly* mythic. It is a theatre of popular desires, a theatre of popular fantasies. It is where we discover and play with the identifications of ourselves, where we are imagined, where we are represented, not only to the audiences out there who do not get the message, but to ourselves for the first time."[15] Or, as Gillespie writes, the manner in which blackness "is always a question, never an answer."[16]

To return to President Trump, while it may appear that the Trump presidency marks the end of the age of colorblindness, it certainly is difficult to see how Hollywood will live up to its recent promises to lead a movement for racial justice. Moreover, while Trump's explicit white supremacy certainly marks a new phase of political discourse, as the history of colorblindness shows, white supremacy has functioned quite effectively through racially coded dog whistles over the last five decades. Trumpism, therefore, marks not a departure but a removal of the thin veil of political rhetorical standards of respect, a bubbling up, or eruption, of the coded discourses that have percolated just below the surface. That Trump, like Ronald Reagan, the man who brought colorblindness to the Oval Office, found considerable success in Hollywood before launching his political career is no coincidence. It also begs the question of whether, despite their public disagreements, Hollywood and the Trump administration, along with its supporters, stand in as stark a contrast as many Hollywood stars wish to believe. As the history of colorblindness and Hollywood's essential role in it illustrate, Hollywood's persistent inability to integrate the industry puts it more in alignment with the white supremacist politics of Donald Trump than those who work in the business realize or care to admit. Ultimately, if Hollywood is to participate in the resistance to Trump's white supremacist politics and contribute more generally toward racial justice, such efforts will not be led by Meryl Streep, Peter Farrelly, or other white Hollywood liberals, but by Ava DuVernay, Jordan Peele, Ryan Coogler, and, perhaps most importantly, Barry Jenkins.

Notes

Introduction

1. Haney López, *Dog Whistle Politics*, 79–81.
2. For more on the history of affirmative action opposition, see Anderson, *Pursuit of Fairness*, chap. 4; Deslippe, *Protesting Affirmative Action*. For anti-busing protests, see Delmont, *Why Busing Failed*, HoSang, *Racial Propositions*, chap. 4; Formisano, *Boston against Busing*.
3. Formisano, *Boston against Busing*, 141, 151–52.
4. Wiegman, "'My Name Is Forrest, Forrest Gump,'" 230.
5. For more on the history of individual versus systemic approaches to scholarly analyses of racism, see Leah Gordon, *From Power to Prejudice*.
6. Guerrero, *Framing Blackness*, 2.
7. Jhally, dir., *Stuart Hall*.
8. Fusco, "Racial Time, Racial Marks, Racial Metaphors."
9. Barthes, *Mythologies*, 129.
10. Barthes, *Mythologies*, 131.
11. Wright, *Six Guns and Society*, 12.
12. Wright, *Six Guns and Society*, 12.
13. See Haney López, *Dog Whistle Politics*; Haney López, *White by Law*; Bonilla-Silva, *Racism without Racists*; Michelle Alexander, *New Jim Crow*.
14. See Lassiter, *Silent Majority*; Kruse, *White Flight*.
15. Nilsen and Turner, *Colorblind Screen*; Squires, *Post-Racial Mystique*.
16. Lipsitz, *Possessive Investment in Whiteness*.
17. Omi and Winant, *Racial Formation in the United States*, 55–56.
18. Hall, "On Postmodernism and Articulation," 141.
19. Hall, "Gramsci's Relevance for the Study of Race and Ethnicity," 431.
20. Hall, "Gramsci's Relevance for the Study of Race and Ethnicity," 431.
21. Ryan and Kellner, *Camera Politica*, 12–13.
22. Rogin, "'Sword Became a Flashing Vision,'" 151.

Chapter 1

1. For more on the legal history of colorblindness, see Haney López, *White by Law*, chap. 8; Brown et al., *Whitewashing Race*, 1–34.
2. Ture and Hamilton, *Black Power: The politics of Liberation*, 54.
3. Graham, "High Court Lets Hiring Plan Stand," *New York Times*, October 13, 1971.

4. See, for example, Philip Gass's letter in response to David Simpson, *New York Times*, August 6, 1972.

5. "Cleaver Arrives for Algiers Fete," *Reuters*, July 15, 1969.

6. "Busing Foes Cite High Court Ruling," *New York Times*, October 14, 1970.

7. "Color-Blind Regime Vowed by Governor of South Carolina," *New York Times*, January 20, 1971.

8. "Letters to the Editor," *New York Times*, July 10, 1972.

9. "Racism of Quotas," *New York Times*, March 14, 1969.

10. Although affirmative action programs benefited many groups other than African Americans, including white women, opponents to such programs almost exclusively cite blacks as the beneficiaries of these programs.

11. For an overview of the 1970s, see Borstelman, *The 1970s*; Schulman, *The Seventies*; Berkowitz, *Something Happened*.

12. See Joseph, *Waiting 'til the Midnight Hour*; Bloom and Martin, *Black against Empire*; Carmichael and Hamilton, *Black Power*; Ongiri, *Spectacular Blackness*.

13. Schatz, "The New Hollywood," 8–36.

14. Guerrero, *Framing Blackness*, 69–70.

15. Biskind, *Easy Riders, Raging Bulls*, 17.

16. Nystrom, *Hard Hats, Rednecks, and Macho Men*, 27.

17. See, for example, Ross, "How Hollywood Became Hollywood," 255–76.

18. Hoberman, *Dream Life*, 330–31; Roger Ebert, "Review: *Dirty Harry*," *Chicago Sun Times*, January 1, 1971, www.rogerebert.com/reviews/dirty-harry-1971. For a complete discussion of the reviews criticizing the racism of the film upon its release, see McGilligan, *Clint: The Life and Legend*.

19. Ongiri, *Spectacular Blackness*, chap. 5; Guerrero, *Framing Blackness*, chap. 3; Bogle, *Toms, Coons, Mulattoes*, chap. 8; Robinson, "Blaxploitation and the Misrepresentation of Liberation."

20. For more on the New Left, see Gitlin, *The Sixties*; Perlstein, *Nixonland*.

21. See McGilligan, *Clint*, 211.

22. Johnson and Ossei-Owusu, "'From Fillmore to No More,'" 75–92. See also Jackson and Jones, "Remember the Fillmore," 57–74.

23. *Joe*, directed by John Avildsen, 1970.

24. For more on *Joe*, see Nystrom, *Hard Hats*, chap. 1.

25. For more on the progressive politics of San Francisco in the late nineteenth century, see Walker, "San Francisco's Haymarket." For more on the counterculture revolution in San Francisco in the 1960s, see Gitlin, *The Sixties*. For a history of queer San Francisco prior to the 1960s, see Boyd, *Wide Open City*.

26. For more on the history of San Francisco's Potrero Hill neighborhood, see Brechin, *Imperial San Francisco*, chap. 3.

27. Oscar Lewis originally developed the "culture of poverty" thesis in his work on Latin America. The Moynihan Report and Charles A. Murray's *Losing Ground* are the two most prominent texts that applied the thesis to America's urban black poor in the 1960s and 1970s. For a more thorough discussion of these works and the emergence of the "culture of poverty" thesis, see Wilson, *The Truly Disadvantaged*, 13–18; Roberts, *Killing the Black Body*, 8.

28. The final version of the script is dated February 8, 1971. Margaret Herrick Library, Los Angeles, CA.

29. This early draft of the script is dated only "1971." The final script is dated February 8, 1971. Therefore, this draft must have been written sometime between January 1, 1971, and February 7, 1971. Both scripts are housed at the Margaret Herrick Library in Los Angeles, CA.

30. Early *Dirty Harry* script draft, 1971.

31. Baldwin, *The Cross of Redemption: Uncollected Writings*, 225

32. Guerrero, *Framing Blackness*, 127.

33. For more on the police and the 1960s, see Sugrue, *Sweet Land of Liberty*; Bloom and Martin, *Black against Empire*; O'Reilly, *Racial Matters*; Perlstein, *Nixonland*; Gitlin, *The Sixties*.

34. For an overview of civil rights history, see Branch, *Parting the Waters*; Branch, *Pillar of Fire*; and Branch, *At Canaan's Edge*.

35. *Bullitt*, directed by Peter Yates, 1968.

36. Leva, dir., *Dirty Harry*.

37. Leva, dir., *Dirty Harry*.

38. Smith, *Clint Eastwood*, 92.

39. While reading aloud Scorpio's ransom letter projected on his office wall, the mayor cannot bring himself to vocalize the word "nigger," written in the document.

40. Kevin Phillips, a strategist for Richard Nixon during his 1968 presidential campaign, was a key architect of Nixon's Southern Strategy, which sought to exploit racism among southern whites to win their votes for the Republicans. Phillips predicted the drastic political realignment of the south in his book, *The Emerging Republican Majority*. For more on Phillips and Nixon's Southern Strategy and "law and order" campaign, see Lassiter, *Silent Majority*, chaps. 9 and 10; Schulman, *The Seventies*, 35–42, 107–8; Perlstein, *Nixonland*, 277, 366.

41. Leva, dir., *Dirty Harry*.

42. See Smith, *Clint Eastwood*.

43. Whitfield, *Culture of the Cold War*, 35.

44. An early version of the script, dated only "1971" (the year of the film's release), sets the action in New York City.

45. Hoberman, *Dream Life*, 325.

46. For more on the Western genre, see Slotkin, *Gunfighter Nation*.

47. Quoted in Perlstein, *Nixonland*, 567.

48. Zinnemann, dir., *High Noon*.

49. Slotkin, *Gunfighter Nation*, 396. The standard leftist reading of the film is that of an allegory of Hollywood's surrender to McCarthyism. This reading is in line with the intentions of the film's screenwriter, Carl Foreman. The conservative reading that Sloktin offers is one in which "the new aggressions of totalitarian Communism represent a 'return' of totalitarian Fascism." See Slotkin, *Gunfighter Nation*, 391–96.

50. Guerrero, *Framing Blackness*, 94. For more on blaxploitation, see Bogle, *Toms, Coons, Mulattoes*, chap. 8; Ongiri, *Spectacular Blackness*, chap. 5; Robinson, "Blaxploitation and the Misrepresentation," 1–12.

51. Guerrero, *Framing Blackness*, 69–70.

52. Ongiri, *Spectacular Blackness*, 165–66.

53. Huey P. Newton, "He Won't Bleed Me," *Black Panther*, January 19, 1971, A, L.

54. "Blaxploitation," *Black Panther*, October 7, 1972, 7–9.

55. Bobby Seale, *Black Panther*, September 27, 1972, 11.

56. Seale, *Black Panther*, September 27, 1972, 11.

57. Robinson, "Blaxploitation and the Misrepresentation," 5.

58. *Black Panther*, September 27, 1972.

59. For more on *Coffy*, see Simms, *Women of Blaxploitation*; Quinn, "From Oppositional Readers to Positional Producers," 266–86.

60. Guerrero, *Framing Blackness*, 94. "Copycat" *Shaft* films include *Super Fly* (1972), *Across 110th Street* (1972), *Black Cesar* (1973), and *Cleopatra Jones* (1973).

61. Guerrero, *Framing Blackness*, 98–100.

62. Inness, *Tough Girls*.

63. Bogle, *Brown Sugar*, 194.

64. Ongiri, *Spectacular Blackness*, 173.

65. Newton, "He Won't Bleed Me," B.

66. Robinson, "Blaxploitation and the Misrepresentation," 5–6.

67. Newton, "He Won't Bleed Me," B.

68. Robinson, "Blaxploitation and the Misrepresentation," 5, 11. For a more complete analysis of the gender politics of the blaxploitation genre, see Ongiri, *Spectacular Blackness*, chap. 5.

69. Ongiri, *Spectacular Blackness*, 185.

70. Bogle, *Toms, Coons, Mulattoes*, 231.

71. For a more complete discussion of vigilante women protagonists in blaxploitation, see Robinson, "Blaxploitation and the Misrepresentation"; Bogle, *Toms, Coons, Mulattoes*, chap. 8.

72. Lipsitz, *Possessive Investment in Whiteness*, viii.

73. Three white men murdered an African American man named James Byrd on June 7, 1998. The men tied Byrd to the back of a pickup truck and dragged him over four miles.

74. See the James Raker Papers, Margaret Herrick Library, Los Angeles, CA.

75. "Seale—Open Up Government," *Oakland Tribune*, March 21, 1973, 34.

76. Schneider, *Smack*, xiv.

77. Because the United States has no real domestic poppy production, drug traffickers must import heroin. Therefore, the drug is found primarily in cities, where there are markets big enough to entice dealers to import large quantities of the drug.

78. Schneider, *Smack*, 115. See also Tabor, *Capitalism Plus Dope Equals Genocide*, 1, www.marxists.org/history/usa/workers/black-panthers/1970/dope.htm.

79. For a complete discussion of heroin, see Schneider, *Smack*.

80. Tabor, *Capitalism Plus Dope Equals Genocide*, 2.

81. See Schneider, *Smack*, chap. 8.

82. Tabor, *Capitalism Plus Dope Equals Genocide*, 1.

83. Carmichael and Hamilton, *Black Power*, 35.

84. Carmichael and Hamilton, *Black Power*, 44–46.

85. Bloom and Martin, *Black against Empire*, 71.

86. Carmichael and Hamilton, *Black Power*, 41; Bloom and Martin, *Black against Empire*, 13–15.

Chapter 2

1. "Four-Yr.-Struggle behind Filming of Black Comedy-Drama *Claudine*," *Variety*, April 15, 1974, 5.

2. Joan L. Cohen, Program, *International Women Filmmakers*, February 12, 1973; "Bootstrap Project in Heart of Harlem," *Los Angeles Times*, September 15, 1973, 7.

3. Linda Gross, "Woman Producer: She Battles for Minorities," *Los Angeles Times*, July 18, 1977, F14; David Oestriecher, "Bootstrap Project in Heart of Harlem," 7.

4. Cook, *Lost Illusions*, 1.

5. For more on the New Hollywood of the 1970s, see Cook, *Lost Illusions*; Biskind, *Easy Riders, Raging Bulls*.

6. Gross, "Woman Producer," F14; "Bootstrap Project in Heart of Harlem," 7.

7. Blumenthal, "John Berry, 82, Stage and Film Director Who Exiled Himself during Blacklisting of 1950's," *New York Times*, December 1, 1999, www.nytimes.com /1999/12/01/arts/john-berry-82-stage-film-director-who-exiled-himself-during -blacklisting-1950-s.html.

8. "Bootstrap Project in Heart of Harlem," 7.

9. Gordon Armstrong, "*Claudine:* Announcement Story," 20th Century Fox, 1974, Margaret Herrick Library.

10. For more on the LA Rebellion, see Field and Horak, *L.A. Rebellion*.

11. Alexander, *New Jim Crow*, chap. 1.

12. "Bootstrap Project in Heart of Harlem," 7.

13. Alan R. Howard, "Movie Review: *Claudine*," *Hollywood Reporter*, April 5, 1974, 22.

14. Untitled *Claudine* review, *Playboy*, June 1974.

15. Carmichael and Hamilton, *Black Power*, 43.

16. For an example, see "Welfare or 'Workfare,'" *Black Panther*, December 7, 1972; "Winston-Salem Welfare Moms 'Bugged,'" *Black Panther*.

17. "From the Mouth of Reagan," *Black Panther*, September 1972.

18. "Oakland—a Base of Operation! Part XXIII: Our Challenge for 1973," *Black Panther*, December 30, 1972.

19. Kelley, *Yo Mama's DysFUNKtional!*, 18.

20. Lubiano, "Black Ladies, Welfare Queens, and State Minstrels," 337; Roberts, *Killing the Black Body*, 207.

21. Bezusko, "Criminalizing Black Motherhood," 42–44; Sugrue, *Sweet Land of Liberty*, 524–31.

22. Nadasen, Mittelstadt, and Chappell, *Welfare in the United States*, 30.

23. Nadasen, Mittelstadt, and Chappell, *Welfare in the United States*, 46.

24. Weiler, "News of the Screen," *New York Times*, July 8, 1973. Years later, Jones would describe the experience of making the film as "one of my best movie experiences ever."

25. Armstrong, "*Claudine:* Announcement Story."

26. Untitled *Claudine* review, *New Republic*, May 25, 1974.

27. Untitled *Claudine* review, *Product Digest*, May 8, 1974.

28. Guerrero, *Framing Blackness*, 105.

Chapter 3

1. Anderson, *Pursuit of Fairness*, chap. 4.

2. By "bigot" I mean someone who holds personal animosity or hatred toward another group, particularly one defined by race, or believes someone to be inferior simply because of the person's membership in a particular racial group.

3. For more on the history of neoliberal thought, see Burgin, *Great Persuasion*; Jones, *Masters of the Universe*. For more on the rise of neoliberal politics in the United States, see Stein, *Pivotal Decade*.

4. Lipman, "Landscape of Education 'Reform' in Chicago," 4–5.

5. Lipsitz, "Introduction: A New Beginning," 11.

6. See Haney López, *Dog Whistle Politics*, 29–33.

7. See, most notably, Lipman, *New Political Economy of Urban Education*, 12.

8. Pierce, *Racing for Innocence*, 21. See also Delmont, *Why Busing Failed*, chap. 8.

9. Lipsitz, *Possessive Investment in Whiteness*, vii.

10. See, for example, Cowie, *Stayin' Alive*, 334–37; Biskind, "Blue Collar Blues."

11. Herbert, "Impossible, Ridiculous, Repugnant," *New York Times*, October 6, 2005.

12. Haney López, *Dog Whistle Politics*, 24.

13. Haney López, *Dog Whistle Politics*, 23.

14. Edsall and Edsall, *Chain Reaction*, 129.

15. Formisano, *Boston against Busing*, 75.

16. Formisano, *Boston against Busing*, 80.

17. Formisano, *Boston against Busing*, 150.

18. Formisano, *Boston against Busing*, 150.

19. Delmont, *Why Busing Failed*, 3.

20. Delmont, *Why Busing Failed*, 49–53.

21. Raskin, *Overruling Democracy*, chap. 4.

22. Delmont, *Why Busing Failed*, 21. For a more detailed critique of the "backlash" thesis, see Haney López, *Dog Whistle Politics*, 31–33.

23. For more on California's antibusing initiatives, see HoSang, *Racial Propositions*, chap. 4.

24. Rubio, *A History of Affirmative Action*, 144; Anderson, *Pursuit of Fairness*, 64.

25. Patterson, *Freedom Is Not Enough*, 1; Anderson, *Pursuit of Fairness*, 92.

26. The report chastised the federal government's racist housing and education, concluding, "Our nation is moving toward two societies, one black, one white—separate and unequal."

27. Rubio, *History of Affirmative Action*, 152–53; Anderson, *Pursuit of Fairness*, 108–43.

28. Deslippe, *Protesting Affirmative Action*, chap. 3.

29. Skrentny, *Ironies of Affirmative Action*, 167–71.

30. See Anderson, *Pursuit of Fairness*, chap. 2.

31. The University of Washington agreed to admit DeFunis until the courts decided his case. By the time it reached the Supreme Court, DeFunis was about to graduate, therefore making the case moot in the court's opinion. For a complete history of the DeFunis case, see Deslippe, *Protesting Affirmative Action*, chap. 4.

32. Lassiter, *Silent Majority*, 3.

33. Lassiter, "Suburban Origins of Color-Blind Conservatism," 549–82.

34. Lassiter, "Suburban Origins of Color-Blind Conservatism," 580.

35. Lassiter, "Suburban Origins of Color-Blind Conservatism," 152.

36. "No Policy for School Integration," *New York Times*, October 13, 1974.

37. "Letters to the Editor," *New York Times*, October 28, 1974.

38. Formisano, *Boston against Busing*, 141, 151–52.

39. For example, a man named Phillip Gass wrote to the *New York Times* in 1972 arguing this point. "Letters to the Editor: Toward Colorblind Politics," *New York Times*, August 6, 1972. More nuanced arguments, such as that of William Julius Wilson, who opposed affirmative action on the basis that the program helped only the black middle class, thereby neglecting the black urban "underclass" or the "truly disadvantaged," also received little public attention amid the vitriolic opposition to affirmative action of any sort. See Wilson, *Truly Disadvantaged*, 110–20.

40. Oster, "Growing Debate: Discrimination—Has it Gone Too Far?," *U.S. News and World Report*, March 29, 1976.

41. George Will, "Civil Rights: Principles and Confusion," *Washington Post*, November 18, 1976.

42. Howard A. E. Dick, "The High-Court's Road in the Bakke Case," *Washington Post*, October 9, 1977.

43. George Will, "Freedom and the Busing Quagmire," *Newsweek*, July 12, 1976.

44. Will, "Freedom and the Busing Quagmire."

45. Will, "Civil Rights: Principles and Confusion," A19.

46. For more on this, see Raskin, *Overruling Democracy*, 76–82.

47. *Village of Arlington Heights v. Metropolitan Housing Development Corp.* (1977) involved a Chicago development corporation that wanted to build subsidized housing in a predominantly white suburb with zoning laws prohibiting multiple-family dwellings. When the city council refused to rezone the proposed site, the developer and several individuals sued, claiming that because blacks constituted 40 percent of the Chicago-area residents eligible for subsidized housing, the city's refusal discriminated against them. A district court sided with the developer, ruling that although the city's rezoning refusal was not deliberately racist, it nonetheless discriminated against African Americans.

48. George Will, "Common Sense on Race," *Newsweek*, January 24, 1977.

49. For more on the *Bakke* case, see Anderson, *Pursuit of Fairness*, 150–55; Pierce, *Racing for Innocence*, 19–22.

50. Cowie, *Stayin' Alive*, 328.

51. Cowie, *Stayin' Alive*, 328.

52. Zirin, *What's My Name, Fool?*, 55.

53. Zirin, *What's My Name, Fool?*, 56.

54. Zirin, *What's My Name, Fool?*, 58.

55. Zirin, *What's My Name, Fool?*, 62.

56. Jacobson, *Roots Too*, 7.

57. Jacobson, *Roots Too*, 9.

58. Jacobson, *Roots Too*, 101.

59. Pierce, *Racing for Innocence*, 22.

60. Cowie, *Stayin' Alive*, 328.

61. Cowie, *Stayin' Alive*, 329.

62. Cowie, *Stayin' Alive*, 329.

63. Canby, "Review: Rocky (1976)," *New York Times*, November 22, 1976; Gallantz, "Critical Dialogue: Rocky's Racism," 191; Biskind and Ehrenreich, "Machismo and Hollywood's Working Class."

64. See Edsall and Edsall, *Chain Reaction*; Deslippe, *Protesting Affirmative Action*; Kruse, *White Flight*; Formisano, *Boston against Busing*; Lassiter, *Silent Majority*.

65. George Will, "Sears Non-Rebellion," *Newsweek*, February 19, 1979.

66. Harvey, *Brief History of Neoliberalism*, 2.

67. Hall, "The Neo-Liberal Revolution," 706.

68. See Wacquant, "Three Steps to a Historical Anthropology," 71; Lipman, *New Political Economy of Urban Education*; Melamed, *Represent and Destroy*.

69. Hardin, "Finding the 'Neo' in Neoliberalism," 214.

70. Brown, *Undoing the Demos*, 17.

71. Brown, *Undoing the Demos*, 24–26.

72. Giroux, "Terror of Neoliberalism," 2.

73. Giroux, "Terror of Neoliberalism," 14.

74. Harvey, *Brief History of Neoliberalism*, 160–65.

75. Peck, *Constructions of Neoliberal Reason*, 4.

76. Peck, *Constructions of Neoliberal Reason*, 9.

77. Omi and Winant, *Racial Formation in the United States*, 213.

78. Williams, *Capitalism and Slavery*; Robinson, *Black Marxism*.

79. Lipman, "Landscape of Education 'Reform'"; Lipsitz, "Introduction: A New Beginning."

80. Lipman, *New Political Economy of Urban Education*, 12.

81. Friedman, *Capitalism and Freedom*, 108.

82. Burgin, *Great Persuasion*, 202.

83. Goldwater, *Conscience of a Conservative*, 20.

84. Friedman, *Capitalism and Freedom*, 110.

85. Friedman, "Created Equal."

86. Harvey, *Brief History of Neoliberalism*, 37.

87. Friedman and Friedman, *Free to Choose*, 110.

88. Friedman and Friedman, *Free to Choose*, 110.

89. Sowell, *Markets and Minorities*, 87.

90. Sowell, *Markets and Minorities*, 87.

91. Sowell, "Stereotypes versus the Market," 264.

92. Roithmayr, *Reproducing Racism*, 29.

93. Roithmayr, *Reproducing Racism*, 30.

94. Roithmayr, *Reproducing Racism*, 35–37. See also chap. 3.

95. Milton Friedman, "Whose Intolerance?," *Newsweek*, October 6, 1975.

96. Milton Friedman, "Bureaucracy Scorned," *Newsweek*, December 29, 1975.

97. Harvey, *Brief History of Neoliberalism*, 5.

98. Harvey, *Brief History of Neoliberalism*, 41–42.

99. Gordon, *From Power to Prejudice*, 3.

100. Rodgers, *Age of Fracture*, 133.

101. Rodgers, *Age of Fracture*, 134.

102. Rodgers, *Age of Fracture*, 136–37.

103. Will, "Common Sense on Race."

104. For more on the decline of unions in the 1970s, see Cowie, *Stayin' Alive*; Cowie, "'Vigorously Left, Right, and Center,'" 75–106; Lichtenstein, *State of the Union*, chap. 4; Stein, *Pivotal Decade*; Stein, *Running Steel, Running America*, chaps. 7–11.

105. See Schulman, *The Seventies*, chap. 4.

106. See Lichtenstein, *State of the Union*, chap. 4.

107. For more on the liberal opposition to affirmative action, see Deslippe, *Protesting Affirmative Action*, chap. 2.

108. Deslippe, *Protesting Affirmative Action*, 48.

109. *Blue Collar* script, Universal Pictures. This early version of the *Blue Collar* script is dated May 10, 1978, at the Margaret Herrick Library in Los Angeles, CA.

110. Knight, "Review: *Blue Collar*," April 1978.

111. Tom Wolfe characterized the 1970s as the "Me Decade" in the August 23, 1976, cover story of *New York* magazine. The moniker refers to, in Wolfe's estimation, the replacement of the communal New Deal progressivism of previous decades with a self-centered me-first, take-the-money-and-run American ethos in the 1970s.

112. Frank Capra's "everyman" in films like *Mr. Smith Goes to Washington* (1939) is a hallmark example.

113. Schulman, *The Seventies*, 145.

114. Norman Mailer, "Mailer on the '70s—Decade of 'Image, Skin Flicks, and Porn,'" *U.S. News and World Report*, December 10, 1979, 57. Quoted in Schulman, *The Seventies*, 145.

115. Hall, *Representation*, 26. This is what Hall refers to as the "constructionist" theory of representation, as opposed to the "reflective" and "intentional" ones, which Hall contests. For more, see Hall, *Representations*, chap. 1.

Chapter 4

1. Anderson, "Strange Career of Affirmative Action," 122–23.

2. Bostdorff and Goldzwig, "History, Collective Memory, and the Appropriation of Martin Luther King, Jr.," 662, 667.

3. Haney López, *Dog Whistle Politics*, ix.

4. Rawls, "Reagan Provides More Aid for Investigation in Atlanta," *New York Times*, March 14, 1981.

5. Anderson, *Pursuit of Fairness*, 155–57.

6. Berger, Opinion of the Court, Fullilove v. Klutznick, 78 U.S. 1007 (1980).

7. Detlefsen, *Civil Rights under Reagan*, 10.

8. Detlefsen, *Civil Rights under Reagan*, 2.

9. See Troy, *Morning in America*, 94, 184–85; Wilentz, *Age of Reagan*, 181–82; O'Reilly, *Nixon's Piano*, 362–64.

10. Patterson, *Restless Giant*, 174.

11. Wilentz, *Age of Reagan*, 188.

12. Wilentz, *Age of Reagan*, 187–88.

13. Wilentz, *Age of Reagan*, 188.

14. Bostdorff and Goldzwig, "History, Collective Memory, and the Appropriation of Martin Luther King, Jr.," 662, 667. While this was not an overnight process, Reagan implemented these personnel changes and imposed his civil rights mandate with a swiftness not typically associated with the federal government. By the Fall of Reagan's first year in office, he had successfully divided the three federal agencies—Justice Department, Labor Department, and the Equal Employment Opportunity Commission (EEOC)—charged with enforcing civil rights laws over their approach to affirmative action. Reagan's first target was the Justice Department, which, by November, had come to oppose any affirmative action program that used numerical goals and timetables for hiring women and people of color. By December 1981, the Justice Department was pushing more forcefully to impose its opposition onto the entire federal government.

15. Robert Pear, "U.S. Agencies Vary on Rights Policy," *New York Times*, November 16, 1981, A1, A16.

16. Pear, "U.S. Agencies Vary on Rights Policy," A1, A16.

17. Pear, "U.S. Agencies Vary on Rights Policy," A1, A16.

18. Robert Pear, "Rights Policy: New Outlook," *New York Times*, December 14, 1981, A21.

19. Pear, "Rights Policy: New Outlook," A21.

20. Conyers, "Justice Dept.'s 'Color-Blind' Policy: Affirmative Action Is Being Attacked Because It Works," *Los Angeles Times*, May 15, 1983, G5.

21. Detlefsen, *Civil Rights under Reagan*, 11.

22. "Equality: A Chill in the Air," *Los Angeles Times*, January 11, 1982, A10.

23. "Equality: A Chill in the Air," A10.

24. O'Reilly, *Nixon's Piano*, 378; Edsall and Edsall, chap. 9.

25. "Two Reagan Policies Assailed," *New York Times*, February 23, 1982, A17.

26. Sheila Rule, "Study Accuses Justice Department of Waging Attack on Civil Rights Laws," *New York Times*, February 24, 1982, B20.

27. "Reagan Civil Rights Policies Are Defended and Criticized," *New York Times*, May 30, 1983, 1, 6.

28. Stuart Taylor, "'Color-Blind' Rights Law," *New York Times*, March 10, 1982, B8.

29. Robert E. Taylor, "Race and Regulation: Reagan Seeks to Better Relations," *Wall Street Journal*, July 28, 1982, 42.

30. Wilentz, *Age of Reagan*, 181; O'Reilly, *Nixon's Piano*, 369; Laham, *Reagan Presidency and the Politics of Race*, chap. 7.

31. Taylor, "Race and Regulation," 42.

32. Taylor, "Race and Regulation," 42.

33. Taylor, "Race and Regulation," 42.

34. Taylor, "Race and Regulation," 42.

35. Robert Pear, "Rights Panel Calls for 'Summit,'" *New York Times*, September 15, 1982, A16.

36. "Flak on Civil Rights," *Wall Street Journal*, September 20, 1982, 30.

37. "Flak on Civil Rights," 30.

38. Edwin Yonder, "Racial Favoritism Only Prolongs Injustice," *Los Angeles Times*, May 15, 1983, G5.

39. "Rights Official Says Race-Based Policies Are 'Morally Wrong,'" *New York Times*, April 30, 1983, 1, 7.

40. "Rights Official Assails Hiring Quotas, Mandatory Busing," *Los Angeles Times*, April 30, 1983, A5.

41. "Reagan Civil Rights Policies Are Defended and Criticized," *New York Times*, May 30, 1983, 1, 6.

42. Robert Pear, "Commission Intends to Reassess Rights," *New York Times*, January 8, 1984, A4.

43. "Panel Blasts Reagan Policy on Job Quotas," *Los Angeles Times*, June 26, 1984, A2.

44. Pear, "Commission Intends to Reassess Rights," A4.

45. Lee May, "Justice Aide Faults Racial Hiring Quotas," *Los Angeles Times*, September 13, 1983, B5.

46. May, "Justice Aide Faults Racial Hiring Quotas," B5.

47. Robert Pear, "Reagan's Rights Stance Called Akin to King's," *New York Times*, September 13, 1983, B17.

48. Lindsey Gruson, "Survey Finds 73% Oppose Racial Quotas in Hiring," *New York Times*, September 25, 1983, A29, www.nytimes.com/1983/09/25/us/survey-finds-73-oppose-racial-quotas-in-hiring.html.

49. Hodding Carter, "When Will Reagan Do Something *for* Minorities?" *Wall Street Journal*, June 2, 1983, 31.

50. Gruson, "Survey Finds 73% Oppose Racial Quotas in Hiring," A29.

51. Robert Pear, "Just How Fair Is Affirmative Action?," *New York Times*, December 11, 1983, E4.

52. "Administration Is Hoping to Force Court to Confront Racial Quotas," *New York Times*, December 5, 1983.

53. "Affirmative Action Is under Fire," *Los Angeles Times*, December 13, 1983, C6.

54. "Affirmative Action Is under Fire," C6.

55. "An Attack without Foundation," *Los Angeles Times*, June 15, 1984, D6.

56. Ann Mariano, "Rights Official Sees No U.S. Role in Integrated Housing," *Washington Post*, July 11, 1984, B1.

57. "The Undermining of Civil Rights," *Los Angeles Times*, July 15, 1984, D4.

58. Troy, *Morning in America*, 97.

59. Diane Camper, "The Reagan Race Phonograph," *New York Times*, July 6, 1984, A22.

60. López, *Dog Whistle Politics*, 58.

61. Alexander, *New Jim Crow*, 48.

62. López, *Dog Whistle Politics*, 59.

63. Alexander, *New Jim Crow*, 48.

64. Alexander, *New Jim Crow*, 199.

65. Reinarman and Levine, "Crack Attack," 19.

66. Reinarman and Levine, "Crack Attack," 19.

67. Reeves and Campbell, *Cracked Coverage*, 3.

68. Reeves and Campbell, *Cracked Coverage*, 18.

69. Reeves and Campbell, *Cracked Coverage*, 160.

70. Reeves and Campbell, *Cracked Coverage*, 98.

71. Reeves and Campbell, *Cracked Coverage*, 73.

72. See Bederman, *Manliness and Civilization*, chap. 1.

73. Reeves and Campbell, *Cracked Coverage*, 100.

74. Riggs, *Color Adjustment*; quoted in Reeves and Campbell, *Cracked Coverage*, 100.

75. Gray, "Remembering Civil Rights," 353.

76. Hodding Carter, "The U.S. Has Yet to Expunge the Stain of Racism," *Wall Street Journal*, April 26, 1984.

77. Philip Hager, "Justice Official Denounces Racial Quotas"; see also "Approach Called 'Colorblind,'" *New York Times*, August 9, 1984, B8.

78. O'Reilly, *Nixon's Piano*, 360–62. For an alternative account praising the work of Reynolds, see Wolters, *Right Turn*.

79. Robert E. Taylor, "Civil Rights Division Head Will Seek Supreme Court Ban on Affirmative Action," *Wall Street Journal*, December 8, 1981, 4.

80. Detlefsen, *Civil Rights under Reagan*, 61.

81. Wilentz, *Age of Reagan*, 181–82.

82. Rodgers, *Age of Fracture*, 134.

83. Reynolds, "Individualism vs. Group Rights," 996.

84. Reynolds, "Individualism vs. Group Rights," 1001.

85. Reynolds, "Individualism vs. Group Rights," 1003.

86. Reynolds, "Individualism vs. Group Rights," 1003.

Chapter 5

1. "Mrs. King Fears Results of Victory by Reagan," *New York Times*, November 3, 1980, D15.

2. "Not a 35-Year Question," *New York Times*, October 21, 1983, A34.

3. Robert Pear, "President, Signing Bill, Praises Dr. King," *New York Times*, November 3, 1983, A1.

4. "Filibuster by Helms on Dr. King Holiday Is Dropped in Senate," *New York Times*, October 5, 1983, A16.

5. "Reagan Sympathetic, but Cautious on a King Holiday," *New York Times*, May 11, 1982, B13.

6. "Reagan's Doubts on Dr. King Disclosed," *New York Times*, October 22, 1983, 7.

7. For example, Reynolds, "Individualism vs. Group Rights."

8. See, for example, Golub, "History Died for Our Sins," 23–45; Madison, "Legitimation Crisis and Containment," 399–416.

9. Wiegman, "'My Name Is Forrest, Forrest Gump,'" 230.

10. "Attorney General Meese," *Wall Street Journal*, February 26, 1985, 34.

11. "Civil Rights Chief Predicts End to Race, Sex Quotas in Hiring," *Los Angeles Times*, February 8, 1985, A2.

12. Anderson, *Pursuit of Fairness*, 179–81.

13. "Civil Rights Chief Predicts End to Race, Sex Quotas in Hiring," A2.

14. "Black Leaders Draw Charge of 'New Racism,'" *Los Angeles Times*, March 5, 1985, A1.

15. "Black Leaders Draw Charge of 'New Racism,'" A1.

16. "Black Leaders Draw Charge of 'New Racism,'" A1.

17. Robert Pear, "Judge Bars Black Firefighters' Promotion Quotas," *New York Times*, April 2, 1985, A10.

18. Robert Pear, "The Courts Try to Sort Out Challenges to Affirmative Action," *New York Times*, April 14, 1985, A4.

19. Pear, "Courts Try to Sort Out Challenges to Affirmative Action," A4; "Affirmative Retreat," *New York Times*, May 5, 1985, A24.

20. "Affirmative Retreat," A24.

21. Anthony Lewis, "'Blatant and Continuous': Reagan Switch on Civil Rights," *New York Times*, May 19, 1985, E21.

22. "Backward Progress," *Los Angeles Times*, April 5, 1985, C4.

23. "Affirmative Retreat," A24.

24. Lewis, "'Blatant and Continuous,'" E21.

25. "Reynolds Hearing Put Off in Senate," *New York Times*, May 8, 1985, B28.

26. "Verbatim: Rights Record," *New York Times*, May 12, 1985, A4.

27. Cart T. Rowan, "Abolish the Civil-Rights Panel—Pendleton Made It a Sham," *Los Angeles Times*, March 11, 1985, C5.

28. John C. Eastman, "Letters to the Times," *Los Angeles Times*, March 21, 1985, C4.

29. Eastman, "Letters to the Times," C4.

30. Dolores Garcia, "Letters to the Times," *Los Angeles Times*, March 21, 1985, C4.

31. "Don't Promote Civil Rights Wrongs," *New York Times*, June 5, 1985, A26.

32. "Reynolds Hearing Put Off in Senate," B28.

33. "Reynolds Hearing Put Off in Senate," B28.

34. "Reynolds Hearing Put Off in Senate," B28.

35. Robert Pear, "Senate Committee Rejects Reynolds for Justice Post," *New York Times*, June 28, 1985, A1; "Red Light for Reynolds, *Los Angeles Times*, June 28, 1985, A12.

36. Pear, "Senate Committee Rejects Reynolds," A1.

37. "Acid Test," *Wall Street Journal*, August 16, 1985, 28; see also Pear, "Reading Tea Leaves on the Civil Rights Uproar," *New York Times*, August 20, 1985, B4.

38. Pear, "Senate Committee Rejects Reynolds," A1.

39. See Laham, *Reagan Presidency and the Politics of Race*, chap. 3.

40. "The Colorblind Vision," *Wall Street Journal*, March 11, 1985, 28.

41. Michael Kinsley, "On Civil Rights, Conservative Can't Means Won't: Viewpoint," *Wall Street Journal*, June 20, 1985, 29.

42. "Civil Rights, Civil Wrongs, and Mr. Reynolds: Letter," *New York Times*, July 11, 1985, A22.

43. Ken Masugi, "Letters to the Times: 'Red Light for Reynolds,'" *Los Angeles Times*, July 12, 1985, 6.

44. HoSang, *Racial Propositions*, 105. For more on Alan Robbins's anti–civil rights activism, see chap. 4.

45. "Letters to the Editor," *Wall Street Journal*, November 11, 1985, 25.

46. "The U.S. Constitution Was Never Color-Blind: Letter," *New York Times*, November 27, 1985, A22.

47. William Bradford Reynolds, "Racial Quotas Hurt Blacks and the Constitution: Letter," *New York Times*, December 9, 1985, A22.

48. The bust was later moved to Statuary Hall.

49. Lou Fintor, "Widow Unveils Bust of King for Capitol," *Los Angeles Times*, January 17, 1986, A22.

50. Laham, *Reagan Presidency and the Politics of Race*, 75.

51. "Reagan Quotes King Speech in Opposing Minority Quotas," *New York Times*, January 19, 1986, A20.

52. "Distortion of History," *Los Angeles Times*, January 21, 1986, B4.

53. "Reagan Hit as 'Rambo' Rights Raider," *Los Angeles Times*, January 23, 1986, A2; Lou Fintor, "Urban League Says Reagan Set Blacks Back a Decade," *Los Angeles Times*, January 24, 1986, A5.

54. Roger Wilkins, "A Dream Still Denied: An Equal Irony: Reagan Becomes Chief Celebrant of King's Birthday," *Los Angeles Times*, January 19, 1986, G1.

55. "President's News Conference on Foreign and Domestic Issues," *New York Times*, February 12, 1986, A12.

56. For evidence of this published in early 1986, see "A Right Path for Equal Rights," *Los Angeles Times*, February 14, 1986, B4; "No Retreat," *Los Angeles Times*, April 3, 1986, C4; Don Edwards, "Keep Affirmative Action," *New York Times*, February 13, 1986, A31.

57. "Going Colorblind Too Slowly," *Wall Street Journal*, April 23, 1986, 30.

58. Brian C. Whitten, "Dr. King's Dream Remembered," *Los Angeles Times*, February 2, 1986, A18.

59. Robert Pear, "Affirmative Action Effort on Amtrak Corridor Praised as Effective," *New York Times*, April 22, 1986, A12.

60. "Reagan Tells of Weighing Plans to Revise Minority Hiring Rules," *New York Times*, February 12, 1986, A13.

61. Melanie Lomax, "Affirmative Action Struggles On," *Los Angeles Times*, July 11, 1986, C5.

62. Phillip Hager, "President Is Rebuffed in Two Rulings," *Los Angeles Times*, July 3, 1986, C1; Phillip Hager, "Justices Uphold Affirmative Action," July 3, 1986, 4; "Justices, in Blow to Reagan, Uphold Affirmative Action: Broad Ruling Endorses Racial Quotas, Timetables," *Los Angeles Times*, July 2, 1986, 1.

63. "The Right to Remedy, Affirmed," *New York Times*, July 3, 1986, A30.

64. "Court Extends Racial Quotas to Promotions," *Los Angeles Times*, February 26, 1987, 7.

65. See Anderson, *Pursuit of Fairness*, 190–92.

66. Don Irwin, "Reynolds Accuses Justice of Misinterpreting 14th Amendment: Rights Enforcer Assails Brennan's View of Constitution," *Los Angeles Times*, September 14, 1986, A4.

67. "Preferential Treatment for Blacks Called Essential by Justice Marshall," *Los Angeles Times*, September 6, 1986, 2.

68. "Antibias Plans Said to Aid Cities," *New York Times*, September 19, 1986, A30.

69. Clarence Thomas, "Colorblindness," *Wall Street Journal*, February 20, 1987, 21.

70. Stuart Taylor, "Supreme Court, 6–3, Extends Preferences in Employment for Women and Minorities," *New York Times*, March 26, 1987, A1.

71. "Reynolds's Remarkable Rise," *New York Times*, October 20, 1987, A32.

72. Charles Mohr, "Marchers Exhorted to Go After 'Deferred Dreams,'" *New York Times*, August 28, 1988, 20.

73. Mohr, "Marchers Exhorted to Go After 'Deferred Dreams,'" 20.

74. Mohr, "Marchers Exhorted to Go After 'Deferred Dreams,'" 20.

75. Hall, *Cultural Representations*, chap. 1.

76. Foucault, "Film and Popular Memory," 7–24.

77. For more on the history of Hollywood slavery dramas, see Williams, *Playing the Race Card*; Robinson, *Forgeries of Memory and Meaning*, chap. 2; Rogin, *Blackface, White Noise*, chap. 2; Guerrero, *Framing Blackness*, chap. 2.

78. Bogle, *Toms, Coons, Mulattoes*, 175–76; Guerrero, *Framing Blackness*, chap. 3.

79. See Bogle, *Toms, Coons, Mulattoes*.

80. Jabir, *Conjuring Freedom*, 130.

81. Horne, "Review: *Glory*," 1141.

82. Manning Marable, "*Glory*—Black History and Struggle," *Indianapolis Recorder*, February 10, 1990, A8.

83. Cullen, *Civil War in Popular Culture*; Turner, *Ceramic Uncles and Celluloid Mammies*; and Ebert have similarly noted the centrality of Shaw rather than the black soldiers in the film.

84. Cullen, *Civil War in Popular Culture*, 164.

85. Cullen, *Civil War in Popular Culture*, 161; Wills, *Gone with the Glory*, 145–46; Blatt, "*Glory*: Hollywood History, Popular Culture, and the Fifty-Fourth Massachusetts Regiment," 221–22; Turner, *Ceramic Uncles and Celluloid Mammies*, 172–76.

86. Jabir, *Conjuring Freedom*, 131.

87. Silverman, *The Subject of Semiotics*, 201.

88. Butler, *Bodies That Matter*, 211.

89. Hartman, *Scenes of Subjection*, 19.

90. Ebert, "Review: *Glory*," *Chicago Sun-Times*, January 12, 1990, www.rogerebert.com/reviews/glory-1989.

91. Cullen, *Civil War in Popular Culture*, 153.

92. Cullen, *Civil War in Popular Culture*, 156.

93. For more on the historical differences between the historical record of the Massachusetts Fifty-Fourth Regiment and *Glory*, see Blight, "Meaning or the Fight," 141–53.

94. In Fuller, "Debating the Present through the Past," 179.

95. Shohat and Stam, *Unthinking Eurocentrism*, 179.

96. David Ansen, "History a la Hollywood," *Newsweek*, January 13, 1991, 54.

97. Ebert, "Review: *The Long Walk Home*," *Chicago Sun-Times*, March 22, 1991. www.rogerebert.com/reviews/the-long-walk-home-1991.

98. Blatt, "*Glory*: Hollywood History, Popular Culture, and the Fifty-Fourth Massachusetts Regiment," 225.

99. "Colorblind," *Los Angeles Times*, January 17, 1989, 47.

100. "Colorblind," 47.

101. Lee May, "Blacks Look Back with Anger at Reagan Years," *Los Angeles Times*, January 20, 1989, B1.

102. May, "Blacks Look Back with Anger at Reagan Years," B1.

103. May, "Blacks Look Back with Anger at Reagan Years," B1.

104. For more on the economic impact of the Reagan Presidency, see Troy, *Morning in America*; Johnson, *Sleepwalking through History*; Patterson, *Restless Giant*; Wilentz, *Age of Reagan*.

105. May, "Blacks Look Back with Anger at Reagan Years," B1.

106. George E. Curry, "Colorblind Economic Parity Urged," *Chicago Tribune*, January 25, 1989, 5.

107. Richard Nixon appointed 232; Jimmy Carter, 262; George H. W. Bush, 194; Bill Clinton, 379; and George W. Bush, 328. "Judgeship Appointments by President," United States Courts, www.uscourts.gov/JudgesAndJudgeships/Viewer.aspx?doc=/uscourts/JudgesJudgeships/docs/appointments-by-president.pdf.

108. Julie Johnson, "Blacks Found Lagging Despite Gains," *New York Times*, July 28, 1989, A6.

109. Johnson, "Blacks Found Lagging Despite Gains," A6.

110. Johnson, "Blacks Found Lagging Despite Gains," A6.

111. Nietzsche, *Use and Abuse of History*, 13.

112. Nietzsche, *Use and Abuse of History*, 15.

113. Du Bois, *Black Reconstruction in America*, 714.

114. Display ad, *New York Times*, December 28, 1990, C10.

Chapter 6

1. For more on the right-wing populism of Orange County and its role in launching the New Right revolution in American politics, see McGirr, *Suburban Warriors*.

2. See, for example, Lipsitz, *Possessive Investment in Whiteness*, chap. 7; Giroux, "Race, Pedagogy, and Whiteness in *Dangerous Minds*," 46–49; Bauer, "Indecent Proposals," 301–17; Farhi, "Hollywood Goes to School," 157–59; Beyerbach, "Social Foundations Classroom," 267–85.

3. Perry, *More Beautiful and More Terrible*, 50.

4. Perry, *More Beautiful and More Terrible*, 50.

5. Winant, *New Politics of Race,* 62; quoted in Perry, *More Beautiful and More Terrible,* 51.

6. "The Court's 'Retreat' on Civil Rights," *Chicago Tribune,* June 19, 1989, 14.

7. "It's Up to Congress Now," *Los Angeles Times,* June 16, 1989, 46. For more on the details of these decisions, see Anderson, *Pursuit of Fairness,* chap. 5.

8. Anderson, *Pursuit of Fairness,* 202.

9. Anderson, *Pursuit of Fairness,* 204.

10. George Will, "The Court Reagan Built Does Much to Roll Back the Racial Spoils System," January 29, 1989, *Los Angeles Times,* 5E.

11. Will, "The Court Reagan Built," 5E.

12. Will, "The Court Reagan Built," 5E.

13. Paul A. Gigot, "Lone Wolf's Work: A Constitution More Color-Blind," *Wall Street Journal,* June 16, 1989, A6.

14. Gigot, "Lone Wolf's Work," A6.

15. William Bradford Reynolds, "Stripping Away the Quota Barnacles," *Los Angeles Times,* June 28, 1989, A7.

16. Reynolds, "Stripping Away the Quota Barnacles," A7.

17. Reynolds, "Stripping Away the Quota Barnacles," A7.

18. Gigot, "Lone Wolf's Work," A6.

19. For more on the Civil Rights Bills of 1990 and 1991, see Anderson, *Pursuit of Fairness,* 206–13; Patterson, *Restless Giant,* 241–54.

20. George Will, "Mocking Civil Rights," *Washington Post,* May 20, 1990, B7.

21. The 1991 Civil Rights Act sought to curb the rising burden of proof placed on plaintiffs, rather than defendants and corporations, in civil rights lawsuits. It therefore expanded the use of jury trials in discrimination cases and added a new section to Title VII, making it less difficult for plaintiffs to prove discrimination by their employer. It also capped potential punitive and compensatory damages. For more, see the EEOC's summary of the act, http://www.eeoc.gov/eeoc/history/35th/1990s /civilrights.html. See also Anderson, *Pursuit of Fairness,* 209–13; Patterson, *Restless Giant,* 241–42.

22. Rowland Evans and Robert Novak, "Scholarships, Quotas," *Washington Post,* December 19, 1990, A23.

23. Evans and Novak, "Scholarships, Quotas," A23.

24. Kenneth J. Cooper, "Administration Revises Race-Based Grant Rule," *Washington Post,* December 19, 1990, A1.

25. Michael Kinsley, "None So Colorblind," *Washington Post,* December 20, 1990, A23.

26. George Will, "Racial Spoils System," *Washington Post,* December 23, 1990.

27. Mike Ashe, "Be Color-Blind," *Chicago Tribune,* April 22, 1989, 10.

28. Ali Webb, "Don't Ask," *Washington Post,* September 8, 1990, A19.

29. Tom Wicker, "Toward the Ideal," *New York Times,* December 26, 1991, A25.

30. George Will, "Let's Hear from Judge Souter," *Washington Post,* September 13, 1990, A23.

31. For more on the Clarence Thomas and Anita Hill hearings, see Morrison, *Race-ing Justice, En-gendering Power.*

32. "'I Emphasize Black Self-Help': Thomas' Thoughts on Quotas, the Work Ethic, and Conservatism," *Washington Post*, July 2, 1991, A7.

33. "Clarence Thomas in His Own Words," *New York Times*, July 2, 1991, A14.

34. Stephen Wermeil and Paul Barrett, "Bush's Court Nominee, a Black Politician, Is Deft Political Choice," *Wall Street Journal*, A1; "Clarence Thomas in His Own Words," A14. For news coverage of Thomas's nomination, see Sharon LaFraniere, "President to Avoid 'Quota System' in Choosing Marshall Successor," *Washington Post*, June 29, 1991, A11; "Review & Outlook: Justice Thomas," *Wall Street Journal*, July 2, 1991, A12; Wermeil and Barrett, "Bush's Court Nominee," A1.

35. John Yang, "'Lord, How Dare We Celebrate?': Bush Hears King's Daughter Decry Setbacks for Blacks' Progress," *Washington Post*, January 18, 1992, A1.

36. Yang, "'Lord, How Dare We Celebrate?,'" A1.

37. "Shaking and Shaping Up the GOP," *Washington Post*, April 12, 1992, C6.

38. Brooks, *Rethinking the American Race Problem*.

39. Robert Weisbrot, "The Future of Civil Rights in America," *Washington Post*, March 10, 1991, 3.

40. "US Elections: How Groups Votes in 1992," Roper Center, www.ropercenter.uconn.edu/elections/how_groups_voted/voted_92.html.

41. For more on the Guinier controversy, see Mukherjee, *Racial Order of Things*, 62–63.

42. Anderson, *Pursuit of Fairness*, 223.

43. Anderson, *Pursuit of Fairness*, 216.

44. Anderson, *Pursuit of Fairness*, 215.

45. Anderson, *Pursuit of Fairness*, 240–43.

46. Anderson, *Pursuit of Fairness*, 232.

47. The Republican momentum continued into 1995. "Race and Rage" declared *Newsweek* in spring of 1995, characterizing the mood of the nation. "The summer of 1995 became the defining moment for affirmative action. The *Adarand* decision, Clinton's speech, and the debate in California resulted in a national reexamination of the policy," argues Terry Anderson. By the mid-1990s, he contends, the belief of "reverse discrimination" was fully ingrained in the minds of a significant number of white males, enough to result in a tipping point for affirmative action. One 1995 poll found that whites opposed affirmative action by a margin of 79 percent to 14 percent.

48. Anderson, *Pursuit of Fairness*, 246–50.

49. Anderson, *Pursuit of Fairness*, 246–50.

50. San Francisco and Alameda County opposed Proposition 209 in the most significant margins—70 percent and 60 percent, respectively—and 54 percent of Los Angeles and Marin County voters voted against it. Santa Clara, Santa Cruz, and San Mateo County all voted against Proposition 209 by a 1 percent margin. https://ballotpedia.org/California_Affirmative_Action,_Proposition_209_(1996).

51. Anderson, *Pursuit of Fairness*, 266–69.

52. Musgrove, "Good at the Game of Tricknology," 9.

53. "Proposition 209: Text of Proposed Law," https://lao.ca.gov/ballot/1996/prop209_11_1996.html.

54. Musgrove, "Good at the Game of Tricknology," 10.

55. Musgrove, "Good at the Game of Tricknology," 14.

56. For more on David Duke's connection to Proposition 209, see Musgrove, "Good at the Game of Tricknology," 215–19.

57. For more on Proposition 209 television ads, see Mukherjee, *Racial Order of Things*, 55–60.

58. See *Grutter v. Bollinger* (2003), *Gratz v. Bollinger* (2003), and *Fisher V. Texas* (2013).

59. Holzer and Neumark, *Assessing Affirmative Action*. See also Anderson, *Pursuit of Fairness*, 278–80; Hartmann, "Who Has Benefited from Affirmative Action in Employment?," 77–96.

60. Harris, "Future of Affirmative Action," 328.

61. McGuinn, *No Child Left Behind and the Transformation of Federal Education Policy*, 28–34, 47–48.

62. McGuinn, *No Child Left Behind*, 41.

63. McGuinn, *No Child Left Behind*, 42.

64. Ross and Gibson, introduction, 4.

65. Ross and Gibson, introduction, 4.

66. Friedman, *Capitalism and Freedom*, 89.

67. Friedman, *Capitalism and Freedom*, 107.

68. See *A Nation at Risk*.

69. Hursh, "Marketing Education," 18.

70. For a more detailed assessment of the legacy of *A Nation at Risk*, see Guthrie and Springer, "*A Nation at Risk* Revisited," 7–35.

71. Lipman, "No Child Left Behind," 35.

72. Lipman, "No Child Left Behind," 45.

73. Lipman, "No Child Left Behind," 65–68.

74. Lipman, "No Child Left Behind," 68.

75. Lipman, "No Child Left Behind," 71.

76. Lipman, "No Child Left Behind," 100.

77. Hursh, "Marketing Education," 15.

78. Hursh, "Marketing Education," 17.

79. Hardin, "Finding the 'Neo' in Neoliberalism," 215.

80. Williams, *Playing the Race Card*, 296–97.

81. Williams, *Playing the Race Card*, 297. For more on the nature of melodrama, see Gledhill, "Melodramatic Field."

82. Grieveson, *Policing Cinema*.

83. Yosso and Garcia, "Who Are These Kids, Rejects from Hell?," 450.

84. As the previous discussion illustrated, the concern of public education was not necessarily driven by a concern over the opportunities of poor pupils of color but, in the context of neoliberal ascent and reform, of wasted tax revenue and the state's inability to function properly or equal to that of private charter schools.

85. See Rose, "Governing Advanced Liberal Democracies," 37–64.

86. Mukherjee, *Racial Order of Things*, 8.

87. *Blackboard Jungle*, dir. Richard Brooks, 1955.

88. Williams, *Playing the Race Card*, 7.

89. Williams, *Playing the Race Card*, 8.

90. Kelley, *Yo Mama's DysFUNKtional!*, 18.

91. Carby, *Cultures in Babylon*, 23.

92. Yosso and Garcia, "Who Are These Kids, Rejects from Hell?," 451.

93. Williams, *Playing the Race Card*, 28.

94. Williams, *Playing the Race Card*, 29.

95. Falola, *End of Colonial Rule*, 170.

96. Márquez, "Black Mohicans," 625–51.

97. Márquez, "Black Mohicans," 629.

98. Márquez, "Black Mohicans," 629–30.

99. Lipsitz, *Possessive Investment in Whiteness*, 142, 145–46.

100. Márquez, "Black Mohicans," 633.

101. Lipsitz, *Possessive Investment in Whiteness*, 228–29.

102. HoSang, *Racial Propositions*, 4.

103. HoSang, *Racial Propositions*, 1–12.

104. HoSang, *Racial Propositions*, 21.

105. Lipsitz, *Possessive Investment in Whiteness*, 229.

Conclusion

1. Donald Trump (@realDonaldTrump), Twitter, January 21, 2019, 7:39 A.M., https://twitter.com/realdonaldtrump/status/1087374046805835776?lang=en.

2. Brandon M. Terry, "MLK Now," *Boston Review*, September 10, 2018, http://bostonreview.net/forum/brandon-m-terry-mlk-now.

3. Terry, "MLK Now."

4. Josh Dawsey, "Trump Derides Protections for Immigrants from 'Shithole' Countries." *Washington Post*, January 12, 2018, www.washingtonpost.com/politics/trump-attacks-protections-for-immigrants-from-shithole-countries-in-oval-office-meeting/2018/01/11/bfc0725c-f711-11e7-91af-31ac729add94_story.html?utm_term=.8bb29afeb878; John Cassidy, "A Racist in the Oval Office, *New Yorker*, January 12, 2018, www.newyorker.com/news/our-columnists/trump-shithole-comment-racist-in-the-oval-office; Roxane Gay, "No One Is Coming to Save Us from Trump's Racism," *New York Times*, January 12, 2018. www.nytimes.com/2018/01/12/opinion/trump-shithole-countries-haiti-el-salvador-african-countries-immigration-racism.html.

5. German Lopez, "Donald Trump's Long History of Racism, from the 1970s to 2019," *Vox*, July 15, 2019, www.vox.com/2016/7/25/12270880/donald-trump-racist-racism-history.

6. Ta-Nehisi Coates, "The First White President," *Atlantic*, October 2017, www.theatlantic.com/magazine/archive/2017/10/the-first-white-president-ta-nehisi-coates/537909.

7. Daniel Victor and Giovanni Russonello, "Meryl Streep's Golden Globes Speech," *New York Times*, January 8, 2017, www.nytimes.com/2017/01/08/arts/television/meryl-streep-golden-globes-speech.html.

8. Stacy L. Smith, Marc Choueiti, and Katherine Pieper, "Inequality in 900 Popular Films," 6–9.

9. Gomer, "Leave the Prejudice, Take the Power."

10. Reggie Ugwu, "The Unreality of Racial Justice Cinema," *New York Times*, October 24, 2018, www.nytimes.com/2018/10/24/movies/racial-justice-cinema.html.

11. Gillespie, *Film Blackness*, 5.

12. Gillespie, *Film Blackness*, 158.

13. Anthony Lane, "Fun in *La La Land*," *New Yorker*, December 4, 2016, www
.newyorker.com/magazine/2016/12/12/dancing-with-the-stars.

14. "Black Art Matters: A Roundtable on the Black Radical Tradition," *Red
Wedge*, July 26, 2016, www.redwedgemagazine.com/online-issue/black-art-matters
-roundtable-black-radical-imaginatio; Kelley, *Freedom Dreams*.

15. Hall, "What Is This 'Black' in Black Popular Culture?," 477.

16. Gillespie, *Film Blackness*, 16.

Bibliography

Archival Collections

The Margaret Herrick Library
UCLA Film & Television Archive

Legal Cases

Adarand Constructors, Inc. v. Pena, 515 U.S. 200 (1995)
Brown v. Board of Education of Topeka, 347 U.S. 483 (1954)
Brown v. Board of Education II, 349 U.S. 294 (1955)
Citizens United v. Federal Election Commission, 558 U.S. 310 (2010)
City of Richmond v. James A. Croson Company, 488 U.S. 469 (1989)
DeFunis v. Odegaard, 416 U.S. 312 (1974)
Escobedo v. Illinois, 378 U.S. 478 (1964)
Firefighters Local Union No. 1784 v. Stotts, 467 U.S. 561 (1984)
Fullilove v. Klutznick, 448 U.S. 448 (1980)
Griggs v. Duke Power Co., 402 U.S. 424 (1971)
Hopwood v. Texas, 78 F.3d 932 (5th Cir. 1996)
Johnson v. Transportation Agency, Santa Clara Cty., 480 U.S. 616 (1987)
Local 28 of the Sheet Metal Workers' International Association v. Equal
    Employment Opportunity Commission, 478 U.S. 421 (1986)
Local 93 Firefighters v. City of Cleveland, 478 U.S. 501 (1986)
Miranda v. Arizona, 384 U.S. 436 (1966)
Plessy v. Ferguson, 162 U.S. 537 (1896)
Regents of the University of California v. Bakke, 438 U.S. 265 (1978)
Swann v. Charlotte-Mecklenburg Board of Education, 402 U.S. 1 (1971)
United States v. Paradise, 480 U.S. 149 (1987)
United Steelworkers of America v. Weber, 443 U.S. 193 (1979)
Village of Arlington Heights v. Metropolitan Housing Development Corp.,
    429 U.S. 252 (1977)
Washington v. Davis, 426 U.S. 229 (1976)

Newspapers and Periodicals

Atlantic
Black Panther
Boston Review

Hollywood Reporter
Los Angeles Times
New Yorker
New York Times
Playboy
U.S. News and World Report
Washington Post

Secondary Sources

Books

Alexander, Michelle. *The New Jim Crow: Mass Incarceration in the Age of Colorblindness.* New York: New Press, 2011.

A Nation at Risk: The Imperative for Educational Reform. Washington, DC: National Commission on Excellence in Education, 1983.

Anderson, Terry H. *The Pursuit of Fairness: A History of Affirmative Action.* Oxford: Oxford University Press, 2004.

Baldwin, James. *The Cross of Redemption: Uncollected Writings.* New York: Vintage, 2011.

Bambara, Toni Cade. *The Black Woman: An Anthology.* Washington, DC: Washington Square Press, 2005.

Barthes, Roland. *Mythologies.* New York: Hill and Wang, 1972.

Bederman, Gale. *Manliness and Civilization: A Cultural History of Gender and Race in the United States, 1880–1917.* Chicago: University of Chicago Press, 1995.

Berkowitz, Edward D. *Something Happened: A Political and Cultural Overview of the Seventies.* New York: Columbia University Press, 2006.

Biskind, Peter. "Blue Collar Blues: Proletarian Cinema from Hollywood." In Biskind, *Gods and Monsters,* 75–78.

———. *Easy Riders, Raging Bulls: How the Sex-Drugs-and-Rock 'n' Roll Generation Saved Hollywood.* New York: Simon & Schuster, 1998.

———. *Gods and Monsters: Thirty Years of Writing on Film and Culture from One of America's Most Incisive Writers.* New York: Nation Books, 2004.

Biskind, Peter, and Barbara Ehrenreich. "Machismo and Hollywood's Working Class." In Biskind, *Gods and Monsters,* 53–74.

Blatt, Martin H. "*Glory*: Hollywood History, Popular Culture, and the Fifty-Fourth Massachusetts Regiment." In *Hope and Glory: Essays on the Legacy of the Fifty-Fourth Massachusetts Regiment,* edited by Martin H. Blatt, Thomas J. Brown, and Donald Yacovone, 215–35. Amherst, MA: University of Massachusetts Press, 2001.

Bloom, Joshua, and Waldo Martin. *Black against Empire: The History and Politics of the Black Panther Party.* Berkeley: University of California Press, 2013.

Bogle, Donald. *Brown Sugar: Over 100 Years of America's Black Female Superstars.* New York: Continuum, 2007.

———. *Toms, Coons, Mulattoes, Mammies, and Bucks: An Interpretive History of Blacks in American Films.* New York: Continuum, 2001.

Bonilla-Silva, Eduardo. *Racism without Racists: Color-Blind Racism and the Persistence of Racial Inequality in America*. Lanham: Rowman & Littlefield, 2010.

Borstelman, Thomas. *The 1970s: A New Global History from Civil Rights to Economic Inequality*. Princeton, NJ: Princeton University Press, 2012.

Boyd, Nan. *Wide Open City: A History of Queer San Francisco to 1965*. Berkeley: University of California Press, 2003.

Branch, Taylor. *At Canaan's Edge: America in the King Years, 1965–1968*. Simon & Schuster, 2006.

———. *Parting the Waters: America in the King Years, 1954–1963*. New York: Simon & Schuster, 1989.

———. *Pillar of Fire: America in the King Years, 1963–1965*. New York: Simon & Schuster, 1998.

Brechin, Gray. *Imperial San Francisco: Urban Power, Earthly Ruin*. Berkeley: University of California Press, 2006.

Brooks, Roy L. *Rethinking the American Race Problem*. Berkeley: University of California Press, 1992.

Brown, Michael K., Martin Carnoy, Elliott Currie, Troy Duster, David B. Oppenheimer, Marjorie M. Shultz, and David Wellman. *Whitewashing Race: The Myth of a Color-Blind Society*. Berkeley: University of California Press, 2003.

Brown, Wendy. *Undoing the Demos: Neoliberalism's Stealth Revolution*. Cambridge, MA: MIT Press, 2015.

Burgin, Angus. *The Great Persuasion: Reinventing Free Markets since the Depression*. Cambridge, MA: Harvard University Press, 2012.

Butler, Judith. *Bodies That Matter: On the Discursive Limits of Sex*. New York: Routledge, 1993.

Cannon, Lou. *President Reagan: The Role of a Lifetime*. New York: Public Affairs, 2000.

Carby, Hazel. *Cultures in Babylon: Black Britain and African America*. New York: Verso, 1999.

Carmichael, Stokely, and Charles V. Hamilton. *Black Power: The Politics of Liberation*. New York: Random House, 1967.

Catanese, Brandi Wilkins. *The Problem of the Color(blind): Racial Transgression and the Politics of Black Performance*. Ann Arbor: University of Michigan Press, 2011.

Cook, David A. *Lost Illusions: American Cinema in the Shadow of Watergate and Vietnam, 1970–1979*. Berkeley: University of California Press, 2000.

Cowie, Jefferson. *Stayin' Alive: The 1970s and the Last Days of the Working Class*. New York: New Press, 2010.

———. "'Vigorously Left, Right, and Center': The Crosscurrents of Working-Class America in the 1970s." In *America in the Seventies*, edited by Beth Bailey and David Farber, 75–206. Lawrence: University of Kansas Press, 2004.

Crouch, Colin. *The Strange Non-death of Neoliberalism*. Malden, MA: Polity Press, 2011.

Cullen, Jim. *The Civil War in Popular Culture: A Reusable Past*. Washington, DC: Smithsonian Institution Press, 1995.

Delmont, Matthew F. *Why Busing Failed: Race, Media, and the National Resistance to School Desegregation*. Berkeley: University of California Press, 2016.

Deslippe, Dennis. *Protesting Affirmative Action: The Struggle over Equality after the Civil Rights Revolution*. Baltimore: Johns Hopkins University Press, 2012.

Detlefsen, Robert R. *Civil Rights under Reagan*. San Francisco: ICS Press, 1991.

Du Bois, W. E. B. *Black Reconstruction in America, 1860–1880*. New York: Harcourt, Brace, 1935.

Duggan, Lisa. *The Twilight of Equality? Neoliberalism, Cultural Politics, and the Attack on Democracy*. Boston: Beacon Press, 2003.

Edsall, Thomas, and Mary Edsall. *Chain Reaction: The Impact of Race, Rights, and Taxes on American Politics*. New York: Norton, 1992.

Ehrman, John. *The Eighties: America in the Age of Reagan*. New Haven, CT: Yale University Press, 2005.

Falola, Toyin, ed. *Africa*. Vol. 4, *The End of Colonial Rule: Nationalism and Decolonization*. Durham, NC: Carolina Academic Press, 2002.

Field, Allyson, and Jan-Christopher Horak, eds. *L.A. Rebellion: Creating a New Black Cinema*. Berkeley: University of California Press, 2015.

Formisano, Ronald P. *Boston against Busing: Race, Class, and Ethnicity in the 1960s and 1970s*. Chapel Hill: University of North Carolina Press, 1991.

Friedman, Milton. *Capitalism and Freedom*, 40th anniversary ed. Chicago: University of Chicago Press, 2002.

Friedman, Milton, and Rose Friedman. *Free to Choose: A Personal Statement*. New York: Harcourt Brace Jovanovich, 1980.

Fuller, Jennifer. "Debating the Present through the Past: Representations of the Civil Rights Movement in the 1990s." In *The Civil Rights Movement in American Memory*, edited by Leigh Raiford and Renee C. Romano, 167–96. Athens, GA: University of Georgia Press, 2006.

Fusco, Coco. "Racial Time, Racial Marks, Racial Metaphors." In *Only Skin Deep: Changing Visions of the American Self*, edited by Coco Fusco and Brian Wallis, 13–50. New York: Harry N. Abrams, 2003.

Gillespie, Michael Boyce. *Film Blackness: American Cinema and the Idea of Black Film*. Durham, NC: Duke University Press, 2016.

Gitlin, Todd. *The Sixties: Years of Hope, Days of Rage*. New York: Bantam Books, 1993.

Gledhill, Christine. "The Melodramatic Field: An Investigation." In *Home Is Where the Heart Is: Studies in Melodrama and the Woman's Film*, edited by Christine Gledhill, 299–325. London: British Film Institute, 1987.

Goldwater, Barry. *The Conscience of a Conservative*. Blacksburg, VA: Wilder, 2009.

Gomer, Justin. "Leave the Prejudice, Take the Power: Race in Hollywood in the 21st Century." In *Race Still Matters: African American Lived Experiences in the Twenty-First Century*, edited by Yuya Kiuchi, 301–20. Albany: State University of New York Press, 2016.

Gordon, Leah N. *From Power to Prejudice: The Rise of Racial Individualism in Midcentury America*. Chicago: University of Chicago Press, 2015.

Gordon, Linda. *Pitied but Not Entitled: Single Mothers and the History of Welfare.* New York: Free Press, 1994.

Gramsci, Antonio. *Selections from the Prison Notebooks.* New York: International Publishers, 2008.

Gray, Herman. "Remembering Civil Rights: Television, Memory, and the 1960s." In *The Revolution Wasn't Televised: Sixties Television and Social Conflict*, edited by Lynn Spigel and Michael Curtin, 349–58. New York: Routledge, 1997.

Grieveson, Lee. *Policing Cinema: Movies and Censorship in Early-Twentieth-Century America.* Berkeley, CA: University of California Press, 2004.

Guerrero, Ed. *Framing Blackness: The African American Image in Film.* Philadelphia: Temple University Press, 1993.

Hall, Stuart. "Gramsci's Relevance for the Study of Race and Ethnicity." In *Stuart Hall: Critical Dialogues in Cultural Studies*, edited by David Morley and Kuan-Hsing Chen, 411–41. London: Routledge, 1996.

———. "New Ethnicities." In *Stuart Hall: Critical Dialogues in Cultural Studies*, edited by David Morley and Kuan-Hsing Chen, 442–51. London: Routledge, 1996.

———. "On Postmodernism and Articulation: An Interview with Stuart Hall." In *Stuart Hall: Critical Dialogues in Cultural Studies*, edited by David Morley and Kuan-Hsing Chen, 131–50. London: Routledge, 1996.

———. "Race, Articulation, and Societies Structured in Dominance." In *Black British Cultural Studies: A Reader*, edited by Houston A. Baker, Manthia Diawara, and Ruth H. Lindeborg, 16–60. Chicago: University of Chicago Press, 1996.

———. *Representation: Cultural Representations and Signifying Practices.* London: Sage Hill, 1997.

———. "What Is This 'Black' in Black Popular Culture?" In *Stuart Hall: Critical Dialogues in Cultural Studies*, edited by David Morley and Kuan-Hsing Chen, 468–78. London: Routledge, 1996.

Haney López, Ian. *Dog Whistle Politics: How Coded Racial Appeals Have Reinvented Racism and Wrecked the Middle Class.* New York: Oxford Press, 2014.

———. *White by Law: The Legal Construction of Race.* New York: New York University Press, 2006.

Harris, Louis. "The Future of Affirmative Action." In *The Affirmative Action Debate*, edited by G. E. Curry, 326–36. Reading, MA: Addison-Wesley, 1995.

Hartman, Saidiya. *Scenes of Subjection: Terror, Slavery, and Self-Making in Nineteenth-Century America.* New York: Oxford University Press, 1997.

Hartmann, Heidi. "Who Has Benefited from Affirmative Action in Employment?" In *The Affirmative Action Debate*, edited by G. E. Curry, 77–96. Reading, MA: Addison-Wesley, 1995.

Harvey, David. *A Brief History of Neoliberalism.* New York: Oxford University Press, 2007.

Hoberman, J. *The Dream Life: Media, Movies, and the Myth of the Sixties.* New York: New Press, 2005.

Holzer, Harry, and David Neumark. *Assessing Affirmative Action*. Cambridge, MA: National Bureau of Economic Research, 1999.

HoSang, Daniel. *Racial Propositions: Ballot Initiatives and the Making of Postwar California*. Berkeley: University of California Press, 2010.

Hursh, David W. "Marketing Education: The Rise of Standardized Testing, Accountability, Competition, and Markets in Public Education." In *Neoliberalism and Education Reform*, edited by E. Wayne Ross and Rich Gibson, 15–34. Cresskill, NJ: Hampton Press, 2007.

Inness, Sherrie A. *Tough Girls: Women Warriors and Wonder Women in Popular Culture*. Philadelphia: University of Pennsylvania Press, 1999.

Jabir, Johari. *Conjuring Freedom: Music and Masculinity in the Civil War's "Gospel Army."* Columbus: Ohio State University Press, 2017.

Jackson, Christina, and Nikki Jones. "Remember the Fillmore: The Lingering History of Urban Renewal in Black San Francisco." In *Black California Dreamin': The Crises of California's African-American Communities*, edited by Ingrid Banks, Gaye Johnson, George Lipsitz, Ula Taylor, Daniel Widener, and Clyde Woods, 57–74. Santa Barbara, CA: UCSB Center for Black Studies Research, 2012.

Jacobson, Matthew Frye. *Roots Too: White Ethnic Revival in Post-Civil Rights America*. Cambridge, MA: Harvard University Press, 2006.

Johnson, Haynes. *Sleepwalking through History: America in the Reagan Years*. New York: Anchor Books, 1991.

Johnson, Jasmine, and Shaun Ossei-Owusu. "'From Fillmore to No More': Black-Owned Business in a Transforming San Francisco." In *Black California Dreamin': The Crises of California's African-American Communities*, edited by Ingrid Banks, Gaye Johnson, George Lipsitz, Ula Taylor, Daniel Widener, and Clyde Woods, 75–92. Santa Barbara, CA: UCSB Center for Black Studies Research, 2012.

Jones, Daniel Stedman. *Masters of the Universe: Hayek, Friedman, and the Birth of Neoliberal Politics*. Princeton, NJ: Princeton University Press, 2012.

Jones, James Earl, and Penelope Niven. *James Earl Jones: Voices and Silences*. New York: Scribner, 1993.

Joseph, Peniel. *Waiting 'til the Midnight Hour: A Narrative History of Black Power in America*. New York: Henry Holt, 2006.

Kael, Pauline. *5001 Nights at the Movies*. New York: Henry Holt, 1991.

Kalman, Laura. *Right Star Rising: A New Politics, 1974–1980*. New York: W. W. Norton, 2010.

Katz, Michael B. *The Undeserving Poor: America's Enduring Confrontation with Poverty*. Oxford: Oxford University Press, 2013.

Kelley, Robin D. G. *Freedom Dreams: The Black Radical Imagination*. Boston: Beacon Press, 2003.

———. *Yo Mama's DysFUNKtional! Fighting the Culture Wars in Urban America*. Boston: Beacon Press, 1997.

Klein, Naomi. *The Shock Doctrine: The Rise of Disaster Capitalism*. New York: Picador, 2007.

Kruse, Kevin M. *White Flight: Atlanta and the Making of Modern Conservatism*. Princeton, NJ: Princeton University Press, 2007.

Laham, Nicholas. *The Reagan Presidency and the Politics of Race: In Pursuit of Colorblind Justice and Limited Government*. Westport, CT: Praeger, 1998.

Larrain, Jorge. "Stuart Hall and the Marxist Concept of Ideology." In *Stuart Hall: Critical Dialogues in Cultural Studies*, edited by David Morley and Kuan-Hsing Chen, 46–70. London: Routledge, 1996.

Lassiter, Matthew. *The Silent Majority: Suburban Politics in the Sunbelt South*. Princeton, NJ: Princeton University Press, 2006.

Lichtenstein, Nelson. *State of the Union: A Century of American Labor*. Princeton, NJ: Princeton University Press, 2002.

Lipman, Pauline. *The New Political Economy of Urban Education: Neoliberalism, Race, and the Right to the City*. New York: Routledge, 2011.

———. "'No Child Left Behind': Globalization, Privatization, and the Politics of Inequality." In *Neoliberalism and Education Reform*, edited by Ross E. Wayne and Ross Gibson, 35–58. Cresskill, NJ: Hampton Press, 2007.

Lipsitz, George. *The Possessive Investment in Whiteness: How White People Profit from Identity Politics*. Philadelphia: Temple University Press, 1998.

Lubiano, Wahneema. "Black Ladies, Welfare Queens, and State Minstrels: Ideological War by Narrative Means." In *Race-ing Justice, En-gendering Power: Essays on Anita Hill, Clarence Thomas, and the Construction of Social Reality*, edited by Toni Morrison, 323–63. New York: Random House, 1992.

McGilligan, Patrick. *Clint: The Life and Legend*. New York: St. Martin's Press, 2011.

McGirr, Lisa. *Suburban Warriors: The Origins of the New American Right*. Cambridge, MA: Harvard University Press, 2001.

McGuinn, Patrick J. *No Child Left Behind and the Transformation of Federal Education Policy, 1965–2005*. Lawrence: University Press of Kansas, 2006.

Melamed, Jodi. *Represent and Destroy: Rationalizing Violence in the New Racial Capitalism*. Minneapolis: University of Minnesota Press, 2011.

Morrison, Toni, ed. *Race-ing Justice, En-gendering Power: Essays on Anita Hill, Clarence Thomas, and the Construction of Social Reality*. New York: Pantheon Books, 1992.

Mukherjee, Roopali. *The Racial Order of Things: Cultural Imaginaries of the Post-Soul Era*. Minneapolis: University of Minnesota Press, 2006.

Nadasen, Premilla. *Welfare Warriors: The Welfare Rights Movement in the United States*. New York: Routledge, 2005.

Nadasen, Premilla, Jennifer Mittelstadt, and Marisa Chappell. *Welfare in the United States: A History with Documents, 1935–1996*. New York: Routledge, 2009.

Nickerson, Michelle. *Mothers of Conservatism: Women and the Postwar Right*. Princeton, NJ: Princeton University Press, 2012.

Nietzsche, Friedrich. *The Use and Abuse of History*. Translated by Adrian Collins. Indianapolis: Liberal Arts Press, 1949.

Nilsen, Sarah, and Sarah E. Turner. *The Colorblind Screen: Television in Post-Racial America*. New York: NYU Press, 2014.

Nystrom, Derek. *Hard Hats, Rednecks, and Macho Men: Class in 1970s American Cinema*. New York: Oxford University Press, 2009.

Omi, Michael, and Howard Winant. *Racial Formation in the United States: From the 1960s to the 1990s*. New York: Routledge, 1994.

Ongiri, Amy Abugo. *Spectacular Blackness: The Cultural Politics of the Black Power Movement and the Search for a Black Aesthetic*. Charlotte: University of Virginia Press, 2010.

O'Reilly, Kenneth. *Nixon's Piano: Presidents and Racial Politics from Washington to Clinton*. New York: Free Press, 1995.

———. *Racial Matters: The FBI's Secret File on Black America, 1960–1972*. New York: Free Press, 1989.

Patterson, James T. *Freedom Is Not Enough: The Moynihan Report and America's Struggle over Black Family Life—from LBJ to Obama*. New York: Basic Books, 2010.

———. *Restless Giant: The United States from Watergate to Bush v. Gore*. Oxford: Oxford University Press, 2005.

Peck, Jamie. *Constructions of Neoliberal Reason*. Oxford: Oxford University Press, 2013.

Perlstein, Rick. *Before the Storm: Barry Goldwater and the Unmaking of the American Consensus*. New York: Bold Type Books, 2009.

———. *The Invisible Bridge: The Fall of Nixon and the Rise of Reagan*. New York: Simon & Schuster, 2014.

———. *Nixonland: The Rise of a President and the Fracturing of America*. New York: Scribner, 2008.

Perry, Imani. *More Beautiful and More Terrible: The Embrace and Transcendence of Racial Inequality in the United States*. New York: New York University Press, 2011.

Phillips, Kevin. *The Emerging Republican Majority*. New Rochelle, NY: Arlington House, 1969.

Phillips-Fein, Kim. *Invisible Hands: The Making of the Conservative Movement from the New Deal to Reagan*. New York: W. W. Norton, 2009.

Pierce, Jennifer L. *Racing for Innocence: Whiteness, Gender, and the Backlash against Affirmative Action*. Stanford, CA: Stanford University Press, 2012.

Raskin, Jamin B. *Overruling Democracy: The Supreme Court vs. the American People*. New York: Routledge, 2003.

Reeves, Jimmie L., and Richard Campbell. *Cracked Coverage: Television News, the Anti-Cocaine Crusade, and the Reagan Legacy*. Durham, NC: Duke University Press, 1994.

Reinarman, Craig, and Harry G. Levine. "The Crack Attack: Politics and the Media in the Crack Scare." In *Crack in America: Demon Drugs and Social Justice*, edited by Craig Reinarman and Harry G. Levine, 18–52. Berkeley: University of California Press, 1997.

Roberts, Dorothy. *Killing the Black Body: Race, Reproduction, and the Meaning of Liberty*. New York: Pantheon Books, 1997.

Robinson, Cedric. *Black Marxism: The Making of the Black Radical Tradition*. Chapel Hill: University of North Carolina Press, 2000.

———. *Forgeries of Memory and Meaning.* Chapel Hill: University of North Carolina Press, 2007.

Rodgers, Daniel T. *Age of Fracture.* Cambridge, MA: Harvard University Press, 2011.

Rogin, Michael. *Blackface, White Noise: Jewish Immigrants in the Hollywood Melting Pot.* Berkeley: University of California Press, 1996.

———. *Ronald Reagan, the Movie: and Other Episodes in Political Demonology.* Berkeley: University of California Press, 1988.

Roithmayr, Daria. *Reproducing Racism: How Everyday Choices Lock in White Advantage.* New York: New York University Press, 2014.

Rose, Nikolas. "Governing Advanced Liberal Democracies." In *Foucault and Political Reason: Liberalism, Neo-Liberalism, and Rationalities of Government,* edited by Andrew Barry, Thomas Osborne, and Nikolas Rose, 37–64. Chicago: University of Chicago Press, 1996.

Ross, E. Wayne, and Rich Gibson. Introduction to *Neoliberalism and Education Reform,* edited by E. Wayne Ross and Rich Gibson, 1–14. Cresskill, NJ: Hampton Press, 2007.

———, eds. *Neoliberalism and Education Reform.* Cresskill, NJ: Hampton Press, 2007.

Ross, Steven. "How Hollywood Became Hollywood: Money, Politics and Movies." In *Metropolis in the Making: Los Angeles in the 1920s,* edited by Tom Sitton, 255–76. Berkeley, University of California Press, 2001.

Rubio, Philip F. *A History of Affirmative Action, 1619–2000.* Jackson: University Press of Mississippi, 2001.

Ryan, Michael, and Douglas Kellner. *Camera Politica: The Politics and Ideology of Contemporary Hollywood Film.* Bloomington: Indiana University Press, 1988.

Schatz, Thomas. "The New Hollywood." In *Film Theory Goes to the Movies,* edited by Jim Collins, Hilary Radner, and Ava Preacher Collins, 8–36. New York: Routledge, 1993.

Schneider, Eric C. *Smack: Heroin and the American City.* Philadelphia: University of Pennsylvania Press, 2008.

Schulman, Bruce J. *The Seventies: The Great Shift in American Culture, Society, and Politics.* New York: Free Press, 2001.

Schulman, Bruce, and Julian Zelizer, eds. *Rightward Bound: Making America Conservative in the 1970s.* Cambridge, MA: Harvard University Press, 2008.

Self, Robert O. *American Babylon: Race and the Struggle for Postwar Oakland.* Princeton, NJ: Princeton University Press, 2003.

Shohat, Ella, and Robert Stam. *Unthinking Eurocentrism: Multiculturalism and the Media.* New York: Routledge, 1994.

Silverman, Kaja. *The Subject of Semiotics.* New York: Oxford University Press, 1983.

Simms, Yvonne D. *Women of Blaxploitation: How the Black Action Film Hero Changed American Popular Culture.* Jefferson, NC: McFarland, 2006.

Skrentny, John David. *The Ironies of Affirmative Action: Politics, Culture, and Justice in America.* Chicago: University of Chicago Press, 1996.

Slotkin, Richard. *Gunfighter Nation: The Myth of the Frontier in Twentieth-Century America*. Norman: University of Oklahoma Press, 1998.

Smith, Paul. *Clint Eastwood: A Cultural Production*. Minneapolis: University of Minnesota Press, 1993.

Sowell, Thomas. *Markets and Minorities*. Oxford: Basil Blackwell for the International Center for Economic Policy Studies, 1981.

———. "Stereotypes versus the Market." In Thomas Sowell, *The Thomas Sowell Reader*, 262–64. New York: Basic Books, 2011.

Squires, Catherine. *The Post-Racial Mystique: Media and Race in the Twenty-First Century*. New York: New York University Press, 2014.

Stein, Judith. *Pivotal Decade: How the United States Traded Factories for Finance in the Seventies*. New Haven, CT: Yale University Press, 2010.

———. *Running Steel, Running America: Race, Economic Policy, and the Decline of Liberalism*. Chapel Hill: University of North Carolina Press, 1998.

Stewart, Jacqueline Najuma. *Migrating to the Movies: Cinema and Black Urban Modernity*. Berkeley: University of California Press, 2005.

Sugrue, Thomas. *Sweet Land of Liberty: The Forgotten Struggle for Civil Rights in the North*. New York: Random House, 2008.

Troy, Gil. *Morning in America: How Ronald Reagan Invented the 1980s*. Princeton, NJ: Princeton University Press, 2005.

Ture, Kwame, and Charles V. Hamilton. *Black Power: The Politics of Liberation*. New York: Vintage, 1992.

Turner, Patricia. *Ceramic Uncles and Celluloid Mammies: Black Images and Their Influences on Culture*. New York: Anchor Books, 1994.

Whitfield, Stephen J. *The Culture of the Cold War*. Baltimore: Johns Hopkins University Press, 1996.

Wiegman, Robyn. "'My Name Is Forrest, Forrest Gump': Whiteness Studies and the Paradox of Particularity." In *Multiculturalism, Postcoloniality, and Transnational Media*, edited by Ella Shohat and Robert Stam, 227–55. New Brunswick, NJ: Rutgers University Press, 2003.

Wilentz, Sean. *The Age of Reagan: A History, 1974–2008*. New York: HarperCollins, 2008.

Williams, Eric. *Capitalism and Slavery*. Chapel Hill: University of North Carolina Press, 1994.

Williams, Linda. *Playing the Race Card: Melodramas of Black and White from Uncle Tom to O.J. Simpson*. Princeton, NJ: Princeton University Press, 2001.

Wills, Brian Steel. *Gone with the Glory: The Civil War in Cinema*. New York: Rowman & Littlefield, 2007.

Wilson, William J. *The Truly Disadvantaged: The Inner City, the Underclass, and Public Policy*. Chicago: University of Chicago Press, 1987.

Winant, Howard. *The New Politics of Race: Globalism, Difference, Justice*. Minneapolis: University of Minnesota Press, 2004.

Wolters, Raymond. *Right Turn: William Bradford Reynolds, the Reagan Administration, and Black Civil Rights*. New Brunswick, NJ: Transaction, 1996.

Wright, Will. *Six Guns and Society: A Structural Study of the Western*. Berkeley: University of California Press, 1975.

Yosso, Tara J., and David G. Garcia. "Who Are These Kids, Rejects from Hell?" In *Handbook of Latinos and Education: Theory, Research and Practice*, edited by Enrique G. Murillo Jr., Sofia A. Villenas, Ruth Trinidad Galvan, Juan Sanchez Munoz, Corinne Martinez, and Margarita Machado-Casas, 450–73. New York: Routledge, 2009.

Zirin, Dave. *What's My Name, Fool? Sports and Resistance in the United States*. Chicago: Haymarket Books, 2005.

Articles

Anderson, Terry H. "The Strange Career of Affirmative Action." *South Central Review* 22 (Summer 2005): 110–29.

Bauer, Dale. "Indecent Proposals: Teachers in the Movies." *College English* 60 (1998): 301–17.

Beyerbach, Barbara. "The Social Foundations Classroom: Themes in Sixty Years of Teachers in Film: Fast Times, Dangerous Minds, Stand on Me." *Educational Studies: A Journal of the American Educational Studies Association* 37 (September 2010): 267–85.

Bezusko, Adriane. "Criminalizing Black Motherhood: How the War on Welfare Was Won." *Souls: A Critical Journal of Black Politics, Culture, and Society* 15, no. 1–2 (2013): 39–55.

Blight, David W. "The Meaning or the Fight: Frederick Douglass and the Memory of the Fifty Fourth Massachusetts." *Massachusetts Review* 36 (Spring 1995): 141–53.

Bostdorff, Denise M., and Steven R. Goldzwig. "History, Collective Memory, and the Appropriation of Martin Luther King, Jr.: Reagan's Rhetorical Legacy." *Presidential Studies Quarterly* 35 (December 2005): 661–90.

Clarke, John. "Living with/in and without Neo-liberalism." *Focaal: Journal of Global and Historical Anthropology* 51 (June 2008): 135–47.

Farhi, Adam. "Hollywood Goes to School: Recognizing the Superteacher Myth in Film. *The Clearing House: A Journal of Educational Strategies, Issues and Ideas* 72 (January–February 1999): 157–59.

Foucault, Michel. "Film and Popular Memory: An Interview with Michel Foucault." *Cathiers du Cinema*, July–August 1974, 24–29.

Gallantz, Michael. "Critical Dialogue: Rocky's Racism." *Jump Cut* 18 (August 1978): 33–34.

Giroux, Henry A. "Race, Pedagogy, and Whiteness in *Dangerous Minds*." *Cineaste* 22 (1997): 46–49.

———. "The Terror of Neoliberalism: Rethinking the Significance of Cultural Politics." *College Literature* 32 (Winter 2005): 1–19.

Golub, Mark. "History Died for Our Sins: Guilt and Responsibility in Hollywood Redemption Histories." *Journal of American Culture* 21 (1998): 23–45.

Guthrie, James W., and Matthew G. Springer. "*A Nation at Risk* Revisited: Did 'Wrong' Reasoning Result in 'Right' Results? At What Cost?" *Peabody Journal of Education* 79, no 1. (2004): 7–35.

Hall, Stuart. "Cultural Studies: Two Paradigms." *Media, Culture and Society* 2 (1980): 57–72.

———. "The Neo-Liberal Revolution." *Cultural Studies* 25, no. 6 (2011): 705–28.

Hardin, Carolyn. "Finding the 'Neo' in Neoliberalism." *Cultural Studies* 28 (December 2012): 199–221.

Harvey, David. "Neoliberalism as Creative Destruction." *Annals of the American Academy of Political and Social Science* 610 (March 2007): 22–44.

Horne, Gerald. "Review: *Glory*." *American Historical Review* 95 (October 1990): 1141.

Lassiter, Matthew. "The Suburban Origins of Color-Blind Conservatism: Middle Class Consciousness in the Charlotte Busing Crisis." *Journal of Urban History* 30 (May 2004): 549–82.

Lipman, Pauline. "The Landscape of Education 'Reform' in Chicago: Neoliberalism Meets a Grassroots Movement." *Education Policy Analysis Archives* 25 (June 2017): 1–32.

Lipsitz, George. "Introduction: A New Beginning," *Kalfou: A Journal of Comparative and Relational Ethnic Studies* 1 (Spring 2014): 7–14.

Madison, Kelly J. "Legitimation Crisis and Containment: The 'Anti-Racist-White-Hero' Film." *Critical Studies in Mass Communications* 16 (1999): 399–416.

Márquez, John D. "The Black Mohicans: Representations of Everyday Violence in Postracial Urban America." *American Quarterly* 64 (September 2012): 625–51.

Musgrove, George D. "Good at the Game of Tricknology": Proposition 209 and the Struggle for the Historical Memory of the Civil Rights Movement." *Souls: A Critical Journal of Black Politics, Culture, and Society* 1, no. 3 (1999): 7–24.

Nickerson, Michelle. "Women, Domesticity and Postwar Conservatism." *OAH Magazine of History* 17 (January 2003): 17–21.

Nora, Pierre. "Between Memory and History: Les Lieux de Memoire." *Representations* 26 (Spring 1989): 7–24.

Phillips-Fein, Kim. "Conservatism: A State of the Field." *Journal of American History* 98 (December 2011): 723–43.

Quinn, Eithne. "From Oppositional Readers to Positional Producers: The Making of Black Female Heroism in *Coffy*." *Screen* 53 (Autumn 2012): 266–86.

Reynolds, William Bradford. "Individualism vs. Group Rights: The Legacy of *Brown*." *Yale Law Journal* 93 (May 1984): 995–1005.

Robinson, Cedric. "Blaxploitation and the Misrepresentation of Liberation." *Race and Class* 40 (July 1998): 1–12.

Rogin, Michael. "'The Sword Became a Flashing Vision': D. W. Griffith's *The Birth of a Nation*." In "American Culture between the Civil War and World War I." Special issue, *Representations* 9 (Winter 1985): 150–95.

Taylor, Keeanga-Yamahtta. "Back Story to the Neoliberal Moment: Race Taxes and the Political Economy of Black Urban Housing in the 1960s." *Souls: A Critical Journal of Black Politics, Culture, and Society* 14 (March 2013): 185–206.

Wacquant, Loic. "Three Steps to a Historical Anthropology of Actually Existing Neoliberalism." *Social Anthropology/Anthropologie Sociale* 20 (February 2012): 66–79.

Zelizer, Julian E. "Reflections: Rethinking the History of American Conservatism." *American Quarterly* 38 (June 2010): 367–92.

Online Sources

California Proposition 209 County Demographics. https://ballotpedia.org /California_Affirmative_Action,_Proposition_209_(1996).

Equal Employment Opportunity Commission's summary of the 1991 Civil Rights Act. www.eeoc.gov/eeoc/history/35th/1990s/civilrights.html.

Grossmen, James. "Lincoln, Hollywood, and an Opportunity for Historians." *Perspectives on History* 50, no. 8 (November 2012), www.historians.org /publications-and-directories/perspectives-on-history/november-2012/lincoln -hollywood-and-an-opportunity-for-historians.

"Historians Respond to Spielberg's Lincoln." *Harvard University Press* (blog). Harvard University Press, November 30, 2012. http://harvardpress.typepad .com/hup_publicity/2012/11/historians-respond-to-spielbergs-lincoln.html.

Holzer, Harold. "What's True and False in *Lincoln* Movie." *Daily Beast,* November 22, 2012. www.thedailybeast.com/articles/2012/11/22/what-s-true -and-false-in-lincoln-movie.html.

"Judgeship Appointments by President." United States Courts. www.uscourts.gov /JudgesAndJudgeships/Viewer.aspx?doc=/uscourts/JudgesJudgeships/docs /appointments-by-president.pdf.

Phillips-Fein, Kim. "Right On." *Nation.* September 28, 2009. www.thenation.com /article/right.

"US Elections: How Groups Votes in 1992." Roper Center. www.ropercenter.uconn .edu/elections/how_groups_voted/voted_92.html.

Walker, Richard. "San Francisco's Haymarket: A Redemptive Tale of Class Struggle." *ACME: An International E-Journal for Critical Geographies* 7, no. 1 (2008): 45–58. http://geog.berkeley.edu/PeopleHistory/faculty/R_Walker /Walker_87.pdf.

Film and Television

Avildsen, John, dir. *Joe.* 1970; Cannon Films.
———. *Rocky.* 1976; United Artists.
———. *Lean on Me.* 1989; Warner Brothers.
Berry, John, dir. *Claudine.* 1974; Third World Cinema Corporation.
Brooks, Richard, dir. *Blackboard Jungle.* 1955; Warner Brothers.
Caple Jr., Steven, dir. *Creed II.* 2018; Mirror Releasing and Warner Brothers.
Coogler, Ryan, dir. *Creed.* 2015; Warner Brothers.
DuVernay, Ava, dir. *Selma.* 2014; Paramount.
Estrada, Carlos Lopez, dir. *Blindspotting.* 2018; Lionsgate.
Farrelly, Peter, dir. *Green Book.* 2018; Universal Pictures.
Friedman, Milton. "Created Equal." In *Free to Choose* television series. 1990; Video Arts TV Production.

Haggis, Paul, dir. *Crash*. 2004; Lionsgate Films.

Hill, Jack, dir. *Coffy*. 1973; American International Pictures.

Jenkins, Barry, dir. *If Beale Street Could Talk*. 2018; Mirror Releasing.

———, dir. *Moonlight*. 2016; A24.

Jhally, Sut, dir. *Stuart Hall: Race; The Floating Signifier*. 1997; Hillside Studios. DVD.

Kramer, Stanley, dir. *Guess Who's Coming to Dinner*. 1967; Columbia Pictures.

LaGravenese, Richard, dir. *Freedom Writers*. 2007; Paramount Pictures.

Leva, Gary, dir. *The Long Shadow of Dirty Harry*. 2008; Leva FilmWorks. DVD.

Mandel, Robert, dir. *The Substitute*. 1996; Orion Pictures.

Menendez, Ramon, dir. *Stand and Deliver*. 1988; Warner Brothers.

Parker, Alan, dir. *Mississippi Burning*. 1988; Orion Pictures.

Parks, Gordon, dir. *Shaft*. 1971; Metro-Goldwyn-Mayer.

Pearce, Richard, dir. *The Long Walk Home*. 1990; Miramax Films.

Reiner, Rob, dir. *Ghosts of Mississippi*. 1996; Columbia Pictures.

Riggs, Marlon, dir. *Color Adjustment*. 1991; California Newsreel.

Ritchie, Michael, dir. *Wildcats*. 1986; Warner Brothers.

Siegel, Don, dir. *Dirty Harry*. 1971; Warner Brothers.

Smith, John N., dir. *Dangerous Minds*. 1995; Buena Vista Pictures.

Spielberg, Steven, dir. *Amistad*. 1997; DreamWorks.

———. *Lincoln*. 2012; Walt Disney Studios.

Stallone, Sylvester, dir. *Rocky III*. 1982; Metro-Goldwyn-Mayer/United Artists.

Taylor, Tate, dir. *The Help*. 2011; Walt Disney Studios.

Van Peebles, Melvin, dir. *Sweet Sweetback's Baadasssss Song*. 1971; Cinema Industries.

Yates, Peter, dir. *Bullitt*. 1968: Warner Brothers.

Zemeckis, Robert, dir. *Forrest Gump*. 1996; Paramount Pictures.

Zinnemann, Fred, dir. *High Noon*. 1952; United Artists.

Zwick, Edward, dir. *Glory*. 1989; TriStar Pictures.

Unpublished Materials

Blue Collar script. Universal Pictures. May 10, 1978. Margaret Herrick Library.

Claudine advertising notes. James Raker Papers, Margaret Herrick Library.

Dirty Harry script (draft). 1971. Margaret Herrick Library.

Dirty Harry script (final). February 8, 1971. Margaret Herrick Library.

Index

Note: Figures are indicated by page numbers in *italics*.

white heroism. *See* heroism

white masculinity, 75, 103, 116–17, 119, 124

whiteness: civil rights and, 146, 155; colorblindness and, 7; "Ellis Island," 78–79; in *Glory*, 150, 152; liberal, 128; in *The Long Walk Home*, 156–57; political, 196; in *Rocky*, 78–79, 116; unions and, 63

whites: affirmative action and, 68, 172, 174; busing and, 65–66, 69–71; in civil rights dramas, 145–46; cocaine and, 116; colorblind rhetoric and, 15–16; neoliberalism and, 63–64; Southern Strategy and, 64–65

"white savior" films, 11, 193, 203

"White Slavery" films, 183

white supremacy: affirmative action and, 143; Ali *vs.* Wepner fight and, 74–75; boxing and, 75; California Proposition 209 and, 175–76; capitalism and, 62, 85; civil rights as veneer for, 2; civil rights programs and, 2–3, 60; "Ellis Island Whiteness" and, 78–79; *Glory* and, 150; John Wayne on, 31; masculinity and, 119; movies and, 5, 202; neoliberalism and, 98; overt, as unacceptable, 71; in *Plessy v. Ferguson*, 1; Reagan and, 108, 162; reverse discrimination and, 69; *Rocky* and, 61; *Rocky III* and, 125;

Trump and, 199; Wayne on, 31; white heroism and, 157

whitewashing, 127–28

Whitfield, Stephen J., 30

Whitten, Brian, 140–41

Wicker, Tom, 169

Wiegman, Robyn, 3, 128

Wilkins, Roger, 140

Will, George, 60, 72–73, 82, 92, 166, 168–70

Williams, Eric, 85

Williams, Linda, 182–83, 190

Williams, Michael, 168

Wilson, William Julius, 213n39

Winant, Howard, 7, 85, 165–66

Wolfe, Tom, 215n111

women: abolition and, 145; affirmative action and, 68, 122, 208n10; in California Proposition 209 vote, 174; pathological home trope and, 186; in teacher films, 194–95; Trump and, 200; welfare and, 49, 54

Wright, Richard, 45

Wright, Will, 6

Wrinkle in Time, A, 202

Yosso, Tara J., 183–84

Youth International Party, 19

Zirin, Dave, 75

Zwick, Edward, 146

CPSIA information can be obtained
at www.ICGtesting.com
Printed in the USA
LVHW111631300621
691479LV00010B/1219

9 781469 655802